How to study law

i:
c

AUSTRALIA
The Law Book Company
Brisbane ● Sydney ● Melbourne ● Perth

CANADA
Carswell
Ottawa ● Toronto ● Calgary ● Montreal ● Vancouver

Agents:
Steimatzky's Agency Ltd, Tel Aviv;
N.M. Tripathi (Private) Ltd, Bombay;
Eastern Law House (Private) Ltd, Calcutta;
M.P.P. House, Bangalore;
Universal Book Traders, Delhi;
Aditya Books, Delhi;
MacMillan Shuppan KK, Tokyo;
Pakistan Law House, Karachi, Lahore

How to study law

Third Edition

ANTHONY BRADNEY, LL.B., B.A.
Lecturer in Law in the University of Leicester
FIONA COWNIE, B.A., L.L.B., L.L.M.
Barrister
JUDITH MASSON, M.A., Ph.D.
Professor, University of Warwick
ALAN C. NEAL, LL.B., LL.M., D.G.L.S., Barrister
Professor of Law in the University of Leicester
DAVID NEWELL, LL.B., M.Phil., Solicitor
Deputy Director, The Newspaper Society

LONDON
SWEET & MAXWELL
1995

First Edition 1989
Second Edition 1991
Third Edition 1995
Reprinted 1997, 1998, 1999

Published in 1995 by Sweet & Maxwell Limited of
100 Avenue Road, Swiss Cottage, London NW3 3PF
http://www.smlawpub.co.uk
Typeset by Selwood Systems,
Midsomer Norton
Printed in England by
Clays Ltd, St Ives plc

No natural forests were destroyed to make this product; only farmed timber was
used and replanted.

**A CIP catalogue for this book is available from the
British Library**

ISBN 0-421-53610-1

PREFACE TO THE THIRD EDITION

The third edition of "How to Study Law" follows the structure established in the second edition. This book is for those who want to acquire the skills necessary to understand law. The book assumes no prior knowledge of law on the part of the reader. We begin in Part 1 by providing the reader with a sketch of law and the English legal system. We then move on to the heart of the book, Parts 2 and 3, which is a series of chapters and exercises which describe the materials which the reader will use in studying law and demonstrate the techniques which are necessary if one is to successfully handle those materials. Part 4 looks at the very varied careers that those versed in law can follow.

"How to Study Law" is written for both the student studying alone and for those working in a group with a tutor. The exercises, which are an essential part of the book, are based on actual law reports, statutes and articles reproduced in their original form in the book. The exercises on primary material are all divided into two sections. The first section has questions with answers at the back of the book. The second section has questions with no answers. The book is thus equally useful for the self-study student, who has no access to a tutor who can correct their work, and the tutor with a large class and a shortage of statutes, law reports or journals.

Chapter 7, on study skills, has been newly written by Fiona Cownie. She has also contributed a new exercise on study skills. Study skills are often neglected by both students and tutors who prefer to concentrate on looking at pure legal skills. We are convinced that most students would benefit from looking at techniques which will help them work not harder but more effectively. Law courses often contain a much larger quantity of material than courses in other disciplines. A student who has not considered how to make the best use of their time will find their studies that much the harder.

We are all conscious that this book is drawn not only from our experience but from the help that our colleagues and our students have given to us over the years. We are very grateful to them for their assistance.

AGDB, FCC, JMM, ACN, DRN

ACKNOWLEDGMENTS

We are particularly grateful to the Law Society, Council of Legal Education, General Council of the Bar, and UCAS for their help with Chapter 8.

The authors and publishers wish to thank the following for permission to reprint material from publications in which they have copyright.

Ian K. McKenzie and Academic Press London for the article "Equal Opportunities in Policing: a Comparative Examination of anti-Discrimination Policy and Practice in British Policing" from the *International Journal of the Sociology of Law 1993*, 159–174.

Butterworth & Co. (Publishers) Ltd. for extracts from the *All England Reports*.

CONTENTS

PART 2

Contents   xi

PART 1

CHAPTER 1

Sources of the law

DISCOVERING THE LAW

We could begin by asking "what is law?". Ordinary people regularly make law for their own circumstances. Freely-negotiated commercial contracts may bind them to behave in particular ways. By becoming members of a sports club or a trade union they agree to comply with a set of rules. Sometimes these forms of law will use the courts to enforce their arrangements. In other cases privately-instituted adjudication bodies are established; a third party being appointed to decide whether an agreement or rule has been broken or not. These kinds of arrangements may seem very different from the normal idea of law, especially if law is thought of mainly in terms of the criminal law. However, it is possible to see law simply as a way of regulating behaviour, of deciding what can be done and what cannot be done.

Most laws are not about something dramatic like murder but, rather, about the everyday details of ordinary life. Every time a purchase is made, a contract is created. Both parties make promises about what they will do; one to hand over the goods, one to pay the price. In this and other ways, everybody is involved in law every day of their lives. In some cases the state steps in to say what people can do, perhaps by saying how they can contract or, more dramatically, by saying when they can kill each other. This is the kind of law, that which comes from the state, we most frequently think about. Most courses involving law are interested only in this one kind of law and that is what this book is about.

There are many generally acknowledged sources of English law. Some are more obvious than others. Thus, "the Queen in Parliament" (the House of Commons, the House of Lords and the monarch) is a vital source of modern English law. Here proposals for legislation (*Bills*) are presented to, debated by, and voted upon

by the House of Commons and the House of Lords, finally receiving
the assent of the monarch and thus becoming legislation (*Statutes*
or *Acts*). It is also indisputable that judges are significant sources
of law, since the English legal system places great emphasis upon
judgments in previous legal cases as guidance for future judicial
decision-making. There are, however, less obvious sources of
English law. Some are direct: for example, in some circumstances
the European Community may make law for England. Others are
more indirect: thus customs of a particular trade may be incorporated into the law by the judges or Parliament or international
law (the law between states) may be a basis for national law.

All of the above are sources of *legal rules*. What precisely it is that
is meant by the term legal rules, is a subject much debated by
philosophers of law. Generally speaking, when the term is used it
indicates that a particular course of action should, or should not,
be followed. Legal rules are said to be *binding*. This means if they
are not followed some action in the courts may result. Some of the
questions about the nature of law are discussed in Chapter 5, "Law
in Action/Law in Books."

It will suffice for present purposes if we consider just two of these
sources of law: Parliament and the judiciary. In so doing, we will
discover the central positions occupied within the English legal
system by "statute law" and "judge-made law." There is a further
explanation of international law and the law of the European
Community in Chapter 2.

PARLIAMENT

Parliament creates law but not all the law that is created through
Parliament is of the same kind. There is a need, in particular, to
distinguish between various levels of legislation.

The legislation with which most people are familiar is statute law.
Bills proposed in Parliament become Acts. These Acts may either
be *General or Personal and Local*. Both of these are sometimes
known as *primary legislation.* General Acts apply to everybody,
everywhere within the legal system. In this context it is important
to remember that there are several different legal systems within
the United Kingdom; one for England and Wales, one for Scotland
and one for Northern Ireland. A legal rule in a statute can only be
changed by another statute. Any statute, no matter how important
it seems, can be changed in the same way as any other.

Some Acts apply to all the legal systems; many apply only to one
or two of them. Personal and local Acts apply either to particular

individuals or (more usually) to particular areas. Thus, before divorce was part of the general law, it was possible to get a divorce by Act of Parliament. The most common example of local legislation is that which applies to individual cities. The law in Leicester is sometimes not the same as the law in London. General legislation is much more common than personal and local legislation.

Most legislation consists of a direct statement about how people should behave or indicates the consequences of certain behaviour. For example, a statute may define a crime and say what the punishment will be for that crime. Sometimes Parliament cannot decide exactly what the law should be on a particular point. It may not have the necessary expertise or it may be that the area is one where frequent changes are needed. In such cases Parliament may pass an Act giving somebody else the power to make law in the appropriate area. Such power is often given to government ministers or to local authorities. This is the most common example of what is known as *delegated* or *secondary legislation*. A person or body to whom legislative power is delegated cannot, as can Parliament, make law about anything. The Act (sometimes called *the parent Act*) will determine the area in which law can be made, it may say something about the content of the law, but the details of that law will be left to the person or body to whom legislative power is delegated. They may also have the power to change that law from time to time. Most delegated legislation is published as *a statutory instrument*. Although people are frequently unaware of this type of legislation it is very important, affecting most people's lives. For example, much of the social security system is based on delegated legislation.

The final type of legislation that we have to consider is the range of directives, circulars, and guidance notes produced by various State agencies and bodies such as the Inland Revenue, the DSS and the Department of Employment. Some of these documents bind the people to whom they are addressed to behave in particular ways. Many are not legally binding. They do not compel people in the way that statutes or statutory instruments do. Even so, such documents are often very influential. In practice officials receiving them may always act in the way they indicate. Thus we might consider them all as a form of legislation.

In Chapter 4 you will find an explanation of how to find statutes and statutory instruments and in Chapter 5 an explanation of how you use them to find out where the law stands about something.

LEGISLATION IN PRACTICE

Even if we can find a statute the question still remains, "What will be its effect?". What will happen when somebody acts in a way which is contrary to the statute?

At this stage it is important to appreciate the relationship between the judges and statute law. The judiciary are bound by and, legally, must apply legislation, whether it is primary legislation or secondary legislation. However, an Act or piece of delegated legislation may be unclear or ambiguous. In some cases the difficulty will be resolved by applying one of the general Interpretation Acts. These are Acts which give a definition of words commonly found in legislation. Thus, for example, one Interpretation Act says that where a piece of legislation uses the word "he" this should be taken to mean "he or she" unless it is plain from the context that this should not be so. Some Acts have their own interpretation section, in which certain important words or phrases used in the Act are defined. However, if a difficulty cannot be resolved by such an Act or section; if the ambiguity or lack of clarity remains, it is for the judiciary to decide what the legislation means.

In order to discover the way in which legislation should be applied, the judges have developed a complex network of principles for statutory interpretation, which are designed to assist in the proper application of the law. These principles of statutory interpretation seek, it is said, to combine an interpretation of the natural meaning of the English language used to frame the particular statutory provisions with common-sense meaning and an avoidance of inconsistency. In particular, where primary legislation is involved, it is said that it is not the task of the judges to make law but merely to apply it. Nevertheless, there have been numerous occasions when the judges have been accused of "perverting the true intention" of Parliament. It must be evident that the very process of statutory interpretation always carries with it the risk of divergence between Parliament and the courts in the eventual conclusion reached.

Some of the principles which the judiciary use are very narrow. For example, they might apply only to the meaning of one phrase in a particular type of statute. Others are much broader. Books are written analysing the judicial approach to the interpretation of difficult legislation. At this point it is sufficient for you to know three broad principles. First, judges normally apply the actual words in the legislation not the words the legislator might have intended to use. Secondly, faced with ambiguity, the judges choose the least absurd meaning. Thirdly, when a statute is designed to remedy a problem, the statute will be interpreted in the light of that intent. Plainly these principles will leave many problems unresolved, including that of when to apply one rather than another principle. Leaving aside the difficulties caused in deciding what these principles of interpretation might mean, it is a matter of controversy whether they act as rules deciding what the judges do or provide rationalisations for what the judiciary have already decided.

JUDGE-MADE LAW

Not all legal rules are laid down in an Act of Parliament or some other piece of legislation. A number of fundamental rules are found in the statements of judges made in the course of deciding cases brought before them. A rule made in the course of deciding cases, rather than legislation, is called a rule of *common law*. A common law rule has as much force as a rule derived from statute.

Many important areas of English law, such as contract, tort, crime, land law and constitutional law, have their origins in common law. Some of the earliest common law rules still survive, though many have been supplemented or supplanted by statute. Common law rules are still being made today, though as a source of new legal rules common law is less important than statute. Strictly speaking, the term common law is confined to rules which have been developed entirely by judicial decisions. It excludes new rules made by judges when they interpret statutes. The term *case law* covers both kinds of new rules.

The application of case law is easiest to understand when the issue presently before the court has been raised in some previous analogous case. In such a situation the court will look to see if there is a potential applicable rule in the reports of previously decided cases. Then they will decide whether they have to, or should, apply that rule. It is therefore vital that accurate and comprehensive records be kept of past court decisions and judicial pronouncements. Thus the importance of the numerous and varied series of Law Reports can be appreciated. Anybody entering a law library in England can hardly help being impressed at the volume of materials falling within this category of Law Reports. Row upon row of bound volumes, containing the judgments in thousands of past cases, dominate the holdings of any major English law library.

More information about the various kinds of Law Reports and how to use them can be found in Chapter 4. An explanation of how cases should be read is found in Chapter 5.

Cases are decided in court. Different kinds of legal disputes are decided in different kinds of courts. Sometimes it is possible to bring a legal dispute before two or more different kinds of court. In some situations, once a court has given judgment, it is possible to appeal against that judgment to another court. Some courts only hear appeals.

Not every judgment in every case is of equal importance. The weight which is to be given to them as guidelines for future judicial activity will depend upon two things. One is the level of the court in which that case was decided. In English law there is a principle of a *hierarchy of precedents.* Judgments given by superior courts in the hierarchy are binding on inferior courts.

A brief overview of the court structure seen from this hierarchical view appears below on page 9.

The highest, and thus most important court is the House of Lords. The results of cases heard in the House of Lords and in the Court of Appeal will normally be fully reported in the series of Law Reports as a matter of course. Other courts' judgments will either be reported only when they are considered important by those compiling the reports or, in the case of very lowly courts, will not be reported at all.

Even if a previous case is said to be binding, only some parts of the judgment are important. Lawyers distinguish two parts of a judgment: (a) the *ratio decidendi* and (b) the *obiter dicta.* Put most simply, the *ratio decidendi* is that part of reasoning in the judgment which is necessary in order to determine the law on the issue in the particular case before the judge. It is this which is binding on other courts in the hierarchy. The *obiter dicta,* on the other hand, is a term used to describe the remainder of the judgment. This is not binding but may be *persuasive.* In the absence of a binding *ratio decidendi* the court may be influenced by *obiter dicta.* These two terms are commonly shortened to *ratio* and *obiter.* There is a further discussion of this and other topics at this point in Chapter 5.

Thus, in asking whether a particular judgment is "important" from the point of view of influencing future decisions, and so representing the "state of the law" on any particular matter, we need to consider both its importance in terms of the court which delivered the judgment and whether the *ratio decidendi* of the case is sufficiently clear and relevant to future issues of law arising in later cases. The identification of the *ratio decidendi* is not always an easy matter. There is also great debate amongst academics as to what importance the *obiter dicta* in a previous case may or should have. Some academics, whilst accepting that terms like *ratio* and *obiter* are used in judgments, and whilst accepting that at least some judges think they construct their judgments on the basis of *ratio* and *obiter* in previous judgments, believe that important influences on decisions made by judges are to be found in the nature of matters such as the social background of judges, the economic circumstances of the time or even the very nature of language itself. In some instances there will be no binding precedent applicable to a problem before the court. No court may have been faced with the same issue or the courts which were faced with the issue may have been at the same point or lower in the hierarchy of courts. Even if a court is not bound by a previous judgment it may still consider that judgment to see whether or not it provides a good answer to the problem. The judgment may be persuasive. The importance of the previous case will then depend not simply on its position within the court hierarchy but upon factors such as the identity and experience of the individual judge or the composition of the bench of judges sitting to hear the case, the detail of the legal arguments put before the court, and whether the line laid down in the case has since been adopted by courts deciding subsequent cases.

When looking for the law created and developed by the judges, it will clearly be important to look at reports of cases decided in the higher levels of courts. Nevertheless, it should not be assumed that these are the only important courts. Only a very small proportion of all cases handled in the court system find their way to the Court of Appeal, let alone the House of Lords. The magistrates' courts are very much more important than the House of Lords in terms of the number of cases with which they deal. Nor would it be correct to assume that it is always the "important" cases which work their way through the appeal system, since much of the motivation for bringing an appeal will depend upon financial considerations which are often totally independent of the merits of the dispute in relation to which the case has been brought or the importance or complexity of the law to be applied to that dispute.

The legislature plainly makes new legal rules. Whether or not, in an effort to meet new developments, problems, and shifts in society's values, genuine departures from established rules of common law actually occur, is a matter of debate. The traditional notion is that common law rules do not alter to meet the requirements of society (or "public opinion"); it is the role of the legislator to remedy this through statutory intervention with specific legislation, and not for the judges to create new rules. The legislature makes law, the judiciary merely apply it. However, many academics and some judges would now argue that the judiciary sometimes do more than simply apply existing law; that in looking for rules of law in previous cases the judiciary subtly change the rules, consciously or otherwise, so that they produce the conclusions which they seek. If this is correct the judiciary are, in this sense, just as much legislators as Parliament.

COMMON LAW AND EQUITY

In the section above the term "common law" is used as a synonym for rules of law derived from judicial decisions rather than statute. This is a proper and common usage of the phrase. However another equally frequent sense of the word is as an antonym to "equity." English law has deep historical roots. The opposition of common law and equity refers to the system of rules which originally develop in different courts within the legal system. Common law rules arose first. Later, these rules were seen as being over-formal and concerned too much with the way a case was presented rather than with the justice in the issues at stake. Thus a less strict system of equitable rules was developed. In time, the rules of equity also became formalised. Eventually, the different courts were merged and now all courts can apply both the rules of common law and equity.

CHAPTER 2

Divisions of law

INTRODUCTION

Legal rules can be divided up in many different ways. This chapter introduces some common ways of classifying law. Not all legal rules are of the same type. They show differences in purpose, in origin and form, in the consequences when the rules are breached, and in matters of procedure, remedies and enforcement. The divisions described below are of the broadest kind, chosen to highlight these kinds of differences in legal rules. One kind of division of legal rules has already been introduced, that between statute and case or common law. This division and the others now described overlap. For example, the legal rule defining murder originates in common law, not statute. It is a rule of criminal law rather than civil law; of public law rather than private law and of national law rather than international law.

There are ways other than those discussed here of dividing up the law. One way is to take the legal rules relating to a given topic, grouping them under a title such as "housing law" or "accountancy law." Categorising rules in this way can be very useful: for example, it is not necessary for a personnel manager to know the whole of the general law of contracts before becoming proficient in essential employment law. However, such subject groupings can also be confusing without some understanding of the basic differences between the rules.

CRIMINAL AND CIVIL LAW

One of the most fundamental divisions in law is the division between criminal and civil law. Newcomers to the study of law tend to assume that criminal law occupies the bulk of a lawyer's caseload and of a law student's studies. This is an interesting by-product of the portrayal of the legal system by the media. Criminal law weighs very lightly in terms of volume when measured against non-criminal (civil) law. There are more rules of civil law than there are of criminal law; more court cases involve breach of the civil law than involve breach of the criminal law. Law degree students will find that criminal law is generally only one course out of 12 to 15 subjects in a three-year law degree, although some criminal offences may be referred to in other courses.

Criminal law means the law relating to crime only. Civil law can be taken to mean all the rest. The distinction relies not so much on the nature of the conduct which is the object of a legal rule but in the nature of the proceedings and the sanctions which may follow. Some kinds of conduct give rise to criminal liability, some to civil liability and some to both civil and criminal liability. The seriousness of the conduct does not necessarily determine the type of liability to which it gives rise; conduct which is contrary to the criminal law is not always "worse" than conduct which is against the civil law. Few people would consider every criminal offence a moral wrong (except, perhaps, in the sense that every breach of the law might be thought to be a moral wrong). Equally, some actions which are purely breaches of the civil law might be considered breaches of morality. Nor is harm, in the sense of damage done to individuals, something which is found to a greater degree in the criminal law as against the civil law. The person who parks on a "double-yellow line" breaches the criminal law. The company which fails to pay for the goods that it has bought, thereby bankrupting another company, commits only a breach of the civil law. Who has done the greater harm? Concepts of morality have had some influence on the development of English law but historical accident, political policy and pragmatic considerations have played just as important a part in developing our law.

Some conduct which might be considered "criminal" gives rise only to civil liability or to no liability at all and some conduct which you may consider "harmless' may rise rise to both criminal and civil liability. It will be easier to see that "harm," "morality" and the division between criminal and civil law do not follow any clear pattern if you consider some fictitious examples. In considering them, ask yourself whether or not the conduct described should give rise to any legal liability; if it should, what form should that liability take and what should the legal consequences be which flow from the conduct described? Should any of the people be compensated for the harm done to them and, if so, by whom and for what? Should any of the characters be punished and, if so, for what reason and how? Who should decide whether or not legal proceedings of any variety should be instigated against any of the individuals? The probable legal consequences that follow from each example are found at the end of the chapter. Do not look at these until you have thought about the examples yourself.

Examples

1. Norman drinks 10 pints of beer. He drives his car into a queue at the bus station injuring a young woman and her child.

2. Sue, who is pregnant, lives with Chris. She smokes 50 cigarettes a day. Sue is also carrying on an occasional affair with Richard.

3. Robert agrees to pay Joan, a professional decorator, £500 if she paints his house. She completes the work to a very high standard. Robert, who is a millionaire, refuses to pay her.

Even when a person's actions clearly infringe either the criminal law or civil law, it does not necessarily mean that any actual legal consequences will follow. In criminal and civil cases persons with the legal right to take any legal action have a discretion as to whether or not they initiate legal proceedings. There is a difference between *liability* and *proceedings*. Conduct gives rise to liability. It is for someone else to decide whether or not to take the matter to court by starting proceedings.

In criminal proceedings *a prosecutor* prosecutes *the defendant*. The case is heard in the magistrates' court or the Crown Court, depending on the seriousness of the offence. The prosecutor will have to prove to the court, *beyond all reasonable doubt*, that the defendant committed the offence charged. The court will have to determine whether or not the defendant is guilty. In the magistrates' court it will be for the magistrates to determine this question, in the Crown Court it will be for the jury to decide questions of fact and for the judge to decide questions of law. A finding of "not guilty" will lead to the defendant's acquittal. A finding of "guilty" will lead to a conviction and may lead to a sentence of imprisonment or some other form of punishment such as a fine or probation.

One of the major objectives of the criminal law is to punish the wrongdoer for action which is deemed to be contrary to the interests of the state and its citizens. Criminal proceedings do not have as a major objective the provision of compensation or support for the victim of crime. It is significant that the exercise of the discretion to prosecute is seldom carried out by the victim of the crime.

Criminal proceedings are normally initiated by the state or its agents and brought in the name of the Queen or the prosecuting official.

In civil proceedings it is generally *the plaintiff* (the party harmed) who sues *the defendant*, although in some areas of the civil law other terms are used. For example, in the case of a divorce *the petitioner* sues the respondent. The case will usually be heard in either the county court or the High Court, depending on the nature of the case and the size of the loss involved. The plaintiff usually has to prove, *on the balance of probabilities*, that the events took place in the manner claimed. This is a lower standard of proof than in criminal cases. If the plaintiff proves their case, the court will make some kind of order. What this will be, will depend upon the kind of case and what the plaintiff has asked for. The basic choice before the court is whether to order the defendant to compensate the plaintiff for their loss by awarding damages, or to order the defendant to act, or refrain from acting, in some specific way in the future, or to make both kinds of orders.

The function of civil law is to provide individuals with remedies which are enforceable in the courts where they have suffered a wrong which is recognised by a statute or decided cases. The civil law creates a framework which delineates the rights and obligations of individuals in their dealings with one another. It is primarily founded on the law of contract and tort, which are mainly areas of common law. The law of contract determines which forms of agreement entered into between individuals are legally binding and on whom they will be binding. The law of tort covers categories of civil wrong, other than breach of contract, which may give rise to legal causes of action. It includes the law of negligence, trespass and libel and slander. Just as a set of facts can give rise to conduct which may result in both civil and criminal proceedings, so a set of facts can give rise to actions in contract and in tort. Most plaintiff's primary motivation for bringing civil proceedings will be to obtain an effective remedy for the civil wrong which has been perpetrated. The fact that there is liability will not necessarily mean that they will take action. For example, there may be no point in suing a person for damages if you know they have no money.

The emphasis of the civil law has changed over the last hundred years with an increase in the role of the state and the importance of legislation as opposed to case law as the major source of law. Civil law does not just regulate relations between individuals covering such matters as their property transactions, but also deals with relations between the state and individuals. It covers unemployment and social benefit entitlement, tax and planning questions, and council tenants' relationships with their local authorities. All of these areas are covered by statute law which has created new rights and obligations. These are often enforced in tribunals as opposed to courts.

Statutory provisions have also been enacted in order to minimise the common law rights which have resulted from the judicial development of contract law and the notion of freedom of contract. For example, employment protection and landlord and tenant legislation give employees and tenants statutory rights which will often modify or override terms in their contracts which give their employers or landlords specific rights to dismiss or evict them.

NATIONAL, INTERNATIONAL AND EUROPEAN COMMUNITY LAW

The term "national" or "municipal" law is used to mean the internal legal rules of a particular country, in contrast to international law which deals with the external relationships of a state with other states. In the United Kingdom, national law is normally unaffected by international legal obligations unless these obligations have been transferred into national law by an Act of Parliament. European Community law, however, cuts across this conventional notion that national and international law operate at different and distinct levels. It is a form of international law in that it is in part concerned with legal relations between Member States, but European Community law may also directly affect the national law of Member States. It will therefore be considered separately from both national and international law.

National law

The system of national law has already been considered in Chapter 1.

International law

Public international law regulates the external relations of states with one another. It is a form of law very different from national law. There is no world government or legislature issuing and enforcing laws to which all nations are subject. The international legal order is essentially decentralised and operates by agreement between states. This means that the creation, interpretation and enforcement of international law lies primarily in the hands of states themselves. Its scope and effectiveness depends on the capacity of states to agree and the sense of mutual benefit and obligation involved in adhering to the rules.

International law is created in two main ways: by treaty and by custom. Treaties are agreements between two or more states, and are binding on the states involved if they have given their consent to be so bound. Customary law is established by showing that states have adopted broadly consistent practices towards a particular matter and that they have acted in this way out of a sense of legal obligation. International law is neither comprehensive nor systematic. Few treaties or customary rules involve the majority of world states. Most are bilateral understandings or involve only a handful of parties to a multilateral agreement.

Disputes about the scope and interpretation of international law are rarely resolved by the use of international courts or binding arbitration procedures of an international organisation. This is because submission to an international court or similar process is entirely voluntary and few states are likely to agree to this if there is a serious risk of losing their case of where important political or national interests are at stake. Negotiation is far more common. International courts are used occasionally, for example where settlement is urgent, or protracted negotiations have failed, where the dispute is minor or is affecting other international relations; in other words, in cases where failure to settle is more damaging than an unfavourable outcome. Where international law has been breached, an injured state must rely primarily on self-help for enforcement. There is no effective international institutional machinery to ensure compliance when the law is challenged. This means that in practice powerful states are better able to protect their rights and assert new claims.

Breaching established rules is one, rather clumsy, way of changing international law. In a decentralised system, change can only be effected by common consent or by the assertion of a new claim being met by inaction or acquiescence by others. The lack of powerful enforcement machinery does not mean that international law is widely disregarded. On the contrary, legal rules are regularly followed, not least because states require security and predictability in the conduct of normal everyday inter-state relations.

International law also plays an important role in the promotion of common interests such as controlling pollution, restricting overfishing, or establishing satellite and telecommunication link-ups.

A large number of global or regional international organisations have been established for the regulation and review of current inter-state activity. The best-known example, though perhaps not the most effective, is the United States, whose primary function is the maintenance of international peace and security.

In the United Kingdom, international law has no direct effect on national law and, on a given matter, national law may in fact be inconsistent with the United Kingdom's international obligations. The Government has authority to enter into treaties which may bind the United Kingdom *vis-a-vis* other states. However a treaty will not alter the law to be applied within the United Kingdom unless the provisions are adopted by means of an Act of Parliament. Customary international law may have been incorporated into national law but will enjoy no higher status than any other provision of national law and is, therefore, liable to be superseded by statute. However, it is a principle of judicial interpretation that, unless there is clear legal authority to the contrary, Parliament does not intend to act in breach of international law. In some other countries, international law is accorded a different status. In Holland and West Germany, for example, international law takes effect in municipal law and where these conflict international law prevails.

The lack of direct application should not be taken to mean that international law is of no importance in United Kingdom courts or for United Kingdom citizens. National courts regularly decide domestic cases having presumed the existence and application of international law. For example, under the Vienna Convention of 1961, diplomats enjoy immunity from criminal prosecution. If a defendant claims immunity, a court must decide whether the defend-ant falls within the terms of the treaty before proceeding further. Secondly, individuals may have rights under international law, enforceable not through national courts but through international institutions. The European Convention on Human Rights gives individuals the right to complain of breaches of the Convention to the European Commission on Human Rights which may then refer the case to the European Court of Human Rights. (These institutions should not be confused with EEC bodies: they are quite separate.) Although the United Kingdom ratified the Convention in 1951, it was only in 1966 that the United Kingdom agreed to the articles of the treaty which recognised the right of individual petition and the compulsory jurisdiction of the Court.

European Community law

In joining the European Communities in 1973, the United Kingdom agreed to apply and be bound by Community law, accepting that Community law would override any conflicting provisions of national law. Unlike other forms of international law, European Community law is capable of passing directly into national law; it is applicable in the United Kingdom without being adopted by an Act of Parliament. These principles were given legal effect by the passage of the European Communities Act 1972. The European Communities are made up of three organisations: the European Economic Community (EEC), the European Coal and Steel Community (ECSC) and the European Community for Atomic Energy (Euratom). This section will concentrate on the implications of membership of the European Community for United Kingdom law.

The European Community is an international organisation established and developed by treaty between Member States. The basic framework is set out in the EEC Treaty of 1957 ("Treaty of Rome"), which defines the objectives of the Community, the powers and duties of Community institutions, and the rights and obligations of Member States. This treaty goes much further than just creating law which binds both Member States and Community institutions. It contains many detailed substantive provisions, some of which create rights for individuals which are enforceable directly in national courts. The EEC Treaty, and certain others which have followed it, are thus primary sources of Community law.

The EEC has four major institutions: the Council of Ministers, the Commission, the Assembly (or European Parliament) and the Court of Justice. The terms of the various treaties give the EEC a powerful legislative, administrative and judicial machinery. The Treaty provides that further legislation may be made by the Council of Ministers and the Commission. This is called secondary legislation and takes three forms.

Regulations, once made, pass into the law of a Member State automatically. Regulations are "directly applicable," which means that Member States do not have to take any action (such as passing an Act of Parliament) to implement them or to incorporate them into national law. Regulations are intended to be applied uniformly throughout the Community, and override any conflicting provisions in national law.

Directives are binding on Member States as to the result to be achieved, but leave each Member State with a choice about the method used to achieve that result. Member States are given a transitional period in which to implement the directive. This may involve passing a new law, making new administrative arrangements, or, where national law already conforms with the directive, taking no action. The Commission can initiate proceedings against a Member State if it believes the steps taken do not achieve the desired result. Although directives are addressed to Member States, in some circumstances an individual may be able to rely directly on certain parts, whether or not the Member State has taken implementing action. This is when the relevant part lays down an unconditional obligation and grants enforceable individual rights.

Decisions can be addressed to Member States, individuals or companies. They are binding only on the person to whom they are addressed and take effect on notification.

Community law is applied in Member States by their system of national courts and tribunals. When a point of Community law is crucial to a court's decision, the court may refer the case to the Court of Justice for a preliminary ruling on the interpretation of the point in question. Courts against whose decision there is no appeal, (e.g., the House of Lords) must make a reference to the Court of Justice when the case hinges on European Community law unless the Court has already ruled on that particular issue. Once the Court of Justice has given a preliminary ruling, the case is referred back to the national court from which it originated, which must then decide the case. The Court of Justice will only answer questions put to it about the interpretation of European Community law; it will not rule on national law or on conflict between national and European Community law or apply its interpretation to the facts of the case. These are all matters for national courts. The Commission may bring an action in the Court of Justice against a Member State for breach of a Community obligation, such as the non-implementation of a directive. Proceedings may be taken against the Commission or the Council for failing to act where the EEC Treaty imposes a duty to act. There are also provisions for annulling legislation adopted by the Commission or Council, for example, where the action has exceeded the powers laid down by treaty.

PUBLIC AND PRIVATE LAW

Another distinction that may be drawn between different types of law is the division between "public" law and "private" law. Public law is concerned with the distribution and exercise of power by the state and the legal relations between the state and the individual. For example, the rules governing the powers and duties of local authorities, the operation of the National Health Service, the regulations of building standards, the issuing of passports and the compulsory purchase of land to build a motorway all fall within the ambit of public law. In contrast, private law is concerned with the legal relationships between individuals, such as the liability of employers towards their employees for injuries sustained at work, consumers' rights against shopkeepers and manufacturers over faulty goods, or owners' rights to prevent others walking across their land. The division of law into public and private law and civil and criminal law are two clear examples of categories which overlap. Thus, for example, some public law is civil and some is criminal.

The significance of the public/private law distinction operates at two levels. First, it is a very useful general classification through which we can highlight some broad differences, such as those in the purpose of law, in sources and forms of legal rules, and in remedies and enforcement. This is the way the idea of public/private law will be discussed here. However, the distinction is also used in a second, narrower sense; as a way of defining the procedure by which claims can be raised in court.

One way of thinking about a legal rule is to consider its purpose. The primary purpose underlying most private law rules is the protection of individual interests, whereas the aim of most public law provisions is the promotion of social objectives and the protection of collective rather than individual interests. The methods used to achieve these purposes also differ. A characteristic feature of public law is the creation of a public body with special powers of investigation, decision-making and/or enforcement in relation to a particular problem, whereas private law achieves its ends by giving individuals the right to take action in defence of their interests.

Many problems are addressed by both public and private law. Sometimes a single statute may include both private rights and liabilities alongside public law provisions. This can be seen both by looking at statutes characteristic of public law and by looking at an example in practice.

The Equal Pay Act and the Sex Discrimination Act both came into force in 1975. These Acts made it unlawful to discriminate on the grounds of sex in many important areas such as employment, education and housing. For the individual who had suffered discrimination, the Acts created new private rights to take complaints to industrial tribunals or county courts and claim compensation or other appropriate remedies. At the same time, the Equal Opportunities Commission was set up, with public powers and duties to investigate matters of sex discrimination and promote equal opportunities.

Example

Ann lives next door to an industrial workshop run by Brenda. The machinery is very noisy and the process discharges fumes which make Ann feel ill. This sort of problem is tackled by both public and private law in a number of different ways.

(i) As a neighbour, Ann may bring a private law action in nuisance, which is a claim that Brenda's activities unreasonably interfere with the use of Ann's land. Ann could claim compensation for the hard she has suffered and could seek an injunction to stop the harmful process continuing.

(ii) There are also public law rules which may be invoked whether or not an individual has or may be harmed, aimed at preventing the problem arising in the first place or controlling the situation for the public benefit. For example, when Brenda first started her workshop she would have needed to get planning permission from the local authority if her activities constituted a change in the use of the land. Planning legislation thus gives the local authority an opportunity to prevent industrial development in residential areas by refusing planning permission, or control it by laying down conditions. Other legislation gives the local authority powers to monitor and control various kinds of pollution and nuisances in their area, including noise and dangerous fumes. A further complex set of private rights and public regulations govern the working conditions of the workshop employees, who would also be affected by the noise and smells.

Public and private law also show differences in their origins and form. Some of the most important principles of private law are of ancient origin and were developed through the common law as individuals took their private disputes to court and demanded a remedy. The rules of private rights in contract, over land and inheritance, to compensation for physical injury or damage to property or reputation, were all first fashioned by judges in the course of deciding cases brought before them.

In contrast, most public law rules are of comparatively recent origin first originating in stature, not judicial decisions. There are obvious exceptions. Criminal law and the criminal justice system itself are prime examples where standards of behaviour are set by the state and enforced by a network of public officials with powers of arrest, prosecution, trial and punishment. Much of the early development of this field of public law lies in common law. An important function of public law has its roots in constitutional theory. The actions of public bodies are only lawful if there is a legal rule granting the body authority to act in a given situation. A private individual needs no legal authority merely to act. It is assumed that a person acts lawfully unless there is a legal rule prohibiting or curtailing that behaviour. Public law therefore has a facilitative function, for which there is no equivalent in private law, permitting a public body to take action that would otherwise be unlawful. A feature of much recent public law is a shift towards the grant of broad discretionary powers to public bodies. This means that the same legislative framework can be used more flexibly, accommodating changes in public policy as to the purposes to which the powers should be put or the criteria for the exercise of these powers. This characteristic form of modern public law contrasts quite sharply with the relatively specific rights and duties to be found in private law, and in turn affects the way public and private law can be enforced. All private law is enforced by granting individuals the right to take action in defence of a recognised personal interest. For example, a householder may make a contract with a builder over the repair of a roof, and may sue the builder if the work or materials are of a lower standard than was specified in the contract. Not all public law can be enforced by way of individual action. The enforcement of public law can be viewed from two perspectives.

First, public law can be enforced as when as official ensures that individuals or companies comply with standards set in statutes or delegated legislation, e.g. public health officials making orders in relation to or prosecuting restaurants. Secondly, the enforcement of public law can also be seen as the matter of ensuring public authorities themselves carry out their duties and do not exceed their legal powers. Here, the form of public law statutes, mentioned above, rarely ties a public body to supplying a particular standard of service, as a contract may tie a builder, but gives a wide choice of lawful behaviour.

Even where legislation lays a duty on a public authority, there may be no corresponding right of individual action. For example, under the Education Act 1944, local education authorities are under a duty to ensure that there are sufficient schools, in numbers, character and equipment, for providing educational opportunities for all pupils in their area. However, nobody can sue the authority if the schools are overcrowded or badly equipped. The only remedy is to complain to the Secretary of State, who can make orders if satisfied that the authority is in default of their duties. The mechanism for controlling standards of public bodies is generally by way of political accountability to the electorate or ministers rather than the legal process.

Some parts of public law do create individual rights and permit individual enforcement. In social security legislation, for example, qualified claimants have a right to certain benefits and may appeal against decisions of benefit to a tribunal. There is a procedure, special to public law, called "judicial review of administrative action" (often referred to simply as *judicial review*), whereby an individual may go to the High Court alleging unlawful behaviour on the part of a public body. However, in order to go to court, the individual must show "sufficient interest" in the issue in question (this being legally defined) and the court has a discretion whether to hear the case or grant a remedy. This is quite different from proceedings in private law, where a plaintiff does not need the court's permission for the case to be heard but has a right to a hearing if a recognised cause of action is asserted and also a right to a remedy of some kind if successful.

CRIMINAL LAW AND CIVIL LAW

Legal consequences in questions 1–3:

1. Norman's actions may give rise to both criminal and civil proceedings. He may be prosecuted for drink driving and related road traffic offences and, if convicted, will have a criminal record. All road traffic offences, including parking offences, are just as much part of the criminal law as murder is. He may also be sued by the woman or child who would wish to recover damages for the personal injuries they have suffered. Such an action would be a civil action. The same set of facts may give rise to both criminal and civil liability.

2. Sue has committed no criminal offence. Neither the unborn child nor Richard have any right of civil action for any harm they may consider Sue has done to them.

3. Robert has not committed any criminal offence. He is in no different a position in law to the person who has no money. Joan will be able to commence civil proceedings against him. She will be able to sue him for breach of contract. Robert's wealth makes it more likely that Joan will consider it worth suing him as she is more likely to be able to recover any damages. However she will also have

to remember that Robert will, if he wishes be able to hire the best lawyers so as to delay Joan's inevitable court victory.

CHAPTER 3

Law in action/Law in books

INTRODUCTION

This chapter is about the different kinds of questions that arise when studying law and the different techniques you need when studying them. You might think that studying law is purely a matter of learning a large number of legal rules. If this were the case only one kind of question would ever arise—what is the content of any particular legal rule? However, simply learning a large number of legal rules is not always a very useful way of learning about law. Learning the rules is like memorising the answers to a set of sums. It is of no help when the sums change. If all you do is learn a set of legal rules, when the rules change, when the law is altered, you are back where you started. At the very least, to use your legal knowledge, you also need to know how to find legal rules and how to find out if they have been changed. Thus, to the question "what is the content of the legal rule?" are added questions about how to find them.

Not everyone interested in law is interested in questions about the content of legal rules. For example, we might ask whether it is ever right to disobey the law. This is a question of ethics which might in part relate to the content of a legal rule but is much more about the nature of moral judgement. Equally questions about how the legal system works in practice are only partially concerned with the content of legal rules. Legal rules are about what should happen. Questions about practice are concerned with what does happen.

The various questions above are not merely different questions, they are different kinds of questions. Because they are questions about different things and because the different questions demand different techniques to answer them they are often put into separate categories. The terms for these categories vary. Some terms are more precise than others. We have taken one commonly drawn distinction, that between the law in action and the law in books, as the title for this chapter. This is because the distinction is a very basic one that can be applied to most areas of law. The law in action is that which actually happens in the legal system and is concerned with people's behaviour. The law in books is the system of legal rules which can be deduced from reading cases and statutes. A question about how defendants are treated in court is a question about the law in action. A question about the definition of theft in English law is a question about the law in books.

Although the distinction between the law in action and the law in books is both easy to see and useful to use it is also limited. Some questions about law seem to fit into neither category. For example, is our earlier question about disobedience to law a question about the law in action or the law in books? Information about that actually happens in the legal system will only tell us what people do, not whether their action is morally correct. Equally, being told what the legal rule says is of little help in helping us assess whether we are correct to obey it or not. The question does not appear to fall into either category.

The distinction between the law in action and the law in books is broad but crude. More sophisticated categories provide narrower, more precise distinctions. Thus questions about the nature of law, which can include whether or not one has a duty to obey it, can be grouped together under the title the philosophy of law. Such categories are not firmly fixed and may be defined by different people in different ways. Thus some people would use the term the sociology of law to refer to all questions about the operation of the legal system in practice. Others would distinguish between questions about the relationship between law and other social forces and questions about how effective a legal rule is. They would see the first kind of question as falling within the sociology of law and the second as coming under the heading socio-legal studies. It is more important to be able to identify the different kinds of questions than give them the labels.

DIFFERENT QUESTIONS MEAN DIFFERENT ANSWERS

Knowing that there are different kinds of questions asked when studying law is of intellectual interest but does it have any further significance? What happens if you fail properly to identify the kind of question that you are asking? We can answer these questions by looking at one way in which different kinds of questions are commonly confused.

For many years it was assumed that legal rules which laid down what should happen were an accurate guide to what actually happened. The law in action was thought to be a reflection of the law in books. It was accepted that there were divergencies but these were thought to be on a small scale and of no importance. However, academics have now shown that there is often a very great difference between legal rules and the practice in the legal system. One example of this can be seen in the area of criminal law when people are being prosecuted.

In the United States it is common practice for a prosecutor to agree to drop some criminal charges in return for a guilty plea from the defendant in respect of others. The defendant benefits because those charges are lesser ones, attracting a lower sentence. The prosecution benefits because the trial takes less time and money is saved. This is the practice known as plea-bargaining. In Great Britain the Court of Appeal has said that the defendant should not be subject to any pressure to plead guilty to a charge by being offered a lower sentence in return for that plea. In particular the Court of Appeal has said, a judge should never indicate a willingness to give a lesser kind of sentence (for example a fine instead of a prison sentence) in return for a guilty plea. The existence of these rules which were intended to prevent plea-bargaining, led many people to assume either that plea-bargaining did not exist in Great Britain or that it was very rare. However, when researchers enquired into this area, questioning defendants and looking at court records, they produced evidence which they thought showed that various forms of plea-bargaining were common in the court they studied.

The difference between the law in action and the law in books in this area is important for several reasons. First, confusing the different kinds of questions resulted in an inaccurate description. People accepted the wrong kind of material as evidence for their answers. Secondly, because of that misdescription, those involved in advising others on the law may have given misleading advice. Finally, those involved in considering whether or not the law and legal system are effective and just looked not at the real legal system but at a shadowy reflection of it.

WHICH KIND OF QUESTION AM I ASKING?

Somebody has been divorced and you are asked how their financial affairs will be settled by the courts. Are you being asked what the relevant rules are, or what will actually happen in court, or both?

Outside your course of study it may be very difficult to sort out what kind of question you are being asked. For study purposes the task will generally be simpler. The kind of question that you are being asked is likely to be indicated by the nature of your course as a while. The title of your course may give you a clue. A course on "the sociology of law" is unlikely to be much concerned with questions about the content of legal rules. Some kinds of courses are more usually taught with one kind of question in mind than another. For example, courses on "land law" or the "law of contract" are more often concerned with the law in books than the law in action. These kinds of courses are sometimes termed black-letter law courses.

Even when it is clear what kind of question your course is generally concerned with problems may still arise. It is not only important to know the kind of question that you are interested in. You must also be able to identify the kind of question that the author of a book or article which you are using is interested in. If you know the type of answer they are trying to give you will be in a better position to judge the quality of their argument and, thus the value of their work. Even when you have identified the kind of question an author is most interested in you will also have to be careful to see that other kinds of question are not introduced. For example, it is not uncommon to find a book largely devoted to discussion of the content of legal rules also including a few remarks on the value or justice of those rules. There is nothing wrong with this if the author realises that a different kind of question is being addressed and uses the appropriate material to answer it. Unfortunately this is not always so.

ARE THERE REALLY DIFFERENT QUESTIONS?

There are some people who would argue that it is misleading to distinguish between different questions in the way we have done above. Some would argue that all the distinctions drawn are wrong. Others would argue that only some of them are invalid.

One argument that might be advanced is about the distinction between the law in action and the law in books. In our earlier example we saw that there was a difference between the legal rule laid down in the Court of Appeal and the actual practice studied. If we assume that the practice of all courts was the same as the court studied, and if this practice continued for many years, what would it mean to say that the legal rule was that which was laid down by the Court of Appeal? People would only be affected by what happened in practice which would always be different from that which the legal rules said should happen. Could we really say that the legal rule had any significance? If the legal rule has no significance, then surely all we ought to study is what happens in practice, ignoring questions about the law in books?

Other more complicated forms of the above argument exist. Some people would argue that when a judge makes a decision that decision is influenced by the judge's social background, political views and education. The result of any case is therefore not solely determined by the neutral application of legal rules but by factors personal to the particular judge in the case. If this is so, then what kinds of questions will discussion about the content of legal rules answer? If we are to advise people how to act so as to win cases in court what we need to discuss is not, or not only, the content of legal rules but, rather, who are the judges and what their background is. If we want to find out what the law is we have to ask a whole series of questions other than those about ratios or statutes.

In a similar fashion not everyone accepts that questions about the morality of law and questions about the content of law are different. For these people, the very idea of an immoral law, which is a law that, because it is immoral, should not be obeyed, is a contradiction in terms. They think that all law must have an irreducible minimum moral content. Without that content the "law," in their view, is merely a collection of words that make a command which may be backed by the physical power of the state but do not have the authority of law.

The authors of this book would accept that the distinctions drawn in previous sections are open to question. The relationship between the different questions, if there are different questions, may be more complicated than the simple divisions above. However most books and most courses in law draw the kinds of distinction outlined. At this early stage in your study of law it will be enough if you understand them. Even if later you come to reject all or some of them, you will still find yourself reading material which is based upon them.

ANSWERING QUESTIONS

This chapter has drawn a distinction between three types of question; those concerned with the nature of law, those concerned with the content of legal rules and those which address the operation of law and legal system in practice. Each type of question has a technique appropriate for answering it.

Questions about the nature of law are those which are most difficult to answer. The questions are basic ones, appearing to be very simple. For example, how is law different from other types of command? What is the difference between a gunman telling me to do something and the state, through law, telling me to do something? Are both simply applications of power or is there something fundamentally different between them? Neither the content of particular legal rules nor the operation of the law in practice provide any answer. Arguments in this area are abstract. In advancing and judging such arguments it is necessary to see that all the terms are explained and that the argument is coherent. They must also match the world they purport to explain. In practice these simple conditions are very difficult to meet.

The ultimate source for answers to questions about the law in books is the law reports and statutes which have already been discussed in Chapter 1. Only these sources will give you a definitive answer to any question you are asked. You are told how to find these materials in Chapter 4 and how to use them in Chapter 5. In some cases you may not have either the time or the resources to consult original materials. In such instance you can look at some of the various commentaries on the law. These vary in size, depth of coverage and price. Different commentaries serve different purposes. Some are student texts. Others are written for specific professions or occupations. Most cover only a limited area of law. However there are some general guides to the law and some encyclopedias of law. The best encyclopedia of general English law is Halsbury's Laws of England. This has a section on almost every area of law. Most good reference libraries will have a copy of this. All commentaries try to explain legal rules. You should select one suitable to your interests. Always remember that a commentary is one person's opinion about the law. It may be wrong. You can only be sure what the rule is if you consult the original cases and statutes.

Finding out how the law works in practice is frequently much more difficult than deciding what a legal rule means. It is easy to find opinions about how things work. Almost everybody who has contact with the law, even if only through reading about it in the newspapers, has an opinion on such questions. However, such opinions have little value. At best they are the experience of one person. That experience may be unusual or misinterpreted by that person. What we are trying to understand is how the legal system works, not the anecdotes of one person. Thus, to answer this kind of question, we need to turn to the materials and techniques of the social scientist.

SEEING THE LAW IN ACTION

One obvious source of detailed information about the legal system
is statistical analyses. "You can prove anything with statistics" is
a hostile comment suggesting that nothing at all can be proved
with statistics. However, is this so? What use are statistics to anyone
studying law?

Information about the number of cases handled by a court shows
in specific terms what the court's workload is, Changes from year
to year may indicate some effects of changes in the law and practice.
Statistics here can be used descriptively to provide a clearer picture
than general phrases such as "some," "many" or "a few." Statistical
tests can establish that there is a relationship, a correlation, between
different things. For example, the length of a sentence for theft
may correlate with the value of the items stolen or the experience
of the judge who heard the case. This means that the sentence will
be longer if, for example, more items are stolen or the judge is
more experienced. Statisticians have produced tests to show
whether, given the number of examples you have, there is a
strong correlation or not. Where this correlation fits with a theory
(sometimes termed a hypothesis) it provides evidence tending to
confirm the theory. Such confirmation is important; without it we
have little to establish the effect the law has, being forced to rely
on personal knowledge of individual instances of its application
and having to assume that these have general truth. Empirical
study of the operation of law may reveal areas for improvement.
It can also confirm that measured by particular standards, the court
are working well.

If we want to use statistics where will we get them from? Government departments collect and print a large number of statistics
relating to their operations. A comprehensive index to these, the
Guide to Official Statistics, is published by the Central Statistical
Office. Some of these official statistics provide background information for the study of the operation of law. Thus the Office of
Population Censuses and Surveys (OPCS) publishes details of
the size, composition and distribution of the United Kingdom
population. This information is essential if one is to be sure
that other changes do not merely reflect population changes. The
Department of Social Security provides figures for the number of
social security claimants and also the number of children in the
care of local authorities. Details of use and expenditure on the
Legal Aid scheme come from the Legal Aid Advisory Committee
reports. The Home Office produces the annual criminal statistics
as well as information about the police forces and immigration.

The Lord Chancellor's Department produces the civil judicial statistics which contain figures for the work of the civil and all appellate courts. Most official statistics are collected from returns filed by local offices of the relevant departments. The content of these is determined by what the department needs to know about its activities and also by what Parliament has asked it to report on. Even minor changes in the collection of official statistics means that it is often impossible to make comparisons over a period of years. The information collected in one year is about something slightly different from that in other years. Moreover, because of the way in which information is collected and the purpose of collecting it, these statistics can only answer a few of the questions about the way the law operates. For example, the judicial statistics list the number of cases brought each year in the County Court, broken down according to the type of claim. They provide little or no information about the applicants, the specific point of law relied on or whether the judgment was successfully enforced.

Official statistics, as a source of information, are limited. They provide information about things of importance to those who collected them. These are not necessarily the things which are important to the researcher. Government departments, the research councils and some private bodies sponsor research into specific areas of law. Small scale research is often undertaken without sponsorship. Although this research may be based upon official statistics it may involve first collecting the necessary statistics and then deciding what they mean. The researchers must collect the data they need for each project. They have to design the study, that is to select the methods they will use and choose the sample to ensure that they have all the information relevant to their chosen topic. There is a more detailed discussion of some of these issues in Chapter 6, "Reading Research Materials."

Researchers will not necessarily be concerned solely with statistics. This is only one way of describing law and the legal system. Statistics are useful for describing things like the number of events but are poor for describing things like motivations. This researchers will also have to decide whether they want to interview people or even directly observe what is happening in the area in which they are interested. In each case they must decide how they can do this so as to ensure that the material they collect is an accurate reflection of the world as a whole.

Whatever kind of question you are dealing with it is important that you decide what the answer is. Merely being able to repeat a passage from a book on legal philosophy, a paragraph from a

PART 2

CHAPTER 4

Finding cases and statutes

In Chapter 1 the importance of cases and statutes as sources of law was explained. This chapter explains how you find reports of cases and copies of statutes and how you make sure that they are up-to-date. As has been explained, these materials are sources of law. From them it is possible to derive the legal rules in which you are interested. Chapter 5 will explain in more detail how this is done.

FINDING CASES

In the following, the task of discovering case reports will be considered for three different sets of circumstances:

(a) Where a well-stocked and supported law library is available.

(b) Where some research or library facilities are available, but without access to a fully-equipped law library.

(c) With the aid of on-line computerised retrieval facilities.

Most readers will have different facilities available at different times. For example, a reader who has access to a fully-equipped law library can only use it during opening hours. Equally, even if computer facilities are available it may not always be appropriate to use them. It is important that you are aware of the different ways in which to find cases so that you can decide which is the best method to use at any particular time.

USING FULL LAW LIBRARY NON-ELECTRONIC RESEARCH FACILITIES

The traditional, and still the most comprehensive, form of research in relation to law reports is performed in law libraries containing a wide selection of materials and a variety of support systems, indexes, catalogues, etc., designed to assist the researcher in the task of locating and using particular items. Such libraries are found in academic institutions, such as Universities, as well as in professional institutions such as the Inns of Court. In many cases, it is possible to use such libraries even if you are not a member of the institution.

What follows in this chapter is an attempt to introduce the reader to the major series of law reports, and to indicate basic methods of locating and checking up-to-date material and of up-dating earlier materials. A helpful guide for those interested in more sophisticated use of the whole range of facilities made available in major law libraries is to be found in *How to Use a Law Library*, by J. Dane and P. Thomas. In particular, that work contains detailed explanations of how to use the various indexes and catalogues available in such libraries, and thus provides a more comprehensive guide on the "mechanics" of locating and using legal materials than is offered here.

Law reports go back over 700 years, although most of the case reports you will find in a normal law library have been decided during the last 150 years. Reports are divided into different series. These series do not necessarily reflect any systematic attempt to present the reports of decided cases. (e.g. by subject-matter covered), but tend, instead, to indicate the commercial means by which such reports have been made available. Thus, older cases can be found in series which bear the title of the name (or names) of the law reporter(s). Such a series is the nineteenth century series of Barnewall and Alderson (Bar & Ald). (All law reports have abbreviations which are customarily used when discussing them. Whenever a series is first mentioned here its usual abbreviation will be given, in brackets, as above. Appendix II to this book is a list of useful abbreviations, including those to the main law reports.) The only necessary coherence these cases have is that the reporter thought it was worthwhile to print them. The range and variety of these older cases is enormous, although some help has now been provided to modern legal researchers with some of the old series reprinted in a new collection under the title of *The English Reports* (E.R.).

In 1865, the Incorporated Council of Law Reporting introduced *The Law Reports*, a series which was divided according to the different courts of the day. The Council has continued the current divisions of the reports, are different. Today one can find the following divisions:

(a) Appeal Cases (A.C.)—reports of cases in the Court of Appeal, the House of Lords and the Privy Council.
(b) Chancery Division (Ch.)—report of cases in the Chancery Division of the High Court and cases appealed from there to the Court of Appeal.
(c) Queen's Bench (Q.B.)—reports of cases in the Queen's Bench Division of the High Court and cases appealed from there to the Court of Appeal.
(d) Family Division (Fam.)—reports of cases in the Family Division of the High Court and cases appealed from there to the Court of Appeal. (Until 1972 the Family Division was the Probate, Divorce and Admiralty Division (P.).)

This series is the closest to an "official" series of case reports. If a case is reported in several different series and there is a discrepancy between the different reports it is *The Law Reports* which should normally be followed.

There is, nowadays, a wide range of privately-published law reports. Most of these series concentrate upon a particular area of legal developments, (e.g., the law relating to industrial relations, or the law concerning road traffic). However, there are two series which publish cases dealing with decisions affecting a wide range of legal issues. These general series, with which most students of law will quickly become familiar, are the *Weekly Law Reports* (W.L.R.) and the *All England Law Reports* (All E.R.).

Each of the series above reports fully any case contained in its volumes. There are, in addition, some sources which provide a short summary of, or extracts from, judgments given. In addition to these general series, it is possible to find short reports of case developments in a variety of sources. The most up-to-date of these sources are those newspapers which print law reports. Most of the quality daily newspapers contain law reports as well as news items on matters of legal interest. *The Times* has contained such reports for the longest time and is regarded as being the most authoritative source of such reports. Case-note sections published in legal periodicals, such as the *New Law Journal* (N.L.J.) or the *Solicitors' Journal* (S.J. or Sol. Jo.), are also a good source of such summaries.

There have always been specialist series of reports concerned either with one area of law or one type of occupation. In recent years, the numbers of such series has increased. If your interest is not in law as a whole but in particular areas of law, one of these series of reports may be a valuable tool. Indeed, sometimes such series are the only source for a report of a particular case. However, such series should be used with caution. First, these reports may not be as accurate as the series discussed above. Secondly, they represent not reports of the law but reports of such law as the publishers of the series think important. Their greater selectivity may be useful in giving you a guide as to what is important, but dangerous if you think cases not reported in the series must be irrelevant. Helpful lists of such reports can be found in law dictionaries.

USING LAW REPORTS

Every case which is reported in a series of law reports can be referred to by way of the names of the parties concerned in the action. Thus, where a court action is brought by somebody called Harriman in dispute with somebody called Martin, the case may be referred to as *Harriman v. Martin*. However referring to a case in this way is of limited usefulness. The reference does not tell the reader the date of the case nor does it indicate the series of reports in which it is found. It does not even tell us to which case involving a Harriman and a Martin the reader is being referred. There may be several. Thus, in addition to its name, each reported case possesses a unique reference indicator. This normally includes (although not always in the same order):

(1) A reference to the title of the series of law reports in which the report is to be found.
(2) A date (year) reference. Some series have a volume number for each year. Where the date reference tells you the year in which the case was decided the date is normally enclosed in square brackets.
(3) A reference to the volume number (if there is more than one volume of the particular law reports series in the year concerned).
(4) A reference to the page or paragraph number at which the report of the case may be located.

If the case of *Harriman v. Martin* is reported in the first volume of the *Weekly Law Reports* for 1962, at page 739, the reference would be [1962] 1 W.L.R. 739. This is sometimes called the *citation* for the case. Knowing this reference or citation, it is possible to go directly to the shelves of the law library which house the volumes containing that reference and to turn directly to the report of the case.

If you know only the names of the parties in the case, you will need first to ascertain the specific reference. Although it would be possible to search the indexes for each individual series of law reports for the names of a case, this would be an inefficient and time-consuming approach. Normally, therefore, recourse is had to a general reference manual, which is known as a *case citator*. Such a case citator is provided with the commercial reference service known as *Current Law*. Other means are also available for locating the references of specific cases but *Current Law* is that which is most readily available. What follows is a brief description of the *Current Law* case citator.

The *Current Law* system of citations for cases works through a combination of three separate reference items:

(1) Two hard-bound citators covering the periods 1947–1976 and 1977–1988.
(2) A laminated volume covering the period from 1989 (a new, up-dated version of this volume is issued every year).
(3) "Monthly Parts," which are issued regularly in pamphlet form, for the current year. These are subsequently replaced by a bound volume for the year.

The importance of using all three items to complement one another will appear when we consider the problem of locating up-to-date references (see below).

Entries in the *Current Law* case citator are listed by title of case, arranged alphabetically. Thus, to find the law reports reference to the case of *Harriman v. Martin* you need to turn to the alphabetical heading under "Harriman." This indicates:

> *Harriman v. Martin* [1962] 1 W.L.R. 739; 106 S.J. 507; [1962] 1 All E.R. 225, C.A. . . . Digested 61/1249: Referred to, 72/2355.

From this information, we discover not only the law reports reference to the first volume of the *Weekly Law Reports* for 1962, at page 739, but also that there are reports of the same case in:

106 S.J. 507	*i.e.* the 106th volume of the Solicitors' Journal at page 507.

and:

[1962] 1 All E.R. 225	*i.e.* the first volume of the All England Reports for 1962 at page 225.

We are also informed that the court which delivered the decision reported at those locations was:

C.A.   *i.e.* the Court of Appeal.

Next, we are told that a "digest" (a brief summary) of the case has been included in a companion volume to the *Current Law Case Citator* at:

62/1249   *i.e.* in the companion year volume of
                                  Current Law for 1962 at paragraph
                                  1249.

Finally, we are told that the case was "referred to" (in another case) and that that case is to be found at:

72/2355   *i.e.* in the companion year volume of
                                  Current Law for 1972 at paragraph
                                  2355.

It now only remains to locate one of these volumes in the law library, and to turn to the appropriate page for a report on the case of *Harriman v. Martin.*

The above is not only a method for finding the reference to a case. If you already have a reference to a case, but you find that volume already in use in the library, you can use the method above to find an alternative citation for the case.

UP-DATING CASES

It is not enough to know merely what was said in a particular case in order to know the importance which should be attached to that case. It is also necessary to know whether such an earlier case has been used or referred to subsequently by the judges, or, indeed, whether it has been expressly approved or disapproved of by a later court.

If a case is approved by a court which is further up the hierarchy of courts than the court originally giving judgment (and that approval is part of the ratio of that later case) then the case will take on the status of the later decision. Thus a decision of the High Court approved by the Court of Appeal will take on the status of the Court of Appeal. Even if the approval forms part of the *obiter* within the later judgment this will be significant, indicating the way in which the court is likely to give judgment once the matter becomes central in a decision at that level. Disapproval of a case will be important in a similar fashion. Such information can be discovered by using the *Current Law* case citator.

We can regard a case as reliable (or, at least, not unreliable) where we are informed that it has been "referred to," "considered," "explained," "followed," "approved" or "applied." On the other hand, considerable care must be taken with a case which has been "distinguished," while cases which have been "disapproved" or "overruled" are unlikely to prove reliable for future purposes.

Example

If, for example, at some time during December 1994, we had looked for information on the case of *Roberts v. Roberts* (which was decided in 1962), we would have found the following:

1. From the *Current Law Case Citator* volume 1947–1976:

Roberts v. Roberts [1962] P. 212; [1962] 3 W.L.R. 448; 126 J.P. 438, 106 S.J. 513; [1962] 2 All E.R. 967; [26 M.L.R. 92], D.C. . . . Digested, 62/996: Considered, 62/995; 69/1124: Followed, 71/3362.

This tells us the various locations of reports of the case, as explained above. When there is a reference enclosed in square brackets it also tells us that there has been a note or article written explaining what the decision means:

[26 M.L.R. 92]   *i.e.* in volume 26 of the *Modern Law Review* at page 92.

The court which decided the case is indicated (as explained previously) as D.C., (*i.e.* the Divisional Court or the High Court exercising its appellate function), and we are told that a digest of the case is to be found in the *Current Law Year Book* for 1962 at paragraph 996.

We are, however, additionally informed that the case has been "considered" by a court on two subsequent occasions, and that we can discover information about the cases in which that happened by turning to the paragraphs indicated in the *Current Law Year Book* series:

62/995   *i.e.* a digest entry for the case of *Smith v. Smith and Brown* [1962] 1 W.L.R. 1218, in the Court of Appeal.

69/1124   *i.e.* a digest for the case of *P v. P* [1969] 1 W.L.R. 898.

We are also informed that the case has been "followed" on one occasion in a case digested at paragraph 3362 of the *Current Law Year Book* for 1971. However, if we turn to that reference, we find that even the compilers of citator volumes are human! There is no reference to our case of *Roberts v. Roberts*, although, if we look above at paragraph 3361, we will find a digest for the case of *Snow v. Snow* (1971) 115 S.J. 566, in the Court of Appeal, which does "follow" the case of *Roberts v. Roberts*.

2. From the supplementary *Current Law Case Citator* 1977–1988:

Roberts v. Roberts [1962] . . . Considered 84/190; 85/168

As in the case of the 1947–1976 volume, we are referred to digest entries where *Roberts v. Roberts* has been "considered".

84/190   *i.e.* a digest entry for the case of *W v. W* which is reported in *The Times* for 3rd November 1984.

85/168   *i.e.* a digest entry for the case of *Willets v. Wells* [1985] 1 W.L.R. 237.

3. From the laminated volume *Current Law Case Citator* 1989/93:

The next thing we would normally do is to consult the annual volume of *Current Law* which brings us up-to-date from 1989 until the end of the last complete year (which, in December 1994, would be the volume for 1989–1993).

There is no reference to the case of *Roberts v. Roberts* in this volume, so that we can deduce that the case was not mentioned in any reported case included in *Current Law* during the period between 1989 and 1993.

4. From the *Current Law Monthly Parts* for the last year

Finally, in order to bring ourselves as up-to-date as possible with the *Current Law* system, we must look at the *Monthly Parts* for 1994. These are cumulative, *i.e.* information in the later Parts refers back to information in the earlier Parts for the same year. Cases are listed alphabetically. Cases which have been previously listed, such as *Roberts v. Roberts*, are noted in italic script.

On looking at the October *Monthly Part* for 1994, which is the most recent Part available by December 1994, we find that there is no reference to our case of *Roberts v. Roberts*. We therefore know that there has been no mention of our case in any reported case contained in *Current Law* up to October 1994.

USING LIMITED LIBRARY FACILITIES

The problems of finding and using cases and law reports where limited resources are available are significant. Clearly, it will not be possible to find reports of all the cases which you may need, since the available reports may only be found in series which are not at your disposal. By the same token, you may not have access to sufficiently comprehensive reference manuals, such as a case law citator or similar.

You may have access to one of the general series of law reports. This will often be a set of *All England Law Reports*. Many public reference libraries possess a set of these law reports. If this is the case, some searching for cases can be done using the indexes contained in those volumes; though this will, of course, be time consuming. Alternatively, if you are concerned only with a limited specialist area you may have access to a specialised series of law reports.

Whatever your source of available material, however, it is of paramount importance that you familiarise yourself with the specific indexing and cross-referencing system adopted by that source. If you do this, you will be able to use the material at your disposal, limited though it may be by comparison with the resources of a fully-equipped and supported law library, in the most efficient manner.

It will also be important to discover whether you can obtain access to some means for updating the material contained in your available sources. The use of a citator, as explained above, is clearly of major benefit, for the consolidation of information within one reference item avoids the necessity of searching through a range of separate volumes and series. Amongst possible sources of updated information might be the general legal periodicals, such as the *New Law Journal* or the *Solicitors Journal* (both of which have been referred to above). Many public libraries subscribe to one of these, or to other relevant periodicals. Where your needs related to a specific area, the periodicals available in relation to that area may be of assistance in obtaining up-to-date information. Thus, for example, many personnel management journals contain information about cases decided by the courts in relation to employment law. All of these will probably refer you to sources of information which you do not have but they will also enable you to make the most efficient use of those sources which are available.

A further common source of information will be text-books on the subject about which you are seeking information. The important rule here is to check that you have access to the latest possible edition of the book, and to bear in mind the possibility that case-law developments may have overtaken the legal position as it was stated at the time of writing of the book. Most books dealing with the law will contain a statement in the "Foreword" stating the date on which the information given in the book is said to be current.

In some instances, you may have access to a *case-book*. This term is something of a misnomer since case books frequently contain not just cases but also statutes and comments on the law. Such books are generally concerned with a specific topic, for example "contract law," and contain edited material relevant to the area. These books can be a very useful source where you have access only to limited library facilities. However, they suffer from several deficiencies. First, the reader relies on the editor of the volume to select the most appropriate material. There is no way in which the quality of the work can be checked. Secondly, the material presented may only be given in part. Again, the reader must trust that the editor has not given misleading extracts. Finally, the reader has no means of up-dating the material. In some areas of law encyclopedias are produced. These are similar to case-books, although they are generally more detailed. Publishers of this kind of work often supply an up-dating service. Increasingly, encyclopedias are produced in a loose-leaf form and the reader will substitute new pages as supplements are issued. (The use of encyclopedias is considered at the end of this chapter.)

USING ELECTRONIC RETRIEVAL FACILITIES

To complete this section on finding and using reports of cases, mention must be made of the important and fast-developing range of computerised information retrieval systems. Two primary formats are considered here: *(i)* so-called "on-line" systems, where the information stored in a large "database" is located on a centrally organised "host" computer, to which individual connections from a desktop computer can be made using a combination of a "modem" and standard telephone or other telecommunication links; and *(ii)* CD-ROM facilities, where the database information, together with the computing software needed to access and to search that information, has been loaded onto a "compact disc" (looking much like the commonly found music compact discs) which can be used on any normal personal computer equipped with a suitable CD-ROM drive.

"On-line" Services

The major "on-line" system relevant to English case-law is the service known as LEXIS. This is a long-established system, which uses traditional computing software to enable researchers to find their way into the huge body of information stored in its centralised databases. Criticisms that the LEXIS system is not very "user-friendly" are compensated for, to a great extent, by the relative completeness of the material available through the system. However, some training on the LEXIS system is a necessary pre-requisite to effective use of its facilities.

It should also be noted that a range of similar "on-line" services are available through various organisations which enable users to gain access to legal materials and case-law from many foreign systems and in a range of foreign languages.

As regards LEXIS, access is made through a terminal located in the office or library of the researcher. This terminal is connected to a large "host" computer, operated by the providers of the service, either by direct telephone-line or by direct communication through a "network" such as the British Telecom PSS system. The "host" computer contains an electronic "database" in which are housed the reports of thousands of cases.

In general, these reports of cases contain exactly the same words as are to be found in traditional series of law reports, although the format for presentation of those words on the computer screen may not reflect the format to be found on the traditional printed page. Thus, the amount of material displayed on the computer screen will, generally, not correspond to a printed page in, for example, a traditional law report series. The absence of pagination corresponding to printed series of law reports, along with an inability to present other important "signposts" contained in tra-ditional law reports (*e.g.* the series of "letters" commonly set out down the vertical margin of a law report page) has also been a factor in relegating "print-outs" from systems such as LEXIS to a marginal role when law reports are used in courts on a day-to-day basis. On the other hand, as a means of academic research, and as a relatively efficient way of speedily "scanning" a wide range of potentially relevant material in relation to a particular problem, such systems offer significant advantages.

Not all law reports found in traditional series are available by electronic means. On the other hand, a variety of "unreported" cases are available on different electronic retrieval services.

Searching for a case using an electronic retrieval system is done on the basis of selecting "key words." Thus, the user may ask the large computer to indicate where a specific term or "string" of letters and/or numbers occurs in its database. The system will respond by telling the user how often that term or "string" has been found and will indicate the number of cases in which that word is to be found. In response to this, the user may attempt to narrow down the number of "responses," by further limiting the selected "key word." This is done by requesting the system to indicate where the original "key word" or "string" is to be found in conjunction with another "string."

Eventually, the number of occasions on which the requested string or strings is to be found on the database will be small enough for the user to take a look at those instances which the computer has discovered. At this stage, it is possible for the user to ask for the text of the reports containing the requested string(s) to be displayed on the terminal. The full text of a law report may be requested, or there may just be a call for a selected portion of the report, such as the title, the decision, or the names of the lawyers acting in the case.

Any information displayed on the user's terminal can be printed simultaneously, and used as a record of the "search." Since the computer which houses the case-law database works on the basis of matching "strings" of text within that database with the "key words" selected by the user, it is possible to search on the basis of names, (*e.g.* asking for the occasions on which "Harriman" appears, with a view to locating the case of *Harriman v. Martin*) dates, courts, or subject-matter. The sophistication of any search undertaken using this method depends in large measure upon the ability of the user to ask for matching of sufficiently specific and relevant "key words."

Access to systems for on-line electronic retrieval of legal information offers the experienced user the possibility of making detailed and exhaustive searches in relation to known cases or around particular subject areas. It also makes possible speedy searches of law reports series, as well as offering access to the facilities of a large, well-equipped and constantly up-dated law library in the comfort of the user's office.

CD-ROM facilities

Rapid growth in the availability of legal materials in CD-ROM format has opened up the possibility of access to large quantities of information stored in databases. Retrieving information stored in this way has the advantage of the speed which comes from increasingly powerful software contained in personal desktop computers. In addition, the elimination of any need to use telephone or other telecommunication links between the user's computer and the "host" database has also been seen as a major advantage by comparison with "on-line" facilities.

Although, at the time of writing in December 1994, there is still only a limited range of domestic legal material in CD-ROM format, mention should be made of a number of products produced under the name of JUSTIS CD-ROMs, which currently include a selection of Statutory Instruments, a collection of case-law contained in the *Weekly Law Reports* series, and various specialised series of law reports, such as the *Industrial Cases Reports*.

FINDING AND UP-DATING STATUTES

Finding and updating statutory material is approached in very much the same manner as that described for case-law. With statutes there are three main problems. Is the statute in force? Has the statute been repealed by Parliament, (*i.e.* replaced by some other statute)? Has the statute been amended by Parliament, (*i.e.* had part of its contents altered by Parliament)?

Having started out with a provision in an Act of Parliament (either in the form in which it was originally passed, or in a form amended subsequently and stated to be effective at a given date), it is necessary to use one of the "citator" systems in order to discover the most up-to-date changes (if any) which have affected that provision. There are several different ways of performing this updating task, all of which are explained in detail in *How to Use a Law Library*. To assist you in the task, the following example shows how to update a relatively recent statutory provision using the *Current Law Legislation Citator*.

Example

Let us take the provision of section 57(3) of the Employment Protection (Consolidation) Act 1978. In its original form, this provision was set out as follows:

General provisions relating to fairness of dismissal

57.—(1) . . .

(2) . . .

(3) Where the employer has fulfilled the requirements of sub-section (1), then, subject to sections 58 to 62, the determination of the question whether the dismissal was fair or unfair, having regard to the reason shown by the employer, shall depend on whether the employer can satisfy the tribunal that in the circumstances (having regard to equity and the substantial merits of the case) he acted reasonably in treating it as a sufficient reason for dismissing the employee.

(4) . . .

Let us now assume that, in December 1994, we wish to discover what has happened subsequently in relation to subsection 3 of section 57. In order to do this, it is necessary first to turn to the most recent available version of the *Current Law Legislation Citator*. In December 1994, this was the Citator for 1972–88.

The *Current Law Legislation Citator* is arranged in chronological order, by year and then by Chapter number for each Act. Chapter numbers are fully explained at page 74 but, briefly, they are a unique way of identifying the statute. Each statute in a year has its own Chapter number. For the Employment Protection (Consolidation) Act 1978 this is Chapter 44. To find our section, we turn to 1978, and eventually reach Chapter 44. Having come this far, we now only have to continue until we reach the required section number (s.57). The entry at this point tells us the following:

> s.57, amended: 1980, c.42, s.6.

From the information contained in this entry, we can now tell that, between 1978 and 1988:

(1) The section was amended in 1980, by section 6 of the statute whose reference is 1980 Chapter 42.

We now need to continue our search beyond 1988. This we do by turning to the most recent continuation volume of the *Legislation Citator*, which, in December 1994, is the *Current Law Legislator Citator 1989/93*. On reaching the entry for Chapter 44 of 1978, we find the following:

> s.57, amended: 1992, c.52. sch.2; 1993, c.19, sch.5.

This informs us that, between 1989 and 1993, in addition to the 1980 amendment which we have already discovered, two further amendments have been made to s.57:

(2) Part of the already amended section was further amended in 1992, by Schedule 2 of the statute whose reference is 1992 Chapter 52; and

(3) A further part of the remainder of the amended section was additionally amended in 1993, by Schedule 5 of the statute whose reference is 1993 Chapter 19.

It is now up to us to find the relevant provisions indicated in the above information. This we can do either by looking up the relevant references on the shelves of statute series in a Law Library, or by turning to the chronological list of entries in the *Current Law Legislation Citator* in order to discover the titles of the Acts whose references we now possess.

Our search will lead us to discover that:

(1) the 1980 amendment was brought about by the Employment Act 1980;

(2) the further amendment in 1992 was effected by the Trade Union and Labour Relations (Consolidation) Act 1992; and

(3) the additional amendment in 1993 was produced by the Trade Union Reform and Employment Rights Act 1993.

We can now turn to the relevant provisions in the statutes which we have discovered and, by applying the amending or repealing provisions to the original version of subsection (3) of section 57 with which we started, we can ascertain what s.57(3) of the Employment Protection (Consolidation) Act 1978 (as amended) now currently provides. By comparison with the original version, that section, in December 1994, had the following content:

General provisions relating to fairness of dismissal

57.—(1) . . .

(2) . . .

(3) Where the employer has fulfilled the requirements of subsection (1), then, subject to sections 57A to 61 and to sections 152, 153 and 238 of the Trade Union and Labour Relations (Consolidation) Act 1992 (provisions as to dismissal on ground of trade union membership or activities or in connection with industrial action), the determination of the question whether the dismissal was fair or unfair, having regard to the reason shown by the employer, shall depend on whether in the circumstances (including the size and administrative resources of the employer's

undertaking) the employer acted reasonably or unreasonably in treating it as a sufficient reason for dismissing the employee; and that question shall be determined in accordance with equity and the substantial merits of the case.

(4) . . .

This method will not only allow us to see whether a statute has been amended. It will also enable us to find out if and when a statute has come into force. Thus, by using the method above, it is possible to see if a relevant "commencement order" has been made, or if part or all of a statute has been brought into effect by means of a Statutory Instrument. Finally, using the method above will also give us the citation of any case interpreting the section in the statute.

HOW TO USE ENCYCLOPEDIAS

Encyclopedias are not, in the strictest sense, a source of law (although they may contain sources of law). Cases and statutes are sources of law. They are what will be used when judges are deciding what the outcome of a case is to be. However, for some people encyclopedias will be the only material they have available. Thus it is important to consider how they can be used most effectively.

Different examples of encyclopedias vary in form and content. They do not all contain the same kind of material nor are they ordered in the same way. Therefore it is not possible to give a series of rules saying how encyclopedias should be used. What follows are points that a reader should consider when first using any encyclopedia.

The first thing to look at is the kind of material that the encyclopedia contains. One advantage of an encyclopedia can be that it brings together a wide variety of material about particular subject matter. Thus, you may find the encyclopedia which you are reading contains all the statutes in a particular area, all the statutory instruments, government circulars and other non-statutory material, references to relevant cases (with some description of their contents) together with some discussion of the application of legal rules in the area. On the other hand the encyclopedia may contain only some of the material or may extract some of it. Thus, for example, instead of having all of a statute you may find that you have only parts of it.

Even if the encyclopedia claims to be fully comprehensive, remember that it is no more than a claim. The editors of the encyclopedia may feel that they have included all relevant statutes; others may disagree with them. It is always as important to be aware of what you do not know as what you do know. Relying on an encyclopedia means that there may be gaps in your knowledge of the particular area of law. However, you may feel it worth relying on the encyclopedia because it is the only source available. Equally, you may find it quicker to use an encyclopedia and consider the advantage of speedy access more important than any element of doubt in your knowledge of the area.

Most encyclopedias extract at least some of the material which they cover. That is to say that they contain extracts of a statute, statutory instrument, or whatever, rather than the whole. Here the problem is that, in extracting their material, the editors of the encyclopedia limit your knowledge of the law. You rely on them to extract that which is relevant and cannot check the matter for yourself. As a source of law, the less comprehensive an encyclopedia is the less useful it will be. However, the more comprehensive an encyclopedia is the slower it may be to use. Before using the encyclopedia you need to consider the kind of question which you are trying to answer. If the question is a very broad and general one about the framework of some area of law you may find an encyclopedia with less detail easier to use. However, if you are trying to answer a very detailed point, perhaps applying the law to a very precise factual situation, you need the most comprehensive encyclopedia that you can find.

Most encyclopedias, and increasingly many other books about law, are now issued in loose-leaf form. This means that the publisher issues supplements to the encyclopedia on a regular basis. These supplements, which contain descriptions of changes in the law, are then substituted for the pages which discuss the out-of-date law. The advantage of the loose-leaf form over ordinary books is that it means the encyclopedia is more likely to be accurate. When using loose-leaf encyclopedias before looking up the point of law that interests you always see when it was last up-dated. You will usually find a page at the front of the first volume of the encyclopedia which tells you when it was last up-dated.

The technique for finding out about points of law in an encyclopedia will vary depending upon the encyclopedia being used. Some are organised according to different areas of law within the subject of the encyclopedia. Others have different volumes for different kinds of material; one volume for statutes, one for discussion of the law and so forth. Most will have both indexes and detailed contents pages. Most encyclopedias have a discussion of how they should be used at the beginning of their first volume. Always consult this when first using an encyclopedia.

FINDING AND USING MATERIAL ON THE LAW OF THE EUROPEAN COMMUNITIES, THE EUROPEAN UNION, AND THE EUROPEAN ECONOMIC AREA

With the changes in membership which take effect on 1 January 1995, what is said here relates to the twelve Master States of the European Union as of December 1994, together with Austria, Finland and Sweden.

All basic material in relation to the European Communities, the European Union, and the European Economic Area is published in English. However, some material is not made available in all of the official languages of the European Communities immediately. What is said here refers specifically to English language versions of such material.

The *Official Journal of the European Communities* is the authoritative voice of the European Communities, and is used to publish daily information. It also contains material relating to the European Economic Area (EEA), which, with effect from 1 January 1995, will relate only to Iceland, Liechtenstein and Norway. The Official Journal (the O.J.) is divided into two major parts (the L and C series). There are also separately published notices of recruitment, notices and public contracts and the like, which are published in a Supplement and in Annexes. Twice a year the O.J. issues a *Directory of Community legislation in force and other acts of the Community institutions.*

LEGISLATION

The L series (Legislation) contains the text of Community legislation. The series is arranged by Volume, starting in 1958, and by issue number sequentially throughout the issue year. Thus, the text of *Council Directive 95/45/EC of 22 September 1994 on the establishment of a European Works Council or a procedure in Community-scale undertakings and Community-scale groups of undertakings for the purposes of informing and consulting employees* is to be found in the *Official Journal* of 30 September 1994.

The Volume number for 1994 is	Volume 37
The issue number of the OJ L series for 30 September 1994 is	L 254

The text of the Directive is set out on page   p.64
64 and thus the page reference is

The official reference for the Directive will
be OJ No L 254, 30.9.1994, p.64

INFORMATION AND NOTICES

The C series (Information and Notices) contains, amongst a host
of other items, key extracts ("the operative part") from judgments
of the Court of Justice of the European Communities (the ECJ,
sitting in Luxembourg) and the Court of First Instance (which also
sits in Luxembourg). Where the language of the particular court
being reported is not English, the C series will include a "provisional
translation": the definitive translation being found in the separately
published *Reports of Cases before the Court.* There is also brief
coverage of actions brought before the ECJ by Member States
against the Council of the European Communities, as well as
questions referred to the ECJ by national courts of Member States.

Also, to be found in the C series will be *Preparatory Acts* in the
course of being made into legislation by the European Communities.
Thus, for example, the *Official Journal* for 19 February 1994
contains the text of an Opinion delivered by the Economic and
Social Committee on a proposal for a Council Regulation on
substances that deplete the ozone layer.

The Volume Number for 1994 is   Volume 37

The issue of the OJ C series for 19 February   C 52
1994 is

The text of the proposed Decision is item 3   03
in issue C 52, and so the reference is

The full reference for the Opinion is OJ 94/C
52/03

OTHER MATERIALS

Whilst the *Official Journal* is the best official source of information
about Community law it should be noted that a wide range of
documentation does not find its way into the *Official Journal* and
other sources may have to be considered for those wanting a
comprehensive list of European materials.

In particular, mention should be made of so-called "COM" documents, which often contain important proposals for future legislation. These are issued by the Commission with a "rolling" numerical reference by sequence of publication during a particular year. Consequently, there is no systematic numbering of such "COM Docs"—a matter which frequently gives rise to criticism about the accessibility of important documentation in the legislative field. By way of example, an important recent *Communication concerning the application of the Agreement on social policy*, presented by the Commission to the Council and to the European Parliament on 14 December 1993, is simply designated:

COM(93) 600 final

Various other series, apart from the "COM" series, are also to be found in relation to a range of spheres of activity within the European Communities.

Judgments of the European Court of Justice are reported in two series of law reports. One series is that "formally" published by the European Communities itself—the *European Court Reports* (E.C.R.). The other series is the privately produced *Common Market Law Reports* (C.M.L.R.). Both can be found in the normal manner. In addition to these specialised law reports series, an increasing number of judgments delivered by the European Court of Justice are now reported as a normal part of general law report series.

Finally, it is worth noting that the European Communities have their own legal database, CELEX, which is updated on a weekly basis. Parts of the CELEX database are also available in CD-ROM format (see above, at p. 48), marketed by a variety of commercial organisations.

COMMUNITY LEGISLATION TRANSPOSED INTO UNITED KINGDOM LAW

Where European Community legislation has been transposed into United Kingdom law by means of Statutory Instruments (S.I.s), it is now possible to discover the relevant references by using a recently introduced addition to the *Current Law* system. This is a separate laminated volume, entitled *Current Law Statutory Instrument Citator*, and the last available version of which is, in December 1994, the volume for 1993.

This part of the *Current Law* system sets out those Statutory Instruments which have been passed in order to give effect in

United Kingdom law to Community provisions, and presents them in chronological order, beginning in 1989.

Since the method of accessing these provisions is from the starting point of the United Kingdom Statutory Instrument reference, the facility is of limited usefulness. In order to discover whether a particular piece of Community legislation has been transposed into United Kingdom law by a Statutory Instrument, it is necessary to read through all of the references until reaching the relevant title of the Community legislation. Nevertheless, this is one of the few generalised methods for linking Community legislation with the relevant United Kingdom counterpart, and will doubtless be improved as researchers increasingly attempt to make use of the *Current Law* facility.

CHAPTER 5

Reading cases and statutes

This chapter will explain how you should use the primary sources for legal rules, cases and statutes. You will find a specimen case report and a specimen statute in each section. Skill in the use of the techniques described here can only be acquired with practice. For this reason there are a series of exercises in Part III of the book.

READING A CASE

The contents of law reports are explained here so that you can start to read cases, understand the law which they contain, and make useful notes about them. You will find the court structure, and how cases are decided, explained in Chapter 1. You will find a copy of a case, *R. v. Terry*, on pp. 60–64. All specific references in this section will be to that case. The copy is taken from the All England Law Reports, which are the most commonly available law reports. However, if you have access to other kinds of law reports you will find that they look very much the same as the All England Law Reports. The techniques discussed here will be just as useful in reading other series of law reports. The different series of law reports and their use has been explained in Chapter 4.

The case is *R. v. Terry*. Lawyers pronounce this Regina (or the Queen, or King, or the Crown) against Terry. Most criminal cases are written like this. In civil cases, the names of the parties are usually given, as in *Donoghue v. Stevenson*, the case being pronounced Donoghue and Stevenson.

Underneath the name of the case at **a** you will see three pieces of information. First, you are told the court in which the case was heard. In this case it was the House of Lords. It is important to know which court heard a case because of the doctrine of precedent (see pages 8–11 for an explanation of the doctrine of precedent).

The report then gives the names of the judges who took part in the case. This information is used to help evaluate the decision. Some judges are known to be very experienced in particular areas of law. Their decisions may be given extra weight. Finally, you are told when the case was heard and when the court gave its decision. In the House of Lords this process is called "delivering opinions," but in other courts it is known as "giving judgment."

The material in italics, at **b** on the first page of the report, is written by the editor of the report. It indicates the subject-matter of the case and the issue which it concerned. The subject index at the front of each volume of law reports includes a similar entry under the first words; in this instance "Road Traffic."

The next section, at **c**, is called the *headnote*. It is not part of the case proper, and is prepared by the law reporter, not by the judges. The headnote should summarise the case accurately giving references to important parts of the court's opinion or judgment and any cases cited. Because it is written when the case is reported, the headnote may stress or omit elements of the case which are later thought to be important. Therefore, care should be taken when using the headnote.

The notes, just below **d**, direct the reader to appropriate volumes of *Halsbury's Laws of England* and *Halsbury's Statutes of England. Halsbury's Laws* provides a concise statement of the relevant law, subject by subject, including references to the main cases and statutes. *Halsbury's Statutes* gives the complete text of all statutes together with annotations which explain them. Although law students and others may need to research the law using *Halsbury* it is not necessary to turn to reference works when reading every case. In most instances, the background law will be sufficiently explained by the judge.

At **e** there is a list of all the cases referred to by the judges. In each case, a list of different places where the cases may be found is given. Where counsel have cited additional cases to which the judges did not refer, to this is given in a separate list under the heading "cases also cited."

At **f** to **g** you will find a full history of the proceedings of the case. This indicates all the courts which have previously considered the case before the present one. The final sentence of this section indicates where a full account of the facts of the case may be found.

Below **h** you will find the names of the counsel (the barristers) who appeared in the case. Senior counsel are called Q.C.s (Queen's Counsel), or K.C.s (King's Counsel) when the monarch is a King.

R v Terry

HOUSE OF LORDS
LORD FRASER OF TULLYBELTON, LORD SCARMAN, LORD BRIDGE OF HARWICH, LORD BRANDON OF
OAKBROOK AND LORD BRIGHTMAN
28 NOVEMBER, 15 DECEMBER 1983

Road traffic – Excise licence – Fraudulent use of licence – Intention to defraud – Intent – What intent must be proved – Whether necessary to prove intent to avoid paying proper licence fee – Whether sufficient merely to prove intent to deceive person performing public duty – Vehicles (Excise) Act 1971, s 26(1).

It is not necessary, on a charge of fraudulently using an excise licence contrary to s 26(1)[a] of the Vehicles (Excise) Act 1971, for the Crown to establish an intent to avoid paying the proper licence fee; it is sufficient merely for the Crown to prove an intent by deceit to cause a person responsible for a public duty to act, or refrain from acting, in a way in which he otherwise would not have done (see p 66 j, p 67 b c and p 68 b to p 69 a, post).

    Welham v DPP [1960] 1 All ER 805 and dicta of Viscount Dilhorne and of Lord Diplock in *Scott v Comr of Police for the Metropolis* [1974] 3 All ER at 1037, 1040 applied.

    R v Manners-Astley [1967] 3 All ER 899 overruled.

Notes

For fraudulent use of vehicle licences, see 40 Halsbury's Laws (4th edn) para 179.

    For the Vehicles (Excise) Act 1971, s 26, see 41 Halsbury's Statutes (3rd edn) 456.

Cases referred to in opinions

R v Manners-Astley [1967] 3 All ER 899, [1967] 1 WLR 1505, CA.

Scott v Comr of Police for the Metropolis [1974] 3 All ER 1032, [1975] AC 819, [1974] 2 WLR 379, HL.

Welham v DPP [1960] 1 All ER 805, [1961] AC 103, [1960] 2 WLR 669, HL.

Appeal

The Crown appealed with leave of the Court of Appeal, Criminal Division against the decision of that court (Dunn LJ, Balcombe and Leonard JJ) on 5 May 1983 allowing an appeal by the respondent, Neil William Terry, against his conviction on 25 February 1982 in the Crown Court at Warrington before Mr Recorder R E Snape and a jury of fraudulently using an excise licence contrary to s 26(1) of the Vehicles (Excise) Act 1971. The Court of Appeal certified, under s 33(2) of the Criminal Appeal Act 1968, that the following point of law of general public importance was involved in the decision: whether, on a charge of fraudulently using an excise licence contrary to s 26(1) of the 1971 Act, the Crown was required to establish an intent to avoid paying the proper licence fee or whether it was sufficient to prove an intent by deceit to cause a person responsible for a public duty to act, or refrain from acting, in a way in which he otherwise would not have done. The facts are set out in the opinion of Lord Fraser.

John M T Rogers QC and *Thomas Teague* for the appellant.
Rhys Davies QC and *Paul O'Brien* for the respondent.

Their Lordships took time for consideration.

15 December. The following opinions were delivered.

LORD FRASER OF TULLYBELTON. My Lords, on 25 February 1982 the respondent was convicted in the Crown Court at Warrington on two counts, viz (1) theft

---

a   Section 26(1), so far as material, is set out at p 65 c, post

of a vehicle excise licence and (2) fraudulently using an excise licence contrary to s 26(1) of the Vehicles (Excise) Act 1971. He appealed against his conviction on the second *a* count. On 5 May 1983 his appeal was allowed by the Court of Appeal, Criminal Division (Dunn LJ, Balcombe and Leonard JJ) on the ground that a person does not 'fraudulently' use an excise licence within the meaning of that section unless he uses it in an attempt to evade paying the proper licence fee, and that the respondent had not been shown to have used it for that purpose. In reaching that decision the Court of Appeal was, as it recognised, bound by its own decision in *R v Manners-Astley* [1967] 3 All ER 899, [1967] *b* 1 WLR 1505. Accordingly, the present appeal is in substance against the decision in *R v Manners-Astley*.

Section 26(1) of the 1971 Act, so far as relevant, provides:

'If any persons forges or fraudulently alters or uses . . . (a) any mark to be fixed or sign to be exhibited on a mechanically propelled vehicle in accordance with section 19 or 21 of this Act; or . . . (c) any licence or registration document under this Act, *c* he shall be liable on summary conviction to a fine . . . or on conviction on indictment to imprisonment . . .'

The relevant provisions of that section are substantially the same as the provisions of s 17(1) of the Vehicles (Excise) Act 1962, which was the section under consideration in *R v Manners-Astley*. *d*

The facts in this case were as follows. On 18 May 1981 the respondent hired a Ford Escort car from a car-hire firm. When he returned it on 22 May 1981 its excise licence disc was missing. On 1 June 1981 he was driving his own car, a Ford Cortina, which had no licence disc displayed on the windscreen. He was stopped by a police officer, who asked him where his excise licence was. The police officer had been riding a motor cycle and at the time he asked the question he had not seen the licence disc. When he looked *e* into the car he saw an excise licence disc lying on the dashboard of the car. The respondent reached into the car, picked up the licence and handed it to the police officer saying, 'I don't think this is the right one'. The police officer at once noticed that the licence did not relate to the respondent's Cortina car. In fact it related to the Escort car which he had hired some days previously. The Crown case is that the respondent stole the excise licence relating to the Escort and that he fraudulently used it on his own Cortina with the *f* intention that a police officer who saw it would wrongly think that the Cortina was properly licensed. The respondent's case was that the licence had fallen off the Escort while on hire to him, and that he had taken it into his house unintentionally and was about to return it to the hire company. Further, he said that by 1 June he had already applied for a new licence for his own Cortina and that he was not using the licence from the Escort in an attempt to avoid paying the licence fee on the Cortina. The recorder *g* directed the jury that they had only to consider two questions on this count: first, whether the licence relating to the Escort had been exhibited on the dashboard of the Cortina, and, if so, second, whether it had been placed there by the respondent with the intention that it would be accepted as a genuine document applicable to the Cortina. The respondent contends that this was a misdirection because it left it open to the jury to convict him even if they accepted his statement that he had already applied for a licence *h* for the Cortina and was therefore not trying to avoid paying the proper licence fee for that car but was merely trying to avoid being charged with using the car without a licence being exhibited in breach of s 12(4) of the 1971 Act. The issue therefore is whether an attempt to avoid paying the licence fee is an essential element of the offence of using a licence fraudulently.

My Lords, the meaning of the words 'with intent to defraud' was considered by this *j* House in *Welham v DPP* [1960] 1 All ER 805, [1961] AC 103. For the purposes of this appeal there is in my opinion no relevant difference of meaning between 'with intent to defraud' and 'fraudulently'. In *Welham v DPP* the appellant was convicted under s 6 of the Forgery Act 1913 on a charge of having 'within intent to defraud' uttered a forged hire-purchase proposal and a forged hire-purchase agreement. His defence was that he

Welham v DPP was considered by the Court of Appeal in *R v Manners-Astley*, where the appellant had been convicted of fraudulently using an excise licence contrary to s 17(1) **a** of the 1962 Act by displaying a vehicle licence issued for one vehicle on another vehicle. The Court of Appeal quashed the conviction on two grounds, one of which was that the jury had not been directed to consider whether the appellant had intended to defraud the Excise by avoiding payment of the licence fee. The Court of Appeal distinguished the decision in *Welham* as being one limited to cases under the Forgery Act 1913. In taking that limited view of the decision the court was, in my respectful opinion, wrong. The **b** speeches in *Welham* were directed to the meaning of 'intent to defraud' in general and were not limited to its meaning in the Forgery Act 1913. I agree with the view expressed by Viscount Dilhorne in *Scott v Comr of Police for the Metropolis* [1974] 3 All ER 1032 at 1037, [1975] AC 819 at 838, where he said:

> 'While the meaning to be given to words may be affected by their context and **c** Lord Radcliffe [in *Welham*] was only considering the meaning of intent to defraud in s 4 of the Forgery Act 1913, the passages which I have cited from his speech are, I think, of general application . . .'

(The passages cited by Viscount Dilhorne were those in the first quotation that I have made above.)

Lord Diplock, who also took part in the decision of *Scott v Comr of Police for the* **d** *Metropolis*, summarised the law in three propositions, of which the third was as follows ([1974] 3 All ER 1032 at 1040, [1975] AC 819 at 841):

> 'Where the intended victim of a "conspiracy to defraud" is a person performing public duties as distinct from a private individual it is sufficient if the purpose is to cause him to act contrary to his public duty, and the intended means of achieving this purpose are dishonest. The purpose need not involve causing economic loss to **e** anyone.'

In the present case I see nothing in s 26(1) of the Vehicles (Excise) Act 1971 which leads me to think that the word 'fraudulently' ought to be given a more limited meaning than that attributed to the words 'intent to defraud' in *Welham v DPP*. On the contrary the context indicates that they should bear a wide meaning. One of the offences created **f** by s 26(1)(a) is fraudulently using any mark (ie a number plate) which is required to be fixed to a vehicle: see s 19(1). It is easy to imagine cases where false number plates might be used by dishonest persons for the purpose of deceiving police officers and causing them to act in the way that they would not otherwise have acted, without any intention of evading payment of the licence fee, and I have no doubt that s 26(1) is applicable to such cases. There is nothing in the section to exclude the application of the general rule **g** stated in *Welham*.

I am accordingly of opinion that the decision in *R v Manners-Astley* was erroneous and should now be overruled. It follows that the decision of the Court of Appeal, Criminal Division in the present appeal was wrong.

For these reasons I would allow the appeal and restore the conviction of the respondent. The first alternative in the certified question should be answered in the negative, and the **h** second alternative in the affirmative.

LORD SCARMAN. My Lords, I agree with the speech of my noble and learned friend Lord Fraser. I would allow the appeal and answer the certified question as he proposes.

LORD BRIDGE OF HARWICH. My Lords, for the reasons given in the speech of **j** my noble and learned friend Lord Fraser, I agree that this appeal should be allowed and the certified question answered in the manner he indicates.

LORD BRANDON OF OAKBROOK. My Lords, I have had the advantage of reading in draft the speech prepared by my noble and learned friend Lord Fraser. I agree

a had no intention of defrauding the finance companies which advanced money and that the reason for bringing the forged documents into existence was to evade credit restrictions by misleading the relevant authorities into thinking that the finance companies were advancing money not as straight loans (which would have been illegal) but under hire-purchase agreements (which would have been legal). His appeal against conviction was dismissed by the Court of Criminal Appeal, whose decision was affirmed by this House. The grounds of decision by this House were that 'with intent to defraud'

b was not confined to the idea of depriving a person by deceit of some economic advantage or inflicting on him some economic loss, but that they applied where a document was brought into existence for no other purpose than of deceiving a person responsible for a public duty into doing something that he would not have done but for the deceit, or not doing something that but for it he would have done. I shall cite two passages from the speech of Lord Radcliffe (see [1960] 1 All ER 805 at 808, [1961] AC 103 at 123–124),

c with whose speech Lord Tucker, Lord Keith and Lord Morris agreed. The first is as follows:

> 'Now I think that there are one or two things that can be said with confidence about the meaning of this word "defraud". It requires a person as its object; that is, defrauding involves doing something to someone. Although in the nature of things
d > it is almost invariably associated with the obtaining of an advantage for the person who commits the fraud, it is the effect on the person who is the object of the fraud that ultimately determines its meaning ... Secondly, popular speech does not give, and I do not think ever has given, any sure guide as to the limits of what is meant by "to defraud". It may mean to cheat someone. It may mean to practise a fraud on someone. It may mean to deprive someone by deceit of something which is regarded
e > as belonging to him or, though not belonging to him, as due to him or his right.'

In the second passage, after referring to a dictionary definition and to the writings of Rudyard Kipling, Lord Radcliffe went on:

> 'There is nothing in any of this that suggests that to defraud is, in ordinary speech, confined to the idea of depriving a man by deceit of some economic advantage or
f > inflicting on him some economic loss. Has the law ever so confined it? In my opinion, there is no warrant for saying that it has. What it has looked for in considering the effect of cheating on another person and so in defining the criminal intent is the prejudice of that person ... Of course, as I have said, in ninety-nine cases out of a hundred the intent to deceive one person to his prejudice merely connotes the deceiver's intention of obtaining an advantage for himself by inflicting
g > a corresponding loss on the person deceived. In all such cases, the economic explanation is sufficient. But in that special line of cases where the person deceived is a public authority or a person holding a public office, deceit may secure an advantage for the deceiver without causing anything that can fairly be called either a pecuniary or an economic injury to the person deceived. If there could be no intent to defraud in the eyes of the law without an intent to inflict a pecuniary or
h > economic injury, such cases as these could not have been punished as forgeries at common law, in which an intent to defraud is an essential element of the offence, yet I am satisfied that they were regularly so treated.'

Lord Denning, with whose speech Lord Radcliffe expressed his agreement, said ([1960] 1 All ER 805 at 816, [1961] AC 103 at 134):

j > ... it appears that the appellant on his own evidence had an intent to defraud; because he uttered the hire-purchase documents for the purpose of fraud and deceit. He intended to practise a fraud on whomsoever might be called on to investigate the loans made by the finance companies to the motor dealers. Such a person might be prejudiced in his investigation by the fraud. That is enough to show an intent to defraud.'

a with it, and for the reasons which he gives I would allow the appeal, restore the respondent's conviction, and answer the certified question in the manner proposed.

LORD BRIGHTMAN. My Lords, I agree.

Appeal allowed. Conviction restored. First alternative in certified question answered in the
b *negative, second alternative in the affirmative.*

Solicitors: *Sharpe Pritchard & Co*, agents for *E C Woodcock*, Chester (for the Crown); *Manches & Co*, agents for *Ashalls*, Warrington (for the respondent).

Mary Rose Plummer   Barrister.

c

The appellant, named first in the title of the report, was the Crown (in other words the state), while Terry was the respondent. The names of the solicitors who represented the two parties and instructed the counsel appear at the very end of the report. Academics may use this information to obtain further information about the case. Solicitors may use it in order to find out which are the best counsel to instruct.

Not all series of law reports have marginal letters as this one does. When they do, these letters can be used to give a precise reference to any part of the case. Thus, the beginning of Lord Fraser's opinion is [1984] 1 All E.R. 65j.

Whilst the matters above provide an introduction to the case, the substance is to be found in the judgments. Every law case raises a question or series of questions to be answered by the judge(s). In civil cases, some of these will be questions of fact (in criminal cases these will be answered by the jury). For example, it may be necessary to know at what speed a car was travelling when an accident occurred. In practice, the answers to these factual questions are very important. Once they have been settled, the legal issues in the case may be simple. However, when it comes to the study of law, it is only the legal questions which matter.

Lawyers and students of law are concerned primarily not with the outcome of a case but with the reasoning which the judge gave for the conclusion. The reasoning is important because within it will be found the *ratio decidendi*. The ratio is that part of the legal reasoning which is essential for the decision in the case. It is the ratio which is binding under the doctrine of precedent and which is thus part of the law. The ratio and the reasons for the decision are not necessarily the same thing. Not all the reasons given for the decision will be essential. In courts where there is more than one judge, each may give a separate judgment. If they do, each judgment will have its own reasons, and thus its own ratio. The judges must agree a conclusion to the case (although they may do so only by majority). However, they do not have to have the same reasons for their decision. If they have different reasons the judgments have different ratios and, thus, the case itself may have no ratio. Lawyers will rarely agree that a case has no ratio at all.

Finding the ratio in a case is crucial. It is also the most difficult part of reading cases. particularly when the case involves several judgments. The ratio is the essence of the case and, thus, may not be found simply by quoting from a judgment. Discovering the ratio involves skills of interpretation—understanding and explaining what judges meant, how they reached their conclusions—in order to see the common ground. Although the ratio is the law, it cannot be divorced entirely from the facts. Facts which are essential for a decision provide the conditions for the operation of the rule and are, thus, part of the rule itself. Deciding which are essential, as opposed to subsidiary, facts takes skill and practice. Lawyers frequently disagree on exactly what the ratio to a decision is. Some may view it broadly, seeing the decision as having few conditions but laying down a general rule. Others may take a narrower approach, suggesting that only in very limited circumstances would a decision bind a future court. Subsequent cases often help to clarify what the ratio of a previous case is accepted as being.

The editors of a law report write what they consider the ratio to be in the headnote. They may be wrong. Even if their interpretation is plausible when they write it, a later case may take a different view. For these reasons, statements of law in the headnote cannot be relied on.

If we look at *R. v. Terry* we can see that some of the things that we are told in the judgment are irrelevant for the purposes of constructing the ratio. Thus, for example, the fact that the accused was driving a Ford Cortina rather than a Rolls Royce is of no account. On the other hand, the fact that he was driving a motor car rather than a horse and cart is significant. The Vehicle (Excise) Act 1971 is only concerned, we are told, with something which is "a mechanically propelled vehicle." Particulars of the individuals in a case and details of the time or place where the events relevant to the case took place are rarely important for the ratio.

After giving the facts of the case Lord Fraser, in his judgment, goes on to consider what the word "fraudulently" means. This is the central issue in deciding what the relevant statutory provision requires. Lord Fraser does this by analysing previous judgments which had considered the phrase "with intent to defraud." This phrase, he asserts, is synonymous with the word "fraudulently." He shows that these previous judgments have argued that "with intent to defraud" does not necessarily imply that one is trying to gain an economic advantage (avoiding to pay a bill or whatever) but merely that some species of deceit is involved. However, one previous Court of Appeal decision had held that this line of analysis did not apply to the Vehicles (Excise) Act; it applied only to the statute which the analysis had directly been concerned with, the Forgery Act 1913. Lord Fraser, in his judgment, says that this Court of Appeal decision is wrong. The analysis of "with intent to defraud" was a general one applying to other statutes using this or similar phrases. Since Lord Fraser is sitting in the House of Lords, a court superior to the Court of Appeal, he can overrule a previous Court of Appeal decision providing the majority of his fellow judges in the case agree with him (which they do in this case).

From the above it would seem that it is relatively simple to construct the ratio of *R. v. Terry.* "Fraudulently" in the Vehicle (Excise) Act 1971 implies some deceit on the part of the accused but that deceit need not necessarily be an attempt to gain economic advantage. However, two questions remain. First, is it just in the context of the facts of the present case that "fraudulently" will take on this meaning? Secondly, and much more importantly, will fraudulently (or similar phrases) always have this meaning? Lord Fraser, in his judgment, says "[i]n the present case I see nothing [to suggest that 'fraudulently' does not imply, broadly, some general form of deceit]." "In the present case" could reasonably be taken to imply that in other cases the analysis would be different.

R. v. Terry contains only a single judgment. That judgment is a short one. If one had a longer judgment (and most judgments are longer) or multiple judgments in the same case the task of constructing a ratio would be much more difficult. When one has to consider one judgment and its obscurities in the light of other judgments the process of analysing the law becomes even more uncertain.

A court must follow the ratio of any relevant case which is binding on it under the doctrine of precedent. Thus, the question arises, when is a case relevant? A case in the same area must be followed unless it can be distinguished on the basis of its facts. If the facts of the case cannot be distinguished, if the case is "on all fours," then it must be followed. The process of distinguishing cases is really just another way of deciding what the ratio of the case is. If the material facts necessary for the operation of the legal rule in the first case are not found in the second, or are different, there is no precedent. Just as lawyers differ about what the ratio to a case is, so they differ about whether a case is binding in a particular situation or not. Judges sometimes distinguish cases on flimsy grounds simply to avoid having to follow precedents which they find unwelcome.

That which is not part of the ratio of the case is said to be the *obiter dictum.* This is usually referred to as the *Obiter.* Obiter is said to have persuasive authority. That which was said obiter in a court such as the House of Lords may be very persuasive indeed for a relatively inferior court such as a County Court. Moreover, remarks made obiter may indicate which way the law is developing or which kinds of arguments judges find particularly persuasive.

Equally, judges are not always very careful about differentiating between ratio and obiter.

The remainder of this section provides some guidance on how to study cases. The first question a student should ask about a case is "Why has this case been set?" The purpose of studying cases is to obtain an understanding of the relevance of the case to the area of law being studied. Some cases will be more important than others. A leading House of Lords decision will require more time and closer examination than a decision which is merely illustrative of a point mentioned in a lecture or included in a problem. Where a case has developed or defined an area of law it is usually helpful to start by reading what the textbook writers say about it. Where more than one case has to be read on the same point of law, they should if possible, be read in chronological order and each one digested before moving on to the next. If the subject under consideration is not an area of substantive law, such as tort or contract, but procedure or precedent, different aspects of the case will be important. In reading the case it is essential that the relevance of the case is borne in mind.

A second question to ask when reading cases is, "How much time is available?" Try to spend more time on important decisions and important judgments, even if you have to rely on a headnote or a textbook when it comes to the others. Do not spend the greater proportion of your time reading cases which have been overruled or which have novel or interesting facts but no new point of law. The headnote is helpful when allocating time. Treat judgments in the same way you treat cases. Do not waste your time reading judgments which merely repeat something you have already read. Spend more time on the leading judgments than the others. Again the headnote will be helpful for this. Some judgments are more clearly written than others. Some judgments are shorter than others. Neither clarity nor brevity necessarily mean that the judgment is more important. Choose what you read because it is the best for your purposes, not because it is the easiest.

Notes on any case should start with the case name and any references. They should then include:

    (1) a brief statement of the facts of the case.
    (2) the history of the case.
    (3) the point of law under consideration.
    (4) the decision with the reasons for it, together with any names of cases relied on.

One side of A4 paper should provide enough space for this basic information leaving the reverse side free for individual notes from judgments and, where necessary, any comments. Some students prefer to keep notes of cases on file cards. These are easier to refer to quickly but less can be put on them.

When reading judgments in order to make notes look for agreement and disagreement on each of the points relevant to your study. It is often useful to make separate notes on each of the points raised by the case and then see what different judges said about them. Do not forget to make it clear in your notes whether a judge was dissenting or not.

HOW TO READ A STATUTE

This section will explain how you should read statutes. The way in which statutes are created is explained on pages 4–5. Looking for a particular legal rule in a statute can be confusing. Some statutes are over 100 pages long, although most are shorter. The language they use often appears complicated and obscure. If you understand the structure of a statute and follow a few simple rules in reading them statutes will become much clearer.

A copy of a statute, the Coal Industry Act 1983, is reproduced below. All subsequent references here are to this statute.

You can find statutes in a number of different ways. Not all of the statutes which you find will look the same as the one which we have reproduced for you. One way to find a statute is to buy it from Her Majesty's Stationery Office, the official stockist for Government publications, or one of its agents. These copies look much the same as the one which we have reproduced but they have, in addition, a contents list at the beginning. Statutes are also printed in a number of different series with different volumes for each year. The copy of the Coal Industry Act 1983 which you are referring to is taken from such a series published by the Incorporated Council of Law Reporting. Some series of statutes are printed in an annotated form. This means that the statute is printed with an accompanying explanatory text, telling you what the statute does. If you use an annotated statute, remember that only the words of the statute are definitive. The explanatory text, although often helpful, is only the opinion of the author.

The different parts

1. This is the *short title* of the Act, together with its year of

ELIZABETH II   c. 60   1

[Royal Seal]

Coal Industry Act 1983   ①

1983 CHAPTER 60   ②

An Act to increase the limit on the borrowing powers of the
National Coal Board; and to make further provision   ③
with respect to grants and payments by the Secretary
of State in connection with the coal industry.   ④
[21st December 1983]

B E IT ENACTED by the Queen's most Excellent Majesty, by and
with the advice and consent of the Lords Spiritual and   ⑤
Temporal, and Commons, in this present Parliament
assembled, and by the authority of the same, as follows:—

1. In section 1(3) of the 1965 Act (which, as amended by Borrowing
section 1 of the 1982 Act, provides for a limit of £4,500 million powers of
on the borrowing of the Board and their wholly owned sub- National Coal
sidiaries but enables that limit to be increased by order up to Board.
£5,000 million) for "£4,500 million" and "£5,000 million"   ⑥
there shall be substituted "£5,500 million" and "£6,000 million" respectively.

2.—(1) In subsection (1) of section 3 of the 1980 Act (which, Deficit and
as amended by section 2(1) of the 1982 Act, provides for the operating
payment of grants in respect of group deficits for financial years grants.
of the Board ending in or before March 1984) for the words
from "for a financial year of the Board" onwards there shall
be substituted "for the financial years of the Board ending in
March 1984, 1985 and 1986".

(2) For subsection (4) of that section there shall be substituted—

" (4) The aggregate of the grants made under this section during the financial years of the Board referred to in subsection (1) above shall not exceed £1,200 million, but the Secretary of State may with the approval of the Treasury, on one or more occasions, by order made by statutory instrument increase or further increase that limit up to £2,000 million.

(5) An order shall not be made under subsection (4) above unless a draft of the order has been laid before and approved by a resolution of the House of Commons."

(3) The following enactments shall cease to have effect, namely—

> section 8 of the 1973 Act (grants as respects coking coal supplied during the financial years of the Board ending in March 1980, 1981, 1982 and 1983);
>
> section 2 of the 1977 Act (grants for or by reference to those financial years for promoting the sale of coal to Electricity Boards);
>
> section 3 of the 1977 Act (grants towards costs incurred in those financial years in connection with stocks of coal or coke); and
>
> sections 4 and 5(2) of the 1980 Act (limit on aggregate amount of grants under the above enactments and under section 3 of the 1980 Act).

Grants in connection with pit closures. 3.—(1) Section 6 of the 1977 Act (grants in connection with pit closures) shall be amended as follows.

(2) In subsection (3) (which, as amended by section 6(1)(*a*) of the 1980 Act, provides for such grants to be made towards expenditure of the Board for financial years of the Board ending in or before March 1984) for " and 1984 " there shall be substituted " 1984, 1985 and 1986."

(3) In subsection (5) (which, as amended by section 4(1) of the 1982 Act, provides for a limit of £200 million on the aggregate amount of grants under section 6), for " £200 million " there shall be substituted " £400 million ".

Payments to or in respect of redundant workers. 4.—(1) Section 7 of the 1977 Act (payments to or in respect of redundant workers) shall be amended as follows.

(2) In subsection (1) (which, as amended by section 7(2) of the 1980 Act, provides that the qualifying period for payments under

a scheme under section 7 ends with March 1984) for " 1st April 1984 " there shall be substituted " 30th March 1986 ".

(3) In subsection (5) (which, as amended by section 4(2) of the 1982 Act, provides for a limit of £300 million on the aggregate amount of such payments during the financial years of the Board ending in or before March 1984) for the words from " and 1984 " onwards there shall be substituted " 1984, 1985 and 1986 shall not exceed £1,200 million."

5. In this Act—   Interpretation.

    " the 1965 Act " means the Coal Industry Act 1965 ;   1965 c. 82.

    " the 1973 Act " means the Coal Industry Act 1973 ;   1973 c. 8.

    " the 1977 Act " means the Coal Industry Act 1977 ;   1977 c. 39.

    " the 1980 Act " means the Coal Industry Act 1980;   1980 c. 50.

    " the 1982 Act " means the Coal Industry Act 1982 ;   1982 c. 15.

    " the Board " means the National Coal Board.

6.—(1) This Act may be cited as the Coal Industry Act 1983.   Citation,
                                                                repeals and
(2) This Act and the Coal Industry Acts 1946 to 1982 may be   extent.
cited together as the Coal Industry Acts 1946 to 1983.

(3) The enactments mentioned in the Schedule to this Act (which include certain spent provisions) are hereby repealed to the extent specified in the third column of that Schedule.

(4) This Act does not extend to Northern Ireland.

4   **c. 60**   *Coal Industry Act 1983*

Section 6(3).   SCHEDULE

REPEALS

Chapter	Short title	Extent of repeal
1973 c. 8.	The Coal Industry Act 1973.	Section 8.
1977 c. 39.	The Coal Industry Act 1977.	Sections 2 and 3.
1980 c. 50.	The Coal Industry Act 1980.	Sections 4 and 5. Section 7(2).
1982 c. 15.	The Coal Industry Act 1982.	Sections 1 and 2. Section 4. In section 5, the definitions of " the Act of 1965 " and " the Act of 1980 ".

publication. When you are writing about a statute, it is normal to use the short title and year of publication to describe the statute. Sometimes, when a statute is referred to constantly, the short title is abbreviated. Thus, the Matrimonial Causes Act 1973 is often referred to as the M.C.A.1973. If you work in a particular area of law, you will quickly learn the standard abbreviations for that area.

2. This is the official *citation* for the statute. Each Act passed in any one year is given its own number. This is known as its *chapter number*. Thus you can describe a statute by its chapter number and year. The citation, 1983 Chapter 60, could only mean the Coal Industry Act 1983. Chapter in the official citation may be abbreviated to c. as in the top right hand corner of your copy of the statute. This form of official citation began in 1963. Before that statutes were identified by the regnal year in which they occurred in, followed by their chapter number. A regnal year is a year of a monarch's reign. Thus, "30 Geo 3 Chapter 3" refers to the Treason Act 1790 which was passed in the 30th year of George III's reign. It is much easier to remember and use the short title of an Act rather than its official citation.

3. This is the *long title* of the Act. The long title gives some indication of the purpose behind the Act. It may be of some use in deciding what the Act is all about. However the long title may be misleading. For example the long title of the Parliament Act 1911 indicates that the Act is part of a process of abolishing the House of Lords. The House of Lords is still there. Long titles are sometimes vague and may conflict with the main body of the Act. In the event of such a conflict the legal rule is that expressed in the main body of the Act.

4. This indicates when the *royal assent* was given and the Coal Industry Bill 1983 became an Act. Statutes become law on the date when they receive the royal assent *unless the Act says otherwise.* The statute itself may say that it becomes law on a fixed date after the royal assent or it may give a Government Minister the power to decide when it becomes law. When a Minister brings a statute into effect after the date on which it has been passed a commencement order must be made. This is a form of delegated legislation. Statutes do not have a retrospective effect unless the Act expressly says so.

5. This is known as the *enacting formula*. It is the standard form of words used to indicate that a Bill has been properly passed by all the different parts of the legislature.

6. By each section you will find a short explanation of the content

of that section. These *marginal notes* may help you understand the content of the section if it is otherwise unclear.

The main body of the statute which follows is broken up into numbered *sections*. Each section contains a different rule of law. When you refer to a rule of law contained in a statute, you should say where that rule of law is to be found. This enables others to check your source and to see whether or not they agree with your interpretation of the law. Instead of writing "section," it is usual to abbreviate it to "s." Thus, section 1 becomes s.1. Sections are often further subdivided. These sub-divisions are known as subsections. When you wish to refer to a subsection you should add it in brackets after the main section.

Example

Does the Coal Industry Act 1983 apply to Northern Ireland? No. See s.6(4) Coal Industry Act 1983.

In larger statutes, sections may be grouped together into different *Parts*. Each Part will deal with a separate area of law. Looking for the correct Part will help you to find the particular legal rule that you want.

Some statutes have one or more *Schedules* at the end. The content of these varies. Some contain detailed provisions which are not found in the main body of the Act. Others are merely convenient reminders and summaries of legal rules, and changes to legal rules, found elsewhere in the Act. In the Coal Industry Act 1983, for example, there is one Schedule to say which sections of previous statutes have been repealed by the 1983 Act. However this Schedule is just there as a reminder. The actual repeals have already been detailed in the main body of the Act. References to Schedules are often abbreviated as "Sched." Where a Schedule is divided up, the divisions are known as *paragraphs* and can be abbreviated as "para.".

USING A STATUTE

Your use of statutory material will vary. Sometimes you will be referred to a particular section or sections of a statute in a case, article, or book that you are reading. In other instances, a new statute will be passed which you need to assess as a whole in order to see how it affects those areas of law that you are interested in. In either case, when first reading statutory material, you may be able to gain some help in deciding what it means from commentaries.

Commentaries are explanations of the law written by legal academics or practitioners. Annotated statutes, which were discussed earlier, are one useful source of such commentaries. You may also find such commentaries in books and articles on the area of law in which the statute falls. Always remember that a commentary represents only one author's opinion of what the statute says. In the case of a very new statute there will probably be no commentary. Therefore, you will need to be able to read a statute yourself, so that you can assess the value of other's opinions and form your own view when there is no other help available.

When reading a statute, do not begin at the beginning and then work your way through to the end, section by section. Statutes do not necessarily use words to mean the same thing that they do in ordinary conversation. Before you can decide what a statute is about you need to know if there are any special meanings attached to words in it. These special meanings can be found in the Act, often in sections called *definition* or *interpretation sections.* These are frequently found towards the end of the Act. For example, in the Coal Industry Act 1983, definitions of some of the phrases used in the Act are found in section 5. An Act may have more than one definition section. Sometimes Parliament, when laying down a particular meaning for a word will say that that meaning will apply in all statutes in which that word appears. Unless a statute specifically says this, you should assume that a definition in a statute applies only to the use of the word in that statute.

You are now in a position to decide what new legal rules the statute creates. Some people begin this task by reading the long title of the Act to give themselves some idea of the general aim of the statute. Although this can be helpful, as we saw above in the section on the different parts of the Act, it can also be misleading.

Statutes should be read carefully and slowly. The general rule is that a statute means precisely what it says. Each word is important. Because of this, some words which we use loosely in ordinary conversation take on special significance when found in a statute. For example, it is important to distinguish between words like "may" and "shall," one saying you can do something and the other saying you must do something. Conjunctives, such as "and," joining things together, must be distinguished from disjunctives, such as "or," dividing things apart.

Example

Part of one process of getting a divorce involves showing that a husband and wife have been separated for 2 years and that they both consent to the divorce. (Section 1(2)(d) Matrimonial Causes Act 1973) This would be a very different provision if it said that it was necessary for there to be proof that the couple had been separated for 2 years or that they had both consented to the divorce. As the law stands the couple must show that both requirements are fulfilled. If a disjunctive were substituted, in the law, a couple would need to prove only one or other of the conditions existed.

So far, the emphasis has been upon closely reading the particular statute. You should also remember that the statute should be read in the context of the general Acts, rules and principles of statutory interpretation discussed in Chapter 1.

One further thing to remember when reading a statute is that the fact that it has been printed does not mean that it is part of the law of the land. It may have been repealed. It may not yet be in force. Re-read pages 49–52 if you cannot remember how to find out of a statute has been repealed. Go back and read about the royal assent on page 74 if you cannot remember how to find out if a statute is in force.

STATUTORY INSTRUMENTS

What statutory instruments are, the way in which they are created, and the purposes which they have, are discussed on page 5.

Statutory instruments should be read in the same way as statutes. However, whilst statutes make relatively little reference to other sources, statutory instruments because of their purpose, make very frequent reference either to other statutory instruments or to their parent statute. The legislative power has been given only for a limited purpose, the statutory instrument is a small part of a larger whole. For this reason, you will find it much more difficult to understand a statutory instrument if you do not have access to the surrounding legislation. Before reading a statutory instrument it is vital that you understand the legislative framework into which it fits.

CHAPTER 6

Reading research materials

Chapter 4 explained that one of the ways of answering questions about law was the use of the research methods of the social scientist. Because this kind of research is the only way in which some questions about law can be answered, it is important that those interested in law can understand it.

In order to understand research into law you have to understand how and why it is written in the particular way that it is. Once you can understand the structure of the material, you will be able to see whether or not it helps to answer the questions in which you are interested.

Haphazard approaches to research are likely to be unsuccessful, the information gathered being too unrepresentative of the world at large and, therefore, too inaccurate for any conclusions to be drawn safely. Good research is done systematically. Research methods are highly developed.

There are three sources of information about how and why the law operates: records, people and activities. There are also three principal methods used in socio-legal research. The researcher may read records, interview people (or send questionnaires), or observe activities.

RECORD READING

The researcher reads the records and collects the required information, which is then either written down or noted on a prepared recording sheet. The researchers must ensure that the information collected from each record is as accurate and as complete as possible. This may involve searching through disordered files of letters and notes or simply copying the details from a form, such as a divorce petition.

INTERVIEWS AND QUESTIONNAIRES

Interviews are conducted in person; questionnaires are given, or sent, to the respondents to complete. It is important, in so far as is possible, to ask the same questions in the same way each time so as to get comparable information. Questions may be "open-ended," allowing the respondent to reply in his or her own words, or be "closed," requiring selection of the answer from a choice given by the interviewer. The style and wording of the question is selected to fit the data sought. Whatever the questions, the interview must be recorded. This may be done by using a tape recorder or by the interviewer noting the replies. Interviews are most useful for finding out what reasons people have for what they have done and for exploiting their feelings. If questions are asked about the future, the answers can only indicate what respondents currently think they would do. It has also been established that recollection of past events may be inaccurate, particularly about dates, times and the exact sequence of events. Interview and questionnaire design requires considerable skill, as does interviewing itself. If it is to reflect the respondent's views rather than those of the researcher.

OBSERVATION

The observer attends the event and records what occurs there. The observer may be an outsider, for example, a person watching court proceedings from the public gallery. Alternatively, the observer may be a person actually taking part in the events being described, for example, a police officer researching into the police force. Observation needs to be done systematically and accurately in order to avoid bias. Observers cannot record everything that they see. They must be careful that they do not record only what they want to see and neglect that which is unexpected and, perhaps, thereby unwelcome. One great difficulty in noting observations lies in deciding what to note down and what to omit. What seems unimportant at the time the notes were taken may take on a greater significance when a later analysis is made. It is important that the observer's record is contemporaneous, otherwise the data is weakened by what has been forgotten.

For any particular piece of research, one method may be more suitable than another, because of the nature of the data sources or the approach which the researcher wishes to take. If, for example, you want to research into the reasons magistrates have for their decisions, there is little point in reading records of what those decisions were. Here, the best place to start would be to interview magistrates. No single method can be said to provide the truth about every situation; some would argue that no method can provide the truth about any situation, for no one truth exists. Each method provides information based on the perceptions of the people who provide it, the record keepers, the interviewers or the observers.

Choice of research method depends not only what information is sought but also on practicalities. The researcher may not be given access to records or permitted to carry out interviews. Professional bodies and employers are not always willing to let their members or staff participate in research. This may be because they consider the research unethical (perhaps requiring them to divulge information given in confidence), because they are too busy, because they do not see the value of the research or because they wish to conceal the very information in which the researcher is interested. Thus, for example, it is unusual for researchers to be able to interview judges about cases, although there is nothing to prevent them sitting in the public gallery and watching cases from there.

For many research studies more than one method is used to obtain a complete picture. However, practical matters, including budget and time limits, may mean that not every avenue of enquiry is pursued. What is important is that the methods chosen are appropriate to the subject of study, the approach of the researcher and the conclusions drawn.

SAMPLING

Looking at every case is not normally practical in detailed social research. Instead, the researcher takes a *sample* of cases. Thus, one may interview some lawyers or some defendants or observe, or read records at some courts. If a completely random sample is taken, then it should have the characteristics of the population as a whole. A sample of judges should, for example, include judges of the different ages, backgrounds and experience to be found amongst the judiciary. However, if a characteristic is very rare a sample may not contain any example of having that characteristic. Thus, a 10 per cent sample of judges, (*i.e.* contacting every tenth judge) might well fail to include any women judges since there are very few of them. The size of sample and method of sampling must be chosen to fit with the study. In a study of attitudes of clients to lawyers there is clearly no point in interviewing only successful clients. The number of people refusing to take part in a study is also important. Researchers will try to obtain a high *response rate* (over 75 per cent) and also attempt to find out if those who refuse are likely to be different in any material way from those who agree to participate in the study.

RESEARCH FINDINGS

The account of any research will usually include some background information about the subject, the purpose of the study (the questions to be answered) and the methods used. Findings presented in words should cause no difficulty to the reader, but numbers may be quite confusing. Where comparisons are made, it is usually thought better to use either *proportions* or *percentages* rather than actual numbers. It is then important to be clear what the percentage represents: for example, was it 20 per cent of all plaintiffs or 20 per cent of successful plaintiffs. Some researchers do not give the actual figures, but prefer to use words such as "some," "most" or "the majority." This is not very helpful, since a word like "majority" can mean anything from 51 per cent to 99 per cent. There is a variety of ways of presenting figures so as to make them clearer. *Tables* (lists of figures) are commonly used because they make it easier to compare two or more categories or questions. *Graphic presentation*, using bar charts (histograms), pie charts or graphs, can create a clear overall impression of a complex set of figures.

Figure 1 below is a *bar chart*. It shows clearly the different numbers of the three offences where guns were used. It also shows for each the relative proportion in which particular types of gun were used. As can be seen from this example, the greatest advantage of a bar chart is the way in which it makes a quick visual comparison of information easy.

Figure 2 is a *pie chart*. The whole circle represents 100 per cent of the particular group. The segments represent different percentages. In this example, the exact percentages represented in the different segments have been printed on to the chart. This is not always done. Different circles represent both different types of original sentence and different courts in which that sentence was imposed. The segments themselves indicate what happened to people who breached their original sentence: for example, by committing a further crime whilst on probation.

Figure 3 is a *graph*. This is probably the best way of showing a trend over time. The graph is designed to show the rise in the number of females found guilty of indictable (basically, serious offences). There are two major problems in doing this. One is that an increase in numbers caused by an increase in the size of the population as a whole is not very interesting. Thus, rather than

Figure 1 Notifiable offences in which firearms were reported to have been used, by type of offence and type of weapon

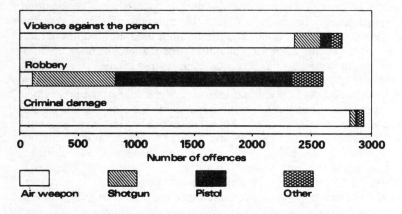

Figures 1, 2 and 3 on pp. 77–78 are from *Criminal Statistics 1982*, HMSO.

Figure 2 Persons breaching their original sentence or order by type of sentence or order imposed for the breach

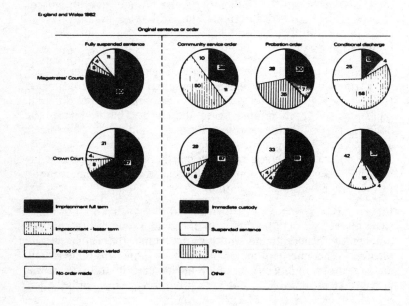

Figure 3 Females found guilty of, or cautioned for, indictable offences[1] per 100,000 population in the age group by age

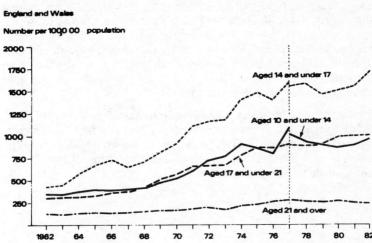

England and Wales

Number per 100,000 population

[1] 1962–76 not adjusted for Criminal Law Act 1977 nor the change in the counting of proceedings.

counting the absolute number of offenders, the graph shows the number of offenders per 100,000 in the population. Secondly, the law relating to who is guilty of an indictable offence was changed in the course of the period which the graph records. Thus, some of the increase in the number of offenders may be due to the fact that the categories of indictable crime have become different. The graph indicates this by showing a dotted vertical line through 1977 (the year in which the change took effect).

As well as graphs and tables, most researchers will state the conclusions that they have drawn from the material and summarise the main findings of the study. It is crucial that the data should establish no more and no less than is stated in the conclusions. Some researchers make great claims for their data, whilst others do not draw out all the answers which it could provide. To avoid being persuaded by poor reasoning, look at the data and see what conclusions seem appropriate, then read the explanation given, and compare it with what you originally thought.

A critical approach to any empirical research should always consider the following three questions. First, are the methods chosen appropriate? This includes both, "have the right questions been asked" and "have the right people (people who should know about the topic) been asked?" There may have been better sources of information available to the researcher, but were the ones used good enough for this study? Secondly, is the sample big enough and has it been properly drawn? Thirdly, does the data justify the conclusions which have been drawn? If it does not, can you see any other conclusions which it would justify?

Research often leaves as many questions raised as answered provided. Further studies may be indicated, interesting new areas which need to be explored. Studying this type of material will, hopefully, increase your interest and insight into the operation of law. It will not provide you with all the answers.

CHAPTER 7

STUDY SKILLS

STUDYING EFFECTIVELY

Whilst you need to be reasonably intelligent in order to be a successful student, you do not have to be a genius. However, if you are not in the genius category, you need to make the most of the ability you have. In other words, you need to study effectively. Studying effectively will not only give you the opportunity to try and improve your academic performance, but will also help to make studying a more enjoyable and satisfying experience. Successful study does not simply involve spending a lot of time reading books. Students who spend a lot of time on their work do not always receive high marks. The purpose of this chapter is to suggest some techniques which you can apply to the tasks which law students are asked to carry out, such as writing essays, reading cases and statutes, participating in seminars and sitting examinations. These techniques are intended to enable you to study effectively. If you are able to study effectively, you should be able not only to be successful in your academic work, but also to have sufficient time for a social life as well.

MANAGING YOUR TIME

One of the most valuable things you can learn as a student is how to manage your time. This, like the other skills discussed in this chapter, is what employers would call a "transferrable skill," a technique which, once you have mastered it, you should be able to apply to numerous other situations.

As a law student, you will be expected to do a number of different things—attend classes or lectures, prepare work for discussion in tutorials, seminars or classes, write essays. Often you will be given several of these tasks at once. Clearly you cannot do them all at the same time. You will have to plan your time, working out how much time is available, identifying what you need to do, how long it will take you and when you are going to do it, so that you can complete all the tasks before the relevant deadline.

Most people find that it is best to plan one or two weeks' activities at a time. Sometimes you will need to plan for longer, for example when you are planning your revision for examinations, but generally speaking it is best to plan for a smaller period. This means that if anything goes wrong with your planning, you do not have to wait for very long before you can adjust your ideas. It is best to make your plan as simple as possible. Your academic timetable gives you a good basis from which to start. You can just extend it into the evenings and the weekends.

Make a list of all the things you want to fit in. There will probably be more things on your list than you have time to do, so you will have to prioritise your list. Highlight those things which you must do, like attending compulsory classes. Then look at other tasks which have to be completed by a particular deadline, such as preparation for essays or tutorials. There may also be practical tasks which are important, such as getting a repair kit for your pushbike. There are then the things you would like to do fairly soon, such as going round to see friends. Finally, there are a number of things which you would like to do at some point when you have time, such as writing to your brother. Number the items on your list, dividing them into three or four levels of priority. Once you have prioritised your list, you can fill in your timetable accordingly, putting the most important items in first. When you are working out your timetable, there are a number of general principles you need to bear in mind:

*Do not try to study for long periods of time without a break.
You will find that making a coffee, going for a brief stroll or reading a newspaper for ten minutes in between periods of study helps to relax you and enables you to extend your total period of study.

*Be realistic when planning your time.
It is counterproductive to set yourself a deadline which you cannot possibly hope to meet. If you do not allow yourself sufficient time to do something, your timetable will not work properly, and you may start to feel depressed and frustrated. If your schedule is realistic, you will gain satisfaction from knowing you have achieved what you set out to do. Of course, everyone underestimates the time they need sometimes, but you should try to avoid this happening to you too often.

*Recognise your own strengths and weaknesses.
If you are the sort of person who can stay in and write your essay on a Saturday afternoon when all your friends are going out together, so you have time to go to a party on Saturday evening, then you can build this into your timetable. On the other hand, if you are the sort of person who cannot wake up before 10.00 a.m., it is unrealistic to plan to write your essay at 8.30 a.m. every morning.

*Find out if there are hidden institutional time constraints.
Your time management can be upset by the arrangements made by your institution. It is all very well planning to do lots of research for an essay during the vacation, but not if the library is going to be closed for three weeks. Equally, you may come across the problem of "bunched deadlines," where several of the courses you are doing require assessed work to be handed in on the same day.

You can alleviate these problems by finding out about the library, computers, and other support services well in advance and by asking tutors to give you assignments in good time, but you may not be able to overcome such difficulties completely. If you are used to planning your time, however, you will be able to deal with the resulting pressure on your time much better than someone who has given no thought to such problems.

*Plan to have some time off each week.
The aim of planning your time is to allow you to do your academic work to the best of your ability, but also to have some time left over to enjoy yourself and to relax.

LECTURES—LISTENING AND NOTETAKING

Lectures are generally seen as a cost-effective way of imparting the main ideas in an area to a large number of people. They also give the lecturer the opportunity to tell students about the latest developments in an area, and to explain any particularly complex parts of a subject. Lectures are often regarded as forming the backbone of a course and it is assumed that most students will attend them.

Lecturing style is closely related to the personality of an individual lecturer, so you are likely to come across a wide variety of lecturers. Some will be excellent, some less so. As a student, you will need to develop a good technique for dealing with lectures, which you can then adapt to cope with the different lecturing styles you come across.

Listening to a lecture can be a very passive experience. Students are not generally expected to interrupt a lecture by asking questions or making comments. It is therefore very easy to "switch off" and lose the thread of the lecture. In order to get the most out of lectures, you need to listen effectively and take good notes. Doing both of these things helps to make the experience less passive and also helps you to record the lecture in a way which will prove useful for future reference.

Listening effectively does not mean merely that you *hear* the lecture. It means that you listen actively. Taking notes will help you listen actively, because it provides the listening activity with a purpose. You should also listen reflectively; in other words, you should try to relate what you are hearing to your existing knowledge of the subject and think how the new information fits into it. A lecture can be very boring if the lecturer has a monotonous delivery, but as an effective listener, you need to train yourself to ignore poor delivery, and concentrate on the content of what is being said.

In order to help you concentrate in lectures, you need to eliminate as many distractions as possible. Make sure you are comfortable; Use a clipboard if there is no desk. Use a convenient size of paper, which gives you enough space to set out your notes clearly. Decide whether you prefer lined or unlined paper. If you have a series of consecutive lectures you may become uncomfortable because you are sitting for long periods; try to move your limbs slightly during the lecture and use any brief gaps between the lectures to get out of your seat and move around a bit.

Taking notes in lectures not only helps you to concentrate; it also means that you have a record of the content of the lecture which you can refer to in the future. Since one of the main purposes of taking notes is to use them in the future, it is important to devise a system of note-taking which produces a clear set of notes which you will understand when you come to look at them again, weeks or months after the original lecture. The following points may help you to achieve that goal:

*Good presentation is important.
Use headings and sub-headings to emphasise the main points made, and to indicate changes in topics. Numbered points can provide a quick way of noting a large quantity of information. Underlining and the use of different coloured pens can direct your attention to particular points.

*Review your notes as soon as possible.
It is important to review your notes while the lecture is still fresh

in your mind. You may need to expand what you have written, or add headings, or do a little research on a point which you have not understood. Some people like to summarise their notes in diagrammatic form at this stage.

*Arrive in reasonably good time.
Handouts and important announcements are often given out at the beginning of lectures; you may be very confused if you miss them.

TUTORIALS AND SEMINARS

Tutorials involve small groups of students who meet regularly with an academic tutor to discuss questions which have generally been set in advance by the tutor. Seminars are similar, but usually involve larger groups of students; sometimes seminars may be led by one or more of the students. In both cases, all the students are generally expected to have prepared the topic under discussion in advance and tutors usually expect that all the students involved in the group will participate, by joining in the discussion. It may be helpful to be aware of the following points:

*Ensure you know what is expected of you.
Many tutors set specific work for tutorials and seminars. Ensure that you obtain this in good time, so that you can prepare the topic properly. If you are unprepared, and unfamiliar with the subject matter, participating in the discussion is more difficult. Different tutors will run these groups in very different ways. You will need to be adaptable, to fit in with different teaching styles. Some tutors will make this easy for you, by having explicit "ground rules," with others you will have to work it out for yourself.

*Try to participate.
Often, you will attend tutorials and seminars with the same group of people for a whole academic year. Clearly, the experience will be more pleasant if the members of the group get on with each other, but this is essentially a learning experience, so you have to balance your desire to be friendly with your learning needs.

No one wants to make a fool of themselves in front of a group of other people, but if you do not try out ideas in discussion, you are not going to develop your thinking, so a little bravery is called for. Try not to be so worried about what the others will think that you do not participate at all. Everyone is in the same situation, so people are generally sympathetic to contributions made by others.

*Consider making a contribution early in the discussion.
If you make a contribution to the discussion at a fairly early stage, it is likelier to be easier than if you delay participating, for a number of reasons. In the early stages of discussion, it is less likely that other people will have made the point you have thought of. Tutors who are keen to involve the whole group may single out people who have not said anything and ask them direct questions; this is much less likely to happen to you if you have already made a contribution. If you are less confident about talking in front of other people, the longer you wait to say something, the more difficult you may find it to join in.

*Think about the art of polite disagreement.
The aim of academic discussion is to try to develop the ideas you are considering. Often, this involves members of the group disagreeing with one another's ideas. Remember that you are challenging the argument which is put forward, not the person who is advancing it. It is also important to remember this when your ideas are challenged.

*Expect to be challenged.
During group discussions, tutors will try to teach you not to make assumptions. Their aim is to help you to think critically and precisely. They will therefore challenge many of the things you say. Most people are not used to being challenged in this way, and the ability of tutors to question almost everything you say can seem unduly negative. However, if you are going to succeed in thinking rigorously, you need to be able to question your own ideas and those of other people, and tutors whose sessions are the most challenging may turn out to be the best ones you have.

*Do not expect to take notes all the time.
If you take notes of everything that goes on in a tutorial or seminar, you will be so busy writing that you will not be able to participate in the discussion. Not only will you not be able to make an oral contribution, but notetaking also detracts from your ability to think about the points that are being made. Try to limit your notetaking to jotting down the main issues raised and the outline of any answer given. You can then read over your notes later and follow up any points of particular interest.

*Take advantage of small group learning situations.
It is much easier to learn in small groups than in huge lectures, because small groups should give you the opportunity to ask questions about aspects of the subject under discussion which you do not understand so well. Clearly, you do not want to

dominate the discussion, or interrupt with too many questions, but small group situations do give you an opportunity to raise issues which are of particular concern to you.

STARTING TO RESEARCH A TOPIC FOR AN ESSAY, TUTORIAL OR SEMINAR

When you are preparing for a tutorial or seminar, or preparing to write an essay or problem answer, you will need to carry out some research, in order to find the information you need. In the case of tutorials and seminars, you will often be given specific reading lists, so some of the research has been done for you, but you will still need to use the information to the best advantage, in much the same way as you need to do when you are writing an essay or problem answer.

Firstly, define the area you are interested in. This task will have been done for you in relation to tutorials and seminars, but you need to work it out for yourself in relation to essays and problems. Next, read the question carefully. Think about what you are being asked to do. Titles which invite you to "discuss" or "critically analyse" mean that you are expected to engage in reasoned argument about the topic; you are not being invited merely to describe something. At this stage, you should make a plan. A plan provides a structure for your argument and allows you to organise your arguments into a coherent whole. It is a vital stage of the research process and you need to produce a plan as soon as possible. You may want to do a bit of basic reading first, but generally, the plan should be one of your first tasks. When preparing for tutorials or seminars, your plan might be just a simple "shopping list" of the topics you have to cover, but if you have been asked questions which require you to look at a particular aspect of the subject, you will need a more elaborate plan, similar to that for an essay. Plans for problem answers are easier to produce than those for essays, because the events which make up the problem give you a structure for your plan. Plan the main points of your answer carefully, fitting in subsidiary points in the most logical places.

Example of the first plan for an essay entitled

"The reform of the legal profession by the Courts and Legal Services Act 1990 was a non-event." Discuss.

Introduction—reasons for reform—refer to relevant reports e.g. Marre

Reforms carried out by Courts and Legal Services Act—brief description

Not a non-event—a) outcry by barristers and judiciary
b) removal of barristers' monopoly in higher courts

Possibly could be said to be an immediate non-event because of delay by designated judges.

However, conclusion = not a non-event, altered face of legal profession radically—quote from articles.

Use your plan flexibly. It is there to help you; you do not have to stick with your original plan too rigidly. If you can see a better way of organising your argument once you have done a bit of reading, then adjust the plan—but do not abandon it. Many students fail to realise that a plan can go through several versions during the research process. It is unlikely that you will come up with the perfect plan immediately, so be prepared to be flexible. The plan in the example above is just a first draft. It provides a basic framework, but it does not contain enough ideas at this stage. The author needs to go and do some more reading before amending the plan in the light of the additional information. However, this is a good start.

Once you have made your plan, you will need to find out some more information about the topic involved. Often, your topic will have been referred to in reading lists or handouts used in classes, so this is a good place to start. Look on the reading lists for books and journal articles relating to your topic. If you are dealing with a completely unknown topic, try looking it up in the relevant student textbooks. Either way, you will come up with some information to get you started. You can then look at the footnotes in the part of the book or the article which is most relevant to your topic, and look up these references to give you some more information.

You also need to find out if there are any books or journal articles which are relevant to your topic. Use the library catalogues to help you do this. You may also find electronic databases or CD Roms which are relevant. You need to ensure that you are using your library as effectively as possible. There may be leaflets designed to help readers find their way around the different catalogues; see if any of these are relevant to you. Some libraries have specialist librarians who are immensely knowledgeable and helpful. Try to help yourself first, but do not ignore the experts whose job it is to help you.

If you are researching a topic which many other people are working on at the same time, you need not be particularly skilled in using the library. Perhaps the most obviously helpful books are all out on loan. Do not despair! Consider the following techniques:

*Use bibliographic sources.

There are a number of publications which give details of all British books in print, arranged by subject, as well as by author and title. The Index to Legal Periodicals will help you to find articles in legal journals and there are similar publications relating to social science literature.

*Work backwards in time.

Start with the most recent literature on your chosen topic, *i.e.* the latest books and the most recent issues of relevant journals. These items may not appear on reading lists, so may have been missed by others.

*Search other nearby libraries.

Many libraries now have the facility to allow you to search the catalogues of other libraries. Think of other libraries in the area which you could use and have a look in their catalogues to see if it would be worthwhile visiting them. Perhaps their students are not all doing the essay on offences against the person which your year has been set.

*Use the references in the text.

Academic writing contains a lot of references and footnotes. At first, this can be confusing, and you may tend to ignore them. However, when you are researching a topic, footnotes and references are an important source of further information. If you look up the material referred to in parts of an article or book that are directly relevant to your work, you will find that footnotes serve some important purposes.

a) They give full references to articles or books which are just mentioned or summarised in the text. This is useful if the material referred to is relevant to your work, because you can then read the full text.

b) They give references to other books or articles on the same topic, which put forward a similar argument (or the opposite one—often indicated by the word *contra* in front of the reference). Again, you can extend your knowledge by following up the references.

c) They give further explanation about points made in the text.

When you are gathering and using written materials, remember that you must always read things for yourself. The insertion of a footnote in a piece of academic writing does not necessarily mean that the footnote is accurate. Sometimes, when you find the article or case report which is referred to, you discover that it cannot possibly be used as justification for the proposition which you have just read. In order to find out whether a footnote is accurate, you will need to look up the reference for yourself. You should not merely replicate a reference without looking it up for yourself.

When you are copying down references from the library catalogue, or any other source, it is important that you take down all the information which you will need. For a book, you will need the author, title, date of publication and edition, plus the reference number—usually a Dewey decimal reference number. Your reference should look something like this:

Bradney et al *How to Study Law* 1995 3rd edition 340.07 HOW

If you are finding a journal article, your reference will be something like:

Addison & Cownie "Overseas Law Students: Language Support and Responsible Recruitment" (1992) 19 JLS p467 PER 340 J 6088

If you do not take down a proper reference for items that you consult, you may find that you waste a lot of time desperately trying to remember which chapter of which book contained that really good quotation, which you now want to use to finish off your essay.

READING

Once you have used your reading list or some of the other bibliographic sources indicated above, you will have to decide whether the references you have found are going to be useful for you. As far as books are concerned, the catalogue will give you some basic information, such as the date of publication and the edition. Legal textbooks go out of date very quickly, so this is important information. If a book is old, it may be inaccurate. Equally, you should generally use the latest edition of a book; often your tutors will refer you to a particular edition, and this is the one you should use; you cannot merely substitute another edition. Not all older books will be relevant; you will need to make up your own mind in each case.

You will have to develop a strategy for dealing with the large amount of reading you will have to do. All students have to face this problem, but if you are studying law, you have a particular problem, because although by this stage you are an expert reader, you are unlikely to have had much experience, if any, of reading legal materials, such as case reports and statutes, so in this respect you are a novice again. The chapters in this book which deal with reading cases and statutes will help you develop an effective method of reading these new types of text, and once you have practised a bit, you will find that you can process them as quickly as other types of text, such as articles or textbooks, with which you are already familiar.

There are many different ways of reading; for example, you can skim quickly through something, or you can read it slowly and carefully. In order to decide what kind of reading you should be doing at any particular time, you need to think about the purpose of your reading. You also need to be aware of the different techniques of reading and be able to use each type as it becomes relevant.

*Titles are there to help you.
When looking at a book, the title and contents pages will give you a broad outline of the information you will find. Subheadings within an article perform the same function.

*Scan the text first.
To check the relevance of a text, skim through it, looking for the key words and phrases which will give you the general sense of the material and enable you to decide whether it is relevant for your purposes.

*Approach the text gradually.
Even when you have decided that a particular chapter of a book or an article is relevant, check it out before you begin to take notes; you may not need to take notes on the whole chapter, but only a part of it; similarly, with an article. It is often suggested that you should read the first sentence of each paragraph to find out more precisely what the text is about.

*Reading Statutes.
As you have discovered in Chapter 5 of this book, statutes must be read carefully and precisely. At first, they can seem very complicated to read, because they are so detailed. When you read a section of a statute, try to establish the main idea first, then you can re-read it and fill in the details on the second reading. You might find it helpful to photocopy the parts of the

statute which you have to read, so that you can use a pen or highlighter to mark the main idea. There is an example below:

Sale of Goods Act 1979 Section 11 (3)

Whether a stipulation in a contract is a condition, the breach of which may give rise to a right to treat the contract as repudiated, **or a warranty**, the breach of which may give rise to a claim for damages but not to a right to reject the goods and treat the contract as repudiated, **depends in each case on the construction of the contract**; and a stipulation may be a condition, though called a warranty in the contract.

The main point which is being made is quite simple, and can be identified by reading the phrases in bold type "Whether a stipulation in a contract is a condition or a warranty depends in each case on the construction of the contract." Having established what the section is basically about, you can now go back and find out what the section says about the effect of a stipulation in a contract being classified as either a condition or a warranty.

NOTETAKING

Your next task is to extract the information which is relevant to the task you have to carry out. You will probably have gathered a number of different sources, and clearly you will not be able to remember everything they contain, so you are going to have to make notes. It is important that your notes are accurate and clear; if they are not, you will waste a lot of time trying to work out what they mean, and where you found a particular piece of information.

Always begin by asking yourself why you are taking notes. Look back at your plan and refresh your memory as to the question you are trying to answer. Remember that you can take different types of notes on different parts of a text—detailed notes on the directly relevant parts, outline notes on other parts, while sometimes you will be able to read through without taking any notes at all.

Your notes will be more use to you if they are reasonably neat. Try to develop a standard way of recording the source you are taking the notes from, perhaps always putting it at the top right-hand corner of the page, or in the margin. You can use this reference for your bibliography, or for footnotes, or for your own use if you need to clarify a point at some later stage. In order to make it even easier to find your way around the original text, you might like to make a note of the actual page you have read, either in the margin, or in brackets as you go along. Here is an example of some notes on the first few pages of a chapter of a book:

> *H. Genn*
> Hard Bargaining *1st Edn.*
> *Oxford Uni. Press. 1987.*
> *344.6 GEN*

Chapter 3 *"Starting Positions" p.34.*

Structural imbalance between the parties.
One-shotter pl. v Repeat-player def.
(Exceptions, e.g. class action)
cf Galanter 1974
Repeat players—advance intelligence, expertise, access to specialists, economies of scale.
cf Ross 1980
Distribution of personal injury work *(p.35)*
Pls—huge variety of firms.
Defs—insurance co/specialist firm
Defs solicitors allowed few mistakes (p.36 top)
Defs solicitors nurture relationship w insurance co.
Contrast position of general practitioner.

When making notes, it might help to keep the following general points in mind:

*Keep notes and comments separate.
It is a good idea to think critically about the content of what you are reading. However, if you want to make comments, keep these separate in some way, preferably on a separate sheet of paper. Otherwise, when you come back to the notes, you might find it impossible to distinguish your great thoughts from those of the original author.

*Good presentation is important.
Remember that clear presentation of your notes is just as important when you are taking notes for an essay or seminar as it is when you are taking lecture notes. Use headings and subheadings, and remember that underlining and the use of different coloured pens can direct your attention to particular points.

*Consider using a different technique for noting cases.
Many tutors recommend that you help yourself to take brief notes of cases by using filecards, one card for each case. You can note the citation, the facts and the main points of the judgment using two sides of a card and then your notes of cases

are in a very flexible form, so you can arrange them alphabetically, or by topic, or by date, depending on your particular needs.

*Do you need to photocopy the bibliography?

When you are taking notes, you will often note down references to other articles or books referred to in the text you are reading. You will have to decide later whether you need to look these up, but many people find that it disturbs their train of thought to look up the full reference for each of these as they occur in the text. If that is the case, it is important to photocopy the bibliography of your source, so that you have a copy of the full reference in case you need to refer to it later.

WRITING ASSIGNMENTS

You will have begun to prepare your essay long before you start to write it. The first stage was to read the question carefully and make a suitable plan. You will have used this plan to help you when you were carrying out the research for your assignment. When you have gathered all the relevant materials and made the necessary notes, it is time to review your plan in the light of what you have discovered. Read through your notes, bearing in mind all the time the question you have been asked. Now you will be able to make a new plan, indicating not only the main points you are going to make, but also any arguments or pieces of information drawn from your research which you wish to include. Once you are satisfied with your revised plan, you can embark on the first draft of your essay. Before you start, consider the following points:

*Make sure all your points are relevant

Look at your plan. Every argument you make should relate to the question you have been asked. This is what makes it relevant. Here is an example of a first plan for an essay whose title is "Settlement of major litigation is a necessary evil." Discuss.

Settlement—definition.

Settlement is necessary because—a) saves court time b) saves expense c) saves litigants' time.

But settlement is an "evil" because—a) litigants are not equally experienced and do not have equal resources b) inexperienced litigants often go to lawyers who are not specialists in the relevant field—& are not well advised c) inexperienced litigants can easily be put under pressure, *e.g.* by payment into court, delays (often manufactured by the other side), worries about cost, risk-aversion.

Conclusion—settlement is a necessary evil, but currently is so evil it is immoral and unacceptable.

Every point which is made relates directly to the quotation which is under discussion. This is an initial plan. After some research, you would be able to expand some points, and to insert the names of books or articles which you could use to justify the points being made. But you would still ensure that everything fitted in to the basic plan, and related to the quotation.

*Remember the audience you are writing for.

When you write an academic essay, you can assume that you are writing for a reasonably intelligent reader who knows almost nothing about your subject. That means you have to explain clearly every step of your argument. At first, many students are ignorant of this convention. They know their essay is going to be marked by an expert, so they do not bother to include all the information about a topic, only to be told by their tutor "I cannot give you credit for anything, unless it is down in your essay. It's no use keeping things in your head." Do not assume that your tutor will draw on their own knowledge to fill in any gaps in the assignment you have submitted.

*Do not make assertions.

In academic writing, you must always be able to justify what you say. You cannot make assertions, but you must always be able to give evidence or provide reasons for your statements. If someone writes "Small claims are proceedings involving £1,000 or less" that is an assertion. There is no evidence that the statement is true, the author is just expecting us to take their word for it. After a little research, it is possible to rewrite the sentence in an academically acceptable way. "Under Order 19 Rule 3(1) of the County Court Rules, small claims are proceedings involving £1,000 or less." If this was a particularly important part of your essay, you could even elaborate by quoting from Order 19. "Under Order 19 Rule 3(1) of the County Court Rules, small claims are 'Any proceedings in which the sum claimed or amount involved does not exceed £1,000 . . .'" Notice that you do not need to write out the whole of Order 19 Rule 3(1). You just quote the relevant part of the section *i.e.* the part which defines a small claim.

*What kind of introduction?

The beginning of your essay is very important. Unless you have been instructed that you must have an introduction in a particular form, your essay might have more impact if you start straight away with a comment on the central point. Try to interest your reader by indicating the main issue, but do not rehearse all your arguments in the first sentence or two. Openings such as "This essay discusses . . ." can be very boring. They can also give hostages to fortune. If you tell your reader that you are going to discuss X, Y and Z, they will expect you to do exactly that. Such promises can prove very difficult to fulfil.

*Consider the style of your writing.
An academic essay is a formal piece of writing, so the style in which you write should not be too colloquial. Shortened forms of phrases, such as isn't and mustn't, are inappropriate. So is too much slang. However, pomposity is equally inappropriate. Phrases such as "I submit that . . ." are out of place. Advocates make submissions in court, but you do not make submissions in an academic essay. Aim for a clear, direct style, which conveys your arguments in a way which can be readily understood. Use paragraphs to indicate a change of subject, and keep sentences reasonably short. In general, academic writing, is written in an impersonal style, so writers do not use phrases such as "I think that . . ." They use alternative phrases, such as "This indicates that . . ."

*Be prepared to write several drafts.
Before you arrive at the final version of your essay, you should have produced several drafts. You should reach each draft carefully, making additions and alterations which you then incorporate into the next draft. Although it is important to correct the spelling and the grammar in each draft, the primary reason for having several drafts is to give yourself the opportunity to examine your argument and make sure that it is as convincing as possible. Think about what you are saying. Have you justified all the points you have made? Does the argument flow logically from one point to another? Is the material relevant?

*Do not describe too much.
In general, the object of writing academic essays is to engage in critical analysis, *i.e.* thought and argument. Your tutors are not looking for detailed descriptions of subjects which they could, after all, read in any competent textbook. A certain amount of description is necessary, to explain what you are talking about, but the main emphasis in any academic piece of work will be on analysing. You are interpreting for the reader the significance of what you have described, and it is this process which is most important.

*Acknowledge your sources.
During the course of your writing, you will often put forward arguments and ideas which you have discovered in books or articles. If you do this, you must acknowledge that the idea is

not an original one. You can do this expressly in the text by saying something like "As Bradney argues in 'How to Study Law' . . . or you can use a footnote to indicate the source of the idea. What you must not do is to pass off someone else's idea as if it were something you had thought of for yourself. That is stealing their idea, and it is a practice known as plagiarism. In academic life, where people's ideas are of the utmost importance, plagiarism is regarded as a form of cheating. Ideally, you will use other people's ideas as a base from which to develop thoughts of your own, acknowledging their idea, and then going on to say something original about them. This is the kind of critical thinking which you are trying to develop.

WRITING PROBLEM ANSWERS

Sometimes, instead of setting you an essay to write, your tutors may give you a legal problem to solve. This will usually consist of a fictional scenario, in which a series of events is described. Various different characters appear in the scenario, and you may be asked to advise one or more of the characters, in the light of the events that have happened to them. An example is given below:

> Bill called at Amanda's house, begging. Amanda told him to weed the garden for an hour. When he had finished, she gave Bill an overcoat and said to him, "You've done a good job; come back on Wednesday and I will give you £10."

> When Bill called on Wednesday, Amanda refused to give him any money. Advise Bill.

It is often said that it is easier to answer a problem than to write an essay, but this is largely a matter of personal preference. Problem answers are certainly easier in one sense, because they provide a framework for your answer by posing certain issues which you must answer. You need to carry out the research and planning process described above when you are answering a problem question. You also need to bear in mind the following points:

*Problem answers do not need lengthy introductions.
The convention is that you need to introduce a problem answer by identifying the main issue in the problem, but you do not need a lengthy introduction.

*All points of law must be justified by reference to authority.
Whenever you make a statement about the law, you must give the relevant legal authority, which might be a case or a section

of a statute, for example, "When X wrote to Y saying that if he did not hear from Y, he would assume that Y agreed to the contract, this has no effect, because silence does not imply consent (*Felthouse v. Bindley* (1862) 11 C.B. 869)."

*Socio Legal information is not relevant in a problem answer.
Strictly speaking, problem questions are just asking you to identify the relevant legal rules relating to the issues raised. There may be very interesting research studies on a topic, but these are not relevant to a problem answer.

ASSESSMENT

It is likely that you will experience a number of different forms of assessment, including continuous assessment, based on written work submitted during the course of the academic year, and the traditional three-hour unseen examination. The strategies discussed above will help you to cope with the various forms of continuous assessment which you are likely to meet. This section will therefore concentrate on strategies designed to help you cope with the traditional unseen examination.

*Make a revision timetable in good time.
It is important to make a realistic revision timetable well in advance of the examinations, allocating a certain amount of time for each subject you have to prepare. Most people find it best to study each subject in turn, rather than finishing one before going on to the next one.

*Make sure you get enough rest.
Studying hard for examinations is a very tiring experience. It is important to ensure that you get sufficient sleep and exercise, so that you remain as fresh as possible. Burning the midnight oil is not necessarily a sensible strategy.

*Reduce your notes to a manageable size.
At the beginning of the revision period, you are likely to find that you have a large amount of notes. It is a good idea to precis these, so that you end up with a manageable quantity of material to work with. As the examinations approach, most people reduce their notes, perhaps several times, so that a whole topic can be covered comprehensively, but speedily.

*Question-spotting is a risky strategy.
It is sensible to consider what sort of subjects might come up in the examination. Consulting old examination papers is a useful way of finding out what is expected of you in the

exam. However, it is unwise to "question spot" too precisely. It is unlikely that you will be able to revise the whole course; indeed, this would often be a waste of effort, but you need to cover several subjects in addition to the three or four which you hope will come up, so that you have plenty of choice when it comes to deciding which questions you will answer in the examination. Remember that you need to be familiar with a range of subjects because:

a) Your favourite topics might not come up at all.
b) Some topics might come up, but in a way which is unfamiliar to you.
c) Your favourite topic might be mixed up with another topic which you have not revised.

*Consider practising timed answers.
If you find it difficult to write answers quickly, it is a good idea to practice writing some answers in the same time that you will have in the examination. Use questions from old examination papers.

Before you enter the examination room, make sure you have all the pens, pencils, etc., that you need. Wear something comfortable, preferably several layers of clothing so you can discard some if the room is hot, or add additional layers if you are cold. Check whether you are allowed to take drinks or food into the examination room. If you are allowed to do so, it is a matter of personal choice whether you take advantage of this facility or not; some people find it helps to have a can of drink, others find it a distraction. Check that you know where you have to sit, and whether there are any attendance slips or other forms that you have to fill in. Ensure that you know whether or not you will be told when you can start the examination—you do not want to sit there, waiting for an instruction which never comes.

In the examination, plan your time carefully. Provided that all the questions carry an equal number of marks, you should allow an equal amount of time for answering each question. Subdivide your time into reading the question, planning the answer, writing the answer and checking it. Planning is a very important part of good examination technique. If you spend a few minutes setting out a good plan, it will allow you to write a much fuller answer than if you are thinking out your answer as you go along, because all the basic thinking will be done at the planning stage, and you will be able to concentrate on writing a relevant answer. Bear in mind the following points:

*Read the rubric carefully.
Make sure that you read the instructions at the top of the
examination paper very carefully. The paper may be divided into
different sections and frequently candidates must answer a certain
number of questions from each section. Sometimes you will be
asked to write certain questions in certain answer books.

*Keep to the timing you have worked out.
Do not spend more than the time which you have allocated for
each question. If you run out of time, leave that question and
go on to the next one, returning to the unfinished question if
you have some spare time later.

*Answer the question.
Read the question carefully. To gain the maximum number of
marks, your answer must be relevant to the question you have
been asked. If you are familiar with a topic on which a question
is set, it is tempting to write down a version of your notes, which
includes all you know about that topic, in the hope that you will
get a reasonable number of marks. However, if you merely write
all you happen to know about a topic, it is unlikely that you will
be answering the question. You need to slant your information
to the question, showing how the things you know relate to the
precise question which you have been asked.

*Answer the correct number of questions.
Under pressure of time, some people fail to answer the whole
examination paper by missing out a question. They often use the
last few minutes to perfect their answers to the questions they
have completed. This is not a good strategy. Examiners can only
award marks for what is written on the examination paper. By
not answering a question, you have forfeited all the marks
allocated to that question. However, it is often said that the
easiest marks to gain are the ones awarded for the beginning of
an answer, so if you do run out of time, it is much better to use
those final minutes to start the final question, rather than per-
fecting answers you have already finished.

*Examiners are human.
When you are writing an examination paper, you often feel as if
the examiner is the enemy "out there", determined to fail you.
In fact, examiners do not want candidates to fail. They want to
be fair, but they generally expect students who have done a
reasonable amount of work to pass examinations.

INTERNATIONAL STUDENTS

The study skills discussed in this chapter are required by all law students. However, if English is not your first language you may feel that you would like some extra assistance with studying in the United Kingdom. Most institutions which welcome students from around the world have a support service which offers different classes covering a range of English Language and study skills, and you should try and find out about these at an early stage in your course. Many institutions also offer self-access materials, which you can go and use at a time which is convenient for you.

The support service will also be able to help you familiarise yourself with the particular types of teaching and learning situations which you will find in British educational institutions, what might be termed the "hidden culture" of learning, such as particular ways of writing essays or behaving in seminars, which might be different to those with which you are familiar at home. This sort of information can be very useful, as it is impossible to discover beforehand, however good your English is.

FURTHER READING

If you would like to find out more about any of the topics covered in this chapter, you will find that there are many books on study skills available. The following brief list includes books which cover a wide range of study skills.

M. Smith & G. Smith, *A Study Skills Handbook* (2nd ed., 1990) Oxford University Press

R. Barnes, *Successful Study for Degrees* (1st ed., 1992) Routledge

L. Marshall & F. Rowland, *A Guide to Learning Independently* (2nd ed., 1993) Open University Press

PART 3

EXERCISES

This section of the book will test your understanding of the skills we have just described. Before attempting each exercise reread the appropriate chapter of this book. Each exercise is divided into two sections. Answers to Section A in each exercise are to be found at the back of this book. Do not look at these answers before you have tried to do the questions yourself. There are no answers to Section B in this book. You should discuss your answers to these questions with either your course tutor or with someone else you know who is studying law.

EXERCISE 1

Statutes I

Start by re-reading the appropriate parts of Chapter 5 and then look at the Timeshare Act 1992. Then answer the questions. When answering the questions, make sure that you include the correct statutory reference.

TIMESHARE ACT 1992

(1992 c. 35)

An Act to provide for rights to cancel certain agreements about timeshare accommodation.   [16th March 1992]

Application of Act

1.—(1) In this Act—
(a) "timeshare accommodation" means any living accommodation, in the United Kingdom or elsewhere, used or intended to be used, wholly or partly, for leisure purposes

by a class of person (referred to below in this section as "timeshare users") all of whom have rights to use, or participate in arrangements under which they may use, that accommodation, or accommodation within a pool of accommodation to which that accommodation belongs, for intermittent periods of short duration, and

(b) "timeshare rights" means rights by virtue of which a person becomes or will become a timeshare user, being rights exercisable during a period of not less than three years.

(2) For the purposes of subsection (1)(a) above—

(a) "accommodation" means accommodation in a building or in a caravan (as defined in section 29(1) of the Caravan Sites and Control of Development Act 1960), and

(b) a period of not more than one month, or such other period as may be prescribed, is a period of short duration.

(3) Subsection (1)(b) above does not apply to a person's rights—

(a) as the owner of any shares or securities,

(b) under a contract of employment (as defined in section 153 of the Employment Protection (Consolidation) Act 1978) or a policy of insurance, or

(c) by virtue of his taking part in a collective investment scheme (as defined in section 75 of the Financial Services Act 1986),

or to such rights as may be prescribed.

(4) In this Act "timeshare agreement" means, subject to subsection (6) below, an agreement under which timeshare rights are conferred or purport to be conferred on any person and in this Act, in relation to a timeshare agreement—

(a) references to the offeree are to the person on whom timeshare rights are conferred, or purport to be conferred, and

(b) references to the offeror are to the other party to the agreement,

and, in relation to any time before the agreement is entered into, references in this Act to the offeree or the offeror are to the persons who become the offeree and offeror when it is entered into.

(5) In this Act "timeshare credit agreement" means, subject to subsection (6) below, an agreement, not being a timeshare agreement—

(a) under which a person (referred to in this Act as the "creditor" provides or agrees to provide credit for or in respect of a person who is the offeree under a timeshare agreement, and

(b) when the credit agreement is entered into, the creditor knows or has reasonable cause to believe that the whole or part of the credit is to be used for the purpose of financing the offeree's entering into a timeshare agreement.

(6) An agreement is not a timeshare agreement or a timeshare

credit agreement if, when entered into, it may be cancelled by virtue of section 67 of the Consumer Credit Act 1974.

(7) This Act applies to any timeshare agreement or timeshare credit agreement if—

(a) the agreement is to any extent governed by the law of the United Kingdom or of a part of the United Kingdom, or

(b) when the agreement is entered into, one or both of the parties are in the United Kingdom.

(8) In the application of this section to Northern Ireland—

(a) for the reference in subsection (2)(a) above to section 29(1) of the Caravan Sites and Control of Development Act 1960 there is substituted a reference to section 25(1) of the Caravans Act (Northern Ireland) 1963, and

(b) for the reference in subsection (3)(b) above to section 153 of the Employment Protection (Consolidation) Act 1978 there is substituted a reference to article 2(2) of the Industrial Relations (Northern Ireland) Order 1976.

Obligation to give notice of right to cancel timeshare agreement

2.—(1) A person must not in the course of a business enter into a timeshare agreement to which this Act applies as offeror unless the offeree has received, together with a document setting out the terms of the agreement or the substance of those terms, notice of his right to cancel the agreement.

(2) A notice under this section must state—

(a) that the offeree is entitled to give notice of cancellation of the agreement to the offeror at any time on or before the date specified in the notice, being a day falling not less than fourteen days after the day on which the agreement is entered into, and

(b) that if the offeree gives such a notice to the offeror on or before that date he will have no further rights or obligations under the agreement, but will have the right to recover any sums paid under or in contemplation of the agreement.

(3) A person who contravenes this section is guilty of an offence and liable—

(a) on summary conviction, to a fine not exceeding the statutory maximum, and

(b) on conviction on indictment, to a fine.

Obligation to give notice of right to cancel timeshare credit agreement

3.—(1) A person must not in the course of a business enter into a timeshare credit agreement to which this Act applies as creditor unless the offeree has received, together with a document setting out the terms of the agreement or the substance of those terms, notice of his right to cancel the agreement.

(2) A notice under this section must state—

(a) that the offeree is entitled to give notice of cancellation of the agreement to the creditor at any time on or before the date specified in the notice, being a day falling not less than fourteen days after the day on which the agreement is entered into, and

(b) that, if the offeree gives such a notice to the creditor on or before that date, then—

(i) so far as the agreement relates to repayment of credit and payment of interest, it shall have effect subject to section 7 of this Act, and

(ii) subject to sub-paragraph (i) above, the offeree will have no further rights or obligations under the agreement.

Provisions supplementary to sections 2 and 3

4.—(1) Sections 2 and 3 of this Act do not apply where, in entering into the agreement, the offeree is acting in the course of a business.

(2) A notice under section 2 or 3 must be accompanied by a blank notice of cancellation and any notice under section 2 or 3 of this Act or blank notice of cancellation must—

(a) be in such form as may be prescribed, and

(b) comply with such requirements (whether as to type, size, colour or disposition of lettering, quality or colour of paper, or otherwise) as may be prescribed for securing that the notice is prominent and easily legible.

(3) An agreement is not invalidated by reason of a contravention of section 2 or 3.

Right to cancel timeshare agreement

5.—(1) Where a person—

(a) has entered, or proposes to enter, into a timeshare agreement to which this Act applies as offeree, and

(b) has received the notice required under section 2 of this Act before entering into the agreement,

the agreement may not be enforced against him on or before the date specified in the notice in pursuance of subsection (2)(a) of that section and he may give notice of cancellation of the agreement to the offeror at any time on or before that date.

(2) Subject to subscription (3) below, where a person who enters

into a timeshare agreement to which this Act applies as offeree has not received the notice required under section 2 of this Act before entering into the agreement, the agreement may not be enforced against him and he may give notice of cancellation of the agreement to the offeror at any time.

(3) If in a case falling within subsection (2) above the offeree affirms the agreement at any time after the expiry of the period of fourteen days beginning with the day on which the agreement is entered into—

(a) subsection (2) above does not prevent the agreement being enforced against him, and

(b) he may not at any subsequent time give notice of cancellation of the agreement to the offeror.

(4) The offeree's giving, within the time allowed under this section, notice of cancellation of the agreement to the offeror at a time when the agreement has been entered into shall have the effect of cancelling the agreement.

(5) The offeree's giving notice of cancellation of the agreement to the offeror before the agreement has been entered into shall have the effect of withdrawing any offer to enter into the agreement.

(6) Where a timeshare agreement is cancelled under this section, then, subject to subsection (9) below—

(a) the agreement shall cease to be enforceable, and

(b) subsection (8) below shall apply.

(7) Subsection (8) below shall also apply where giving a notice of cancellation has the effect of withdrawing an offer to enter into a timeshare agreement.

(8) Where this subsection applies—

(a) any sum which the offeree has paid under or in contemplation of the agreement to the offeror, or to any person who is the offeror's agent for the purpose of receiving that sum, shall be recoverable from the offeror by the offeree and shall be due and payable at the time the notice of cancellation is given, but

(b) no sum may be recoverable by or on behalf of the offeror from the offeree in respect of the agreement.

(9) Where a timeshare agreement includes provision for providing credit for or in respect of the offeree, then, notwithstanding the giving of notice of cancellation under this section, so far as the agreement relates to repayment of the credit and payment of interest—

(a) it shall continue to be enforceable, subject to section 7 of this Act, and

(b) the notice required under section 2 of this Act must also state that fact.

Right to cancel timeshare credit agreement

6.—(1) Where a person—
(a) has entered into a timeshare credit agreement to which this Act applies as offeree, and
(b) has received the notice required under section 3 of this Act before entering into the agreement,
he may give notice of cancellation of the agreement to the creditor at any time on or before the date specified in the notice in pursuance of subsection (2)(a) of that section.

(2) Subject to subsection (3) below, where a person who enters into a timeshare credit agreement to which this Act applies as offeree has not received the notice required under section 3 of this Act before entering into the agreement, he may give notice of cancellation of the agreement to the creditor at any time.

(3) If in a case falling within subsection (2) above the offeree affirms the agreement at any time after the expiry of the period of fourteen days beginning with the day on which the agreement is entered into, he may not at any subsequent time give notice of cancellation of the agreement to the creditor.

(4) The offeree's giving, within the time allowed under this section, notice of cancellation of the agreement to the creditor at a time when the agreement has been entered into shall have the effect of cancelling the agreement.

(5) Where a timeshare credit agreement is cancelled under this section—
(a) the agreement shall continue in force, subject to section 7 of this Act, so far as it relates to repayment of the credit and payment of interest, and
(b) subject to paragraph (a) above, the agreement shall cease to be enforceable.

Repayment of credit and interest

7.—(1) This section applies following—
(a) the giving of notice of cancellation of a timeshare agreement in accordance with section 5 of this Act in a case where subsection (9) or that section applies, or
(b) the giving of notice of cancellation of a timeshare credit agreement in accordance with section 6 of this Act.

(2) If the offeree repays the whole or a portion of the credit—
(a) before the expiry of one month following the giving of the notice, or
(b) in the case of a credit repayable by instalments, before the date on which the first instalment is due,

no interest shall be payable on the amount repaid.

(3) If the whole of a credit repayable by instalments is not repaid on or before the date specified in subsection (2)(b) above, the offeree shall not be liable to repay any of the credit except on receipt of a request in writing in such form as may be prescribed, signed by or on behalf of the offeror or (as the case may be) creditor, stating the amounts of the remaining instalments (recalculated by the offeror or creditor as nearly as may be in accordance with the agreement and without extending the repayment period), but excluding any sum other than principal and interest.

Defence of due diligence

8.—(1) In proceedings against a person for an offence under section 2(3) of this Act it shall be a defence for that person to show that he took all reasonable steps and exercised all due diligence to avoid committing the offence.

(2) Where in proceedings against a person for such an offence the defence provided by subsection (1) above involves an allegation that the commission of the offence was due—

(a) to the act or default of another, or

(b) to reliance on information given by another,

that person shall not, without the leave of the court, be entitled to rely on the defence unless he has served a notice under subsection (3) below on the person bringing the proceedings not less than seven clear days before the hearing of the proceedings or, in Scotland, the diet of trial.

(3) A notice under this subsection shall give such information identifying or assisting in the identification of the person who committed the act or default or gave the information as is in the possession of the person serving the notice at the time when he serves it.

Liability of persons other than principal offender

9.—(1) Where the commission by a person of an offence under section 2(3) of this Act is due to the act or default of some other person, that other person is guilty of the offence and may be proceeded against and punished by virtue of this section whether or not proceedings are taken against the first-mentioned person.

(2) Where a body corporate is guilty of an offence under section 2(3) of this Act (including where it is so guilty by virtue of subsection (1) above) in respect of an act or default which is shown to have been committed with the consent or connivance of, or to be attributable to neglect on the part of, a director, manager, secretary

or other similar officer of the body corporate or a person who is purporting to act in such a capacity, he (as well as the body corporate) is guilty of the offence and liable to be proceeded against and punished accordingly.

(3) Where the affairs of a body corporate are managed by its members, subsection (2) above applies in relation to the acts and defaults of a member in connection with his functions of management as if he were a director of the body corporate.

(4) Where an offence under section 2(3) of this Act committed in Scotland by a Scottish partnership is proved to have been committed with the consent or connivance of, or to be attributable to neglect on the part of, a partner, he (as well as the partnership) is guilty of the offence and liable to be proceeded against and punished accordingly.

Enforcement

10.—The Schedule to this Act (which makes provision about enforcement) shall have effect.

Prosecution time limit

11.—(1) No proceedings for an offence under section 2(3) of this Act or paragraph 4(3) or 5(1) of the Schedule to this Act shall be commenced after—

(a) the end of the period of three years beginning with the date of the commission of the offence, or

(b) the end of the period of one year beginning with the date of the discovery of the offence by the prosecutor,

whichever is the earlier.

(2) For the purposes of this section a certificate signed by or on behalf of the prosecutor and stating the date on which the offence was discovered by him shall be conclusive evidence of that fact; and a certificate stating that matter and purporting to be so signed shall be treated as so signed unless the contrary is proved.

(3) In relation to proceedings in Scotland, subsection (3) of section 331 of the Criminal Procedure (Scotland) Act 1975 (date of commencement of proceedings) shall apply for the purposes of this section as it applies for the purposes of that.

General provisions

12.—(1) For the purposes of this Act, a notice of cancellation of an agreement is a notice (however expressed) showing that the offeree wishes unconditionally to cancel the agreement, whether or not it is in a prescribed form.

(2) The rights conferred and duties imposed by sections 2 to 7 of this Act are in addition to any rights conferred or duties imposed by or under any other Act.

(3) For the purposes of this Act, if the offeree sends a notice by post in a properly addressed and pre-paid letter the notice is to be treated as given at the time of posting.

(4) This Act shall have effect in relation to any timeshare agreement or timeshare credit agreement notwithstanding any agreement or notice.

(5) For the purposes of the Consumer Credit Act 1974, a transaction done under or for the purposes of a timeshare agreement is not, in relation to any regulated agreement (within the meaning of that Act), a linked transaction.

(6) In this Act—

"credit" includes a cash loan and any other form of financial accommodation,

"notice" means notice in writing,

"order" means an order made by the Secretary of State, and

"prescribed" means prescribed by an order.

(7) An order under this Act may make different provision for different cases or circumstances.

(8) Any power under this Act to make an order shall be exercisable by statutory instrument containing an order under this Act (other than an order made for the purposes of section 13(2) of this Act) shall be subject to annulment in pursuance of a resolution of either House of Parliament.

Short title, etc.

13.—(1) This Act may be cited as the Timeshare Act 1992.

(2) This Act shall come into force on such day as may be prescribed.

(3) This Act extends to Northern Ireland.

Section 10 SCHEDULE

ENFORCEMENT

Enforcement authority

1.—(1) Every local weights and measures authority in Great Britain shall be an enforcement authority for the purposes of this Schedule, and it shall be the duty of each such authority to enforce the provisions of this Act within their area.

(2) The Department of Economic Development in Northern Ireland shall be an enforcement authority for the purposes of this Schedule, and it shall be the duty of the Department to enforce the provisions of this Act within Northern Ireland.

Prosecutions

2.—(1) In section 130(1) of the Fair Trading Act 1973 (notice to Director General of Fair Trading of intended prosecution by local weights and measures authority in England and Wales), after "the Property Misdescriptions Act 1991" there is inserted "or for an offence under section 2 of the Timeshare Act 1992".

(2) Nothing in paragraph 1 above shall authorise a local weights and measures authority to bring proceedings in Scotland for an offence.

Powers of officers of enforcement authority

3.—(1) If a duly authorised officer of an enforcement authority has reasonable grounds for suspecting that an offence under section 2 of this Act has been committed, he may—
  (a) require a person carrying on or employed in a business to produce any book or document relating to the business, and take copies of it or any entry in it, or
  (b) require such a person to produce in a visible and legible documentary form any information so relating which is contained in a computer, and take copies of it,
for the purposes of ascertaining whether such an offence has been committed.

(2) If such an officer has reasonable grounds for believing that any documents may be required as evidence in proceedings for such an offence, he may seize and detain them and shall, if he does so, inform the person from whom they are seized.

(3) The powers of an officer under this paragraph may be exercised by him only at a reasonable hour and on production (if required) of his credentials.

(4) Nothing in this paragraph requires a person to produce, or authorises the taking from a person of, a document which he·could not be compelled to produce in civil proceedings before the High Court or (in Scotland) the Court of Session.

4.—(1) A person who—
  (a) intentionally obstructs an officer of an enforcement authority acting in pursuance of this Schedule,
  (b) without reasonable excuse fails to comply with a requirement made of him by such an officer under paragraph 3(1) above, or
  (c) without reasonable excuse fails to give an officer of an enforcement authority acting in pursuance of this Schedule any other assistance or information which the officer has reasonably required of him for the purpose of the performance of the officer's functions under this Schedule,
is guilty of an offence.

(2) A person guilty of an offence under sub-paragraph (1) above is liable on summary conviction to a fine not exceeding level 5 on the standard scale.

(3) If a person, in giving information to an officer of an enforcement authority who is acting in pursuance of this Schedule—
  (a) makes a statement which he knows is false in a material particular, or
  (b) recklessly makes a statement which is false in a material particular,
he is guilty of an offence.

(4) A person guilty of an offence under sub-paragraph (3) above is liable—
  (a) on summary conviction, to a fine not exceeding the statutory maximum, and
  (b) on conviction on indictment, to a fine.

Disclosure of information

5.—(1) If a person discloses to another any information obtained in the exercise of functions under this Schedule he is guilty of an offence unless the disclosure was made—
  (a) in or for the purpose of the performance by him or any other person of any such function, or
  (b) for a purpose specified in section 38(2)(a), (b) or (c) of the Consumer Protection Act 1987 (enforcement of various enactments; compliance with Community obligations; and civil or criminal proceedings).

(2) A person guilty of an offence under sub-paragraph (1) above is liable—

(a)   on summary conviction, to a fine not exceeding the statutory maximum, and

(b)   on conviction on indictment, to a fine.

Privilege against self-incrimination

6. Nothing in this Schedule requires a person to answer any question or give any information if to do so might incriminate him.

The Timeshare Act 1992 (Commencement) Order 1992

1. This Order may be cited as The Timeshare Act 1992 (Commencement) Order 1992.

2. The Timeshare Act 1992 shall come into force on 12th October 1992.

SECTION A

1. Does the Act create civil or criminal liability?

2. To which parts of the United Kingdom does the Act apply?

3. How would you find out whether this Act has come into force?

4. John, a student, enters an agreement with Neverland University by which the university agrees to provide him with a flat during term time throughout his 3 year degree course. Is this agreement covered by the Timeshare Act 1992?

5. Vyomesh goes to Spain for a holiday. While he is there he agrees to buy a 10 year timeshare in Ina's villa there. Is Voymesh's agreement covered by the Timeshare Act 1992?

6. Sunhols plc, a UK based timeshare company selling timeshare properties in France includes a clause in all of its contracts stating that they are governed by French law and requires purchasers to agree that they have no rights under the Timeshare Act 1992. Stella signs such an agreement. Can she cancel it?

SECTION B

7. What is the short title of this Act?

8. Why do you think this Act was passed?

9. Megaprop plc develops timeshare properties and sells them to other holiday companies but not to the public. Does it need to change its trading practices because of the implementation of the Act?

10. Meena agrees to buy a timeshare property in London. When she signs the contract she is given a letter which states that she may cancel within 21 days. When she returns home she realises that her decision was a mistake.

She telephones the company and explains this. Her bank has told her that her cheque for the timeshare has been cashed. Advise Meena.

11. Villanova plc sells timeshares through promotional events and competitions. At one event every person who agreed to buy a timeshare was given a Jetski. Frank collected his Jetski and immediately cancelled his agreement. Advise Villanova whether they must repay the full cost of the timeshare to Frank?

12. Following an advertisement for the Jetski promotion, 200 people attending a Villanova sales day signed up for timeshares. The sales team, Lee and Sonia were overwhelmed and failed to give one customer, Peter, a notice of cancellation. Peter complained to his local trading standards officer who has decided to prosecute Villanova.
    (a) Advise Villanova if it has defence and of the penalty for this offence.
    (b) After one visit to his timeshare property Peter wants to cancel the agreement. What rights, if any, has he to do this?

13. When the trading standards officer investigates Peter's complaint she asks Marco, a director of Villanova to give details of all purchasers of timeshares over the last 12 months so she can check whether they received a notice of their right to cancel. Marco provides a list which omits any people who have complained about the services provided by Villanova. Marco subsequently refuses to answer any questions about Villanova. Advise Marco of his rights and liabilities in relation to this investigation.

14. Sebastian bought a timeshare property in St Lucia from Villanova plc with a loan from a finance company, Villoan Ltd. He cancelled the agreement after 10 days but has not yet received any repayment.
    (a) What are Sebastian's liabilities to Villoan?
    (b) What information must Villoan provide if it wishes to charge Sebastian interest on his debt?

EXERCISE 2

Statutes II

DANGEROUS DOGS ACT 1991

(1991 c. 65)

ARRANGEMENT OF SECTIONS

An Act to prohibit persons from having in their possession or custody dogs belonging to types bred for fighting; to impose restrictions in respect of such dogs pending the coming into force of the prohibition; to enable restrictions to be imposed in relation to other types of dog which present a serious danger to the public; to make further provision for securing that dogs are kept under proper control; and for connected purposes.

[25th July 1991]

Dogs bred for fighting

1.—(1) This section applies to—

(a) any dog of the type known as the pit bull terrier;

(b) any dog of the type known as the Japanese tosa; and

(c) any dog of any type designated for the purposes of this section by an order of the Secretary of State, being a type appearing to him to be bred for fighting or to have the characteristics of a type bred for that purpose.

(2) No person shall—

(a) breed, or breed from, a dog to which this section applies;
(b) sell or exchange such a dog or offer, advertise or expose such a dog for sale or exchange;
(c) make or offer to make a gift of such a dog or advertise or expose such a dog as a gift;
(d) allow such a dog of which he is the owner or of which he is for the time being in charge to be in a public place without being muzzled and kept on a lead; or
(e) abandon such a dog of which he is the owner or, being the owner or for the time being in charge of such a dog, allow it to stray.

(3) After such day as the Secretary of State may by order appoint for the purposes of this subsection no person shall have any dog to which this section applies in his possession or custody except—
(a) in pursuance of the power of seizure conferred by the subsection provisions of this Act; or
(b) in accordance with an order for its destruction made under those provisions;
but the Secretary of State shall by order make a scheme for the payment to the owners of such dogs who arrange for them to be destroyed before that day of sums specified in or determined under the scheme in respect of those dogs and the cost of their destruction.

(4) Subsection (2)(b) and (c) above shall not make unlawful anything done with a view to the dog in question being removed from the United Kingdom before the day appointed under subsection (3) above.

(5) The Secretary of State may by order provide that the prohibition in subsection (3) above shall not apply in such cases and subject to compliance with such conditions as are specified in the order and any such provision may take the form of a scheme of exemption containing such arrangements (including provision for the payment of charges or fees) as he thinks appropriate.

(6) A scheme under subsection (3) or (5) above may provide for specified functions under the scheme to be discharged by such persons or bodies as the Secretary of State thinks appropriate.

(7) Any person who contravenes this section is guilty of an offence and liable on summary conviction to imprisonment for a term not exceeding six months or a fine not exceeding level 5 on the standard scale or both except that a person who publishes an advertisement in contravention of subsection 2(b) or (c)—
(a) shall not on being convicted be liable to imprisonment if he shows that he published the advertisement to the order of someone else and did not himself devise it; and
(b) shall not be convicted if, in addition, he shows that he did not know and had no reasonable cause to suspect that it

related to a dog to which this section applies.

(8) An order under subsection (1)(c) above adding dogs of any type to those to which this section applies may provide that subsections (3) and (4) above shall apply in relation to those dogs with the substitution for the day appointed under subsection (3) of a later day specified in that order.

(9) The power to make orders under this section shall be exercisable by statutory instrument which, in the case of an order under subsection (1) or (5) or an order containing a scheme under subsection (3), shall be subject to annulment in pursuance of a resolution of either House of Parliament.

Other specially dangerous dogs

2.—(1) If it appears to the Secretary of State that dogs of any type to which section 1 above does not apply present a serious danger to the public he may by order impose in relation to dogs of that type restrictions corresponding, with such modifications, if any, as he thinks appropriate, to all or any of those in subsection (2)(d) and (e) of that section.

(2) An order under this section may provide for exceptions from any restriction imposed by the order in such cases and subject to compliance with such conditions as are specified in the order.

(3) An order under this section may contain such supplementary or transitional provisions as the Secretary of State thinks necessary or expedient and may create offences punishable on summary conviction with imprisonment for a term not exceeding six months or a fine not exceeding level 5 on the standard scale or both.

(4) In determining whether to make an order under this section in relation to dogs of any type and, if so, what the provisions of the order should be, the Secretary of State shall consult with such persons or bodies as appear to him to have relevant knowledge or experience, including a body concerned with animal welfare, a body concerned with veterinary science and practice and a body concerned with breeds of dogs.

(5) The power to make an order under this section shall be exercisable by statutory instrument and no such order shall be made unless a draft of it has been laid before and approved by a resolution of each House of Parliament.

Keeping dogs under proper control

3.—(1) If a dog is dangerously out of control in a public place—
(a) the owner; and
(b) if different, the person for the time being in charge of the dog,

is guilty of an offence, or, if the dog while so out of control injures any person, an aggravated offence, under this subsection.

(2) In proceedings for an offence under subsection (1) above against a person who is the owner of a dog but was not at the material time in charge of it, it shall be a defence for the accused to prove that the dog was at the material time in the charge of a person whom he reasonably believed to be a fit and proper person to be in charge of it.

(3) If the owner or, if different, the person for the time being in charge of a dog allows it to enter a place which is not a public place but where it is not permitted to be and while it is there—

(a) it injures any person; or
(b) there are grounds for reasonable apprehension that it will do so,

he is guilty of an offence, or, if the dog injures any person, an aggravated offence, under this subsection.

(4) A person guilty of an offence under subsection (1) or (3) above other than an aggravated offence is liable on summary conviction to imprisonment for a term not exceeding six months or a fine not exceeding level 5 on the standard scale or both; and a person guilty of an aggravated offence under either of those subsections is liable—

(a) on summary conviction, to imprisonment for a term not exceeding six months or a fine not exceeding the statutory maximum or both;
(b) on conviction on indictment, to imprisonment for a term not exceeding two years or a fine or both.

(5) It is hereby declared for the avoidance of doubt that an order under section 2 of the Dogs Act 1871 (order on complaint that dog is dangerous and not kept under proper control)—

(a) may be made whether or not the dog is shown to have injured any person; and
(b) may specify the measures to be taken for keeping the dog under proper control, whether by muzzling, keeping on a lead, excluding it from specified places or otherwise.

(6) If it appears to a court on a complaint under section 2 of the said Act of 1871 that the dog to which the complaint relates is a male and would be less dangerous if neutered the court may under that section make an order requiring it to be neutered.

(7) The reference in section 1(3) of the Dangerous Dogs Act 1989 (penalties) to failing to comply with an order under section 2 of the said Act of 1871 to keep a dog under proper control shall include a reference to failing to comply with any other order made under that section; but no order shall be made under that section

by virtue of subsection (6) above where the matters complained of arose before the coming into force of that subsection.

Destruction and disqualification orders

4.—(1) Where a person is convicted of an offence under section 1 or 3(1) or (3) above or of an offence under an order made under section 2 above the court—

(a) may order the destruction of any dog in respect of which the offence was committed and shall do so in the case of an offence under section 1 or an aggravated offence under section 3(1) or (3) above; and

(b) may order the offender to be disqualified, for such period as the court thinks fit, for having custody of a dog.

(2) Where a court makes an order under subsection (1)(a) above for the destruction of a dog owned by a person other than the offender, then, unless the order is one that the court is required to make, the owner may appeal to the Crown Court against the order.

(3) A dog shall not be destroyed pursuant to an order under subsection (1)(a) above—

(a) until the end of the period for giving notice of appeal against the conviction or, where the order was not one which the court was required to make, against the order; and

(b) if notice of appeal is given within that period, until the appeal is determined or withdrawn,

unless the offender and, in a case to which subsection (2) above applies, the owner of the dog give notice to the court that made the order that there is to be no appeal.

(4) Where a court makes an order under subsection (1)(a) above it may—

(a) appoint a person to undertake the destruction of the dog and require any person having custody of it to deliver it up for that purpose; and

(b) order the offender to pay such sum as the court may determine to be the reasonable expenses of destroying the dog and of keeping it pending its destruction.

(5) Any sum ordered to be paid under subsection (4)(b) above shall be treated for the purposes of enforcement as if it were a fine imposed on conviction.

(6) Any person who is disqualified for having custody of a dog by virtue of an order under subsection (1)(b) above may, at any time after the end of the period of one year beginning with the date of the order, apply to the court that made it (or a magistrates' court acting for the same petty sessions area as that court) for a direction terminating the disqualification.

(7) On an application under subsection (6) above the court may—

(a) having regard to the applicant's character, his conduct since the disqualification was imposed and any other circumstances of the case, grant or refuse the application; and

(b) order the applicant to pay all or any part of the costs of the application;

and where an application in respect of an order is refused no further application in respect of that order shall be entertained if made before the end of the period of one year beginning with the date of the refusal.

(8) Any person who—

(a) has custody of a dog in contravention of an order under subsection (1)(b) above; or

(b) fails to comply with a requirement imposed on him under subsection (4)(a) above,

is guilty of an offence and liable on summary conviction to a fine not exceeding level 5 on the standard scale.

(9) In the application of this section to Scotland—

(a) in subsection (2) for the words "Crown Court against the order" there shall be substituted the words "High Court of Justiciary against the order within the period of seven days beginning with the date of the order";

(b) for subsection (3)(a) there shall be substituted—

"(a) until the end of the period of seven days beginning with the date of the order";

(c) for subsection (5) there shall be substituted—

"(5) Section 411 of the Criminal Procedure (Scotland) Act 1975 shall apply in relation to the recovery of sums ordered to be paid under subsection (4)(b) above as it applies to fines ordered to be recovered by civil diligence in pursuance of Part II of that Act."; and

(d) in subsection (6) the words "(or a magistrates' court acting for the same petty sessions area as that court)" shall be omitted.

Seizure, entry of premises and evidence

5.—(1) A constable or an officer of a local authority authorised by it to exercise the powers conferred by this subsection may seize—

(a) any dog which appears to him to be a dog to which section 1 above applies and which is in a public place—

(i) after the time when possession or custody of it has become unlawful by virtue of that section; or

(ii) before that time, without being muzzled and kept on a lead;

(b) any dog in a public place which appears to him to be a dog to which an order under section 2 above applies and in respect of which an offence against the order has been or is being committed; and

(c) any dog in a public place (whether or not one to which that section or such an order applies) which appears to him to be dangerously out of control.

(2) If a justice of the peace is satisfied by information on oath, or in Scotland a justice of the peace or sheriff is satisfied by evidence on oath, that there are reasonable grounds for believing—

(a) that an offence under any provision of this Act or of an order under section 2 above is being or has been committed; or

(b) that evidence of the commission of any such offence is to be found,

on any premises he may issue a warrant authorising a constable to enter those premises (using such force as is reasonably necessary) and to search them and seize any dog or other thing found there which is evidence of the commission of such an offence.

(3) A warrant issued under this section in Scotland shall be authority for opening lockfast places and may authorise persons named in the warrant to accompany a constable who is executing it.

(4) Where a dog is seized under subsection (1) or (2) above and it appears to a justice of the peace, or in Scotland a justice of the peace or sheriff, that no person has been or is to be prosecuted for an offence under this Act or an order under section 2 above in respect of that dog (whether because the owner cannot be found or for any other reason) he may order the destruction of the dog and shall do so if it is one to which section 1 above applies.

(5) If in any proceedings it is alleged by the prosecution that a dog is one to which section 1 or an order under section 2 above applies it shall be presumed that it is such a dog unless the contrary is shown by the accused by such evidence as the court considers sufficient; and the accused shall not be permitted to adduce such evidence unless he has given the prosecution notice of his intention to do so not later than the fourteenth day before that on which the evidence is to be adduced.

Dogs owned by young persons

6. Where a dog is owned by a person who is less than sixteen years old any reference to its owner in section 1(2)(d) or (e) or 3 above shall include a reference to the head of the household, if

any, of which that person is a member or, in Scotland, to the
person who has his actual care and control.

Muzzling and leads

7.—(1) In this Act—

(a) references to a dog being muzzled are to its being securely
fitted with a muzzle sufficient to prevent it biting any person;
and

(b) references to its being kept on a lead are to its being securely
held on a lead by a person who is not less than sixteen years
old.

(2) If the Secretary of State thinks it desirable to do so he may
by order prescribe the kind of muzzle or lead to be used for the
purpose of complying in the case of a dog of any type, with section
1 or an order under section 2 above; and if a muzzle or lead of a
particular kind is for the time being prescribed in relation to any
type of dog the references in subsection (1) above to a muzzle or
lead shall, in relation to any dog of that type, be construed as
references to a muzzle or lead of that kind.

(3) The power to make an order under subsection (2) above shall
be exercisable by statutory instrument subject to annulment in
pursuance of a resolution of either House of Parliament.

Power to make corresponding provision for Northern Ireland

8. An Order in Council under paragraph 1(1)(b) of Schedule 1
to the Northern Ireland Act 1974 (legislation for Northern Ireland
in the interim period) which states that it is made only for purposes
corresponding to the purposes of this Act—

(a) shall not be subject to paragraph 1(4) and (5) of that Schedule
(affirmative resolution of both Houses of Parliament); but

(b) shall be subject to annulment in pursuance of a resolution of
either House.

Expenses

9. Any expenses incurred by the Secretary of State in consequence
of this Act shall be paid out of money provided by Parliament.

Short title, interpretation, commencement and extent

10.—(1) This Act may be cited as the Dangerous Dogs Act 1991.

(2) In this Act—

"advertisement" includes any means of bringing a matter to

the attention of the public and "advertise" shall be construed accordingly;

"public place" means any street, road or other place (whether or not enclosed) to which the public have or are permitted to have access whether for payment or otherwise and includes the common parts of a building containing two or more separate dwellings.

(3) For the purposes of this Act a dog shall be regarded as dangerously out of control on any occasion on which there are grounds for reasonable apprehension that it will injure any person, whether or not it actually does so, but references to a dog injuring a person or there being grounds for reasonable apprehension that it will do so do not include references to any case in which the dog is being used for a lawful purpose by a constable or a person in the service of the Crown.

(4) Except for section 8, this Act shall not come into force until such day as the Secretary of State may appoint by an order made by statutory instrument and different days may be appointed for different provisions or different purposes.

(5) Except for section 8, this Act does not extend to Northern Ireland.

SECTION A

1. When did this Act come into force?

2. To what parts of the United Kingdom does this Act apply?

3. What types of dogs are dangerous dogs within the Dangerous Dogs Act 1991?

4. Darren owns a pit bull terrier. He does not want to have his dog destroyed. Can he legally keep the dog after the Act has come into force?

5. Rosemary has a pet Pekinese called Sally who is very disobedient and loves ice cream. Rosemary takes Sally to the park and lets her off her lead. Sally spots two children eating ice cream with their mother and rushes over to them, jumps up and bites an ice cream. The mother grabs Sally and complains to the police. What offence, if any, has Rosemary committed?

6. On 1 October 1991 Kirk was taking his muzzled pit bull terrier for a walk when he decided to buy a sandwich. He tied the dog securely to some railings outside the shop and

left it. When he returned 5 minutes later the dog had been taken away by the police.

(a) Has Kirk committed any offence?

(b) Can the dog be destroyed lawfully?

SECTION B

7. How would you find out if any other types of dog had been prohibited by all order under s.2?

8. Barbara is the publisher of a magazine called *Dogs Weekly* which includes a large number of advertisements. Tom, who breeds pit bull terriers and other fighting dogs, places an advert which reads: "For Sale rare U.S. very game £500." Barbara has been charged with an offence under s.1(2)(b). Advise Barbara whether she has any defence and of the penalties if she is convicted.

9. What is the difference between an offence and an aggravated offence under s.3(i) for:

(a) the owner?

(b) the dog?

10. George aged 12 has a pet Alsatian, Polo. One day when George is visiting a friend who lives in a block of flats, Polo slips his lead, chases another dog down a corridor and runs into one of the flats. He barks fiercely and frightens the occupant who faints and hits her head.

(a) What offence, if any, has George committed?

(b) Has Martin, his step-father committed any offence?

(c) Would your answer be different if Martin owned the dog and had let George take it out?

11. Michael bought his dog, Cuddles, when it was a puppy from a man he met in a pub. Cuddles has been a great family pet, is always friendly and docile despite its fierce appearance. One day when Michael was taking Cuddles for a walk he was stopped by a dog warden who demanded to know why Cuddles was not muzzled. Despite Michael's protests the dog warden seized Cuddles and told Michael that he would apply for the dog's destruction because it was a pit bull terrier. Advise Michael who wants Cuddles returned.

12. Phil, a R.A.F. dog handler is patrolling the perimeter of an airfield when he hears a man's voice. He lets his dog off the lead and tells it to stop the man. The dog jumps

on the man and bites him on the arm. The man complains that Phil's dog is dangerously out of control and should be put down. Advise Phil.

13. Drafting Exercise

i. There has been considerable confusion about the meaning of the phrase "any dog of the type known as a pit bull terrier." The Secretary of State asks you to draft a provision which will avoid these difficulties.

ii. The problems created by dogs and their owners are not limited to situations where dogs are out of control but include fouling of the streets and excessive noise. Draft legislation which requires owner's and those in charge to control these aspects of their dog's behaviour but exempting owners of guide-dogs and guard dogs where this seems appropriate.

EXERCISE 3

Cases 1

a # R v Crown Court at Knightsbridge, ex parte Dunne
Brock v Director of Public Prosecutions

b QUEEN'S BENCH DIVISION
GLIDEWELL LJ AND CRESSWELL J
25 JUNE, 2 JULY 1993

Animals – Dog – Dangerous dog – Pit bull terrier – Dog of the type known as pit bull
terrier – Type – Whether 'type' synonymous with 'breed' – Whether evidence of
c *behavioural characteristics of dog conclusive in determining whether it is of 'the type*
known as the pit bull terrier' – Dangerous Dogs Act 1991, s 1.

On its true construction s 1[a] of the Dangerous Dogs Act 1991, which prohibits,
inter alia, allowing 'any dog of the type known as the pit bull terrier' to be in
d public without being muzzled and kept on a lead, does not just apply to the breed
of dogs known as pit bull terriers, since the word 'type' is not synonymous with
the word 'breed'. Instead, giving the phrase 'any dog of the type known as the pit
bull terrier' its ordinary meaning, s 1 applies to any dog having a substantial
number or most of the physical characteristics of a pit bull terrier. Whether a dog
is 'of the type known as the pit bull terrier' is a question of fact for the court to
e decide, but in making that determination a court is entitled to use the standards
established by the American Dog Breeders' Association, which lists the basic
bodily and behavioural characteristics of the pit bull terrier. However, the fact
that a dog does not exhibit the behavioural characteristics of a pit bull terrier is
not conclusive in determining that it is not 'of the type known as the pit bull
f terrier' but neither is it irrelevant in proving that it is not a dog of the type of the
pit bull terrier (see p 496 *j* to p 497 *a h* to p 498 *a e* to *j*, post).
Dictum of the Lord Justice General (Hope) in *Parker v Annan* 1993 SCCR 185 at
190–191 adopted.

Notes
g For dangerous dogs generally, see 2 *Halsbury's Laws* (4th edn reissue) paras 373–
374, and for cases on the subject, see 2 *Digest* (Reissue) 423–426, *2358–2386*.
For the Dangerous Dogs Act 1991, s 1, see 2 *Halsbury's Statutes* (4th edn) (1992
reissue) 559.

h **Case referred to in judgments**
Parker v Annan 1993 SCCR 185, HC of Just.

Case also cited or referred to in skeleton arguments
Annan v Troup 1993 SCCR 192, HC of Just.

j **Application for judicial review**

R v Crown Court at Knightsbridge, ex p Dunne
Gary Dunne applied, with the leave of Laws J given on 8 September 1992, for
judicial review of the decision of Judge Mendl and two justices made on 5 June

a   Section 1, so far as material, is set out at p 494 *a* to *c*. post

1992 in the Crown Court at Knightsbridge whereby they allowed his appeal
against his conviction in the Wells Street Magistrates' Court on 30 December 1991   *a*
on a charge of being the owner of a dog to which s 1 of the Dangerous Dogs Act
1991 applied, namely a dog of the type known as the pit bull terrier, who allowed
the dog to be in a public place without being muzzled, contrary to s 1(2)(d) of that
Act. The relief sought was a declaration that in so far as the judgment of the
Crown Court held that the applicant had failed to displace the presumption under   *b*
s 5(5) of the 1991 Act that his dog was a dog of the type known as the pit bull
terrier the Crown Court had erred in its interpretation of the phrase 'any dog of
the type known as the pit bull terrier', and that on a proper construction of the
1991 Act the word 'type' should be defined in its technical sense of being
equivalent to 'breed', rather than given a broad, popular meaning. The facts are
set out in the judgment of Glidewell LJ.   *c*

Brock v DPP

Karen Brock appealed by way of a case stated by the Crown Court at Wood Green
(Judge Zucker QC and two justices) in respect of its adjudication on 9 December
1992 whereby, on an appeal from justices sitting at Barnet Magistrates' Court on
4 August 1992, the Crown Court upheld the conviction of the appellant of having   *d*
in her possession or custody a dog called 'Buster' to which s 1 of the Dangerous
Dogs Act 1991 applied, namely a dog of the type known as the pit bull terrier,
contrary to s 1(3) of that Act. The questions for the opinion of the High Court
were whether the Crown Court was correct in deciding that, in determining
whether a dog was 'of the type known as the pit bull terrier', the behaviour of the
dog, such as whether or not it had shown dangerous proclivities, was irrelevant,   *e*
whether the Crown Court was correct in deciding that s 1(1) of the 1991 Act
raised the questions 'Known to whom; and in accordance with what criteria?' and
that the answer was 'Known to those experienced in identifying pit bull terriers
in accordance with a recognised and accepted standard' and whether the Crown
Court was correct in deciding that the American Dog Breeders Association   *f*
(ADBA) standard provided a criterion by which it could be determined whether
or not a dog was of the type known as the pit bull terrier. The facts are set out in
the judgment of Glidewell J.

William Locke (instructed by *Winstanley-Burgess*) for Dunne.
Peter Ader (instructed by the *Crown Prosecution Service*, North London) for the   *g*
    respondent in *Dunne's* case.
John H Trumpington (instructed by *Landau & Cohen*, Edgware) for Brock.
Andrew Brierley (instructed by the *Crown Prosecution Service*, Wood Green) for the
    respondent in *Brock's* case.

                                                              Cur adv vult   *h*

2 July 1993. The following judgments were delivered.

GLIDEWELL LJ. In these two cases, although somewhat different questions are
raised, essentially the same point is in issue, namely the proper interpretation of   *j*
the phrase 'any dog of the type known as the pit bull terrier' in s 1(1)(a) of the
Dangerous Dogs Act 1991. We heard argument in the two cases consecutively. It
is convenient to deal with them both in this one judgment.

Mr Dunne
    The applicant, Mr Gary Dunne, was charged that on 26 November 1991—

a   'being the owner of a dog to which Section 1 of the Dangerous Dogs Act 1991 applied, namely a dog of the type known as the pit bull terrier, [he] allowed such dog to be in a public place ... without being muzzled'

contrary to s 1(2)(d) of the 1991 Act. He was convicted at the Wells Street Magistrates' Court on 30 December 1991. He appealed to the Crown Court at Knightsbridge. On 5 June 1992 that court (Judge Mendl and magistrates) decided
b   that (1) the applicant had failed to prove that his dog was not of the type known as the pit bull terrier, but (2) the prosecution had failed to prove that the dog was unmuzzled. The court therefore allowed the applicant's appeal.

The applicant has been advised that he cannot appeal against the Crown Court's conclusion that he had failed to prove that the dog was not of the type
c   known as the pit bull terrier. He therefore seeks judicial review of that decision, for which he has been given leave. The relief he seeks is:

'A declaration that in its judgment of 5 June 1992, the Crown Court erred in its interpretation of the phrase "any dog of the type known as the pit bull terrier", and that on a proper construction of the statute the word "type" in
d   the phrase should be defined in its technical sense—here equivalent to "breed"—rather than given a broad, popular meaning.'

The procedure

For the determination of this question procedure by way of judicial review is
e   not wholly satisfactory. In particular, we do not have any clear findings of fact by the Crown Court upon which it based its conclusion. Moreover, I am not satisfied that Mr Dunne did not have a right of appeal by way of case stated. So far as is material, s 28(1) of the Supreme Court Act 1981 provides:

'... any order, judgment or other decision of the Crown Court may be
f   questioned by any party to the proceedings, on the ground that it is wrong in law or is in excess of jurisdiction, by applying to the Crown Court to have a case stated by that court for the opinion of the High Court.'

It is in my view arguable that the interpretation placed by the Crown Court on the meaning of the words 'of the type known as the pit bull terrier' was a decision
g   which could properly have been the subject of a case stated.

However, both parties were agreed that procedure by way of judicial review was appropriate in the circumstances, and we therefore assumed jurisdiction to hear Mr Dunne's application.

h   *The legislation*

The 1991 Act was brought into force by a commencement order made by the Secretary of State for the Home Department on 12 August 1991. The long title is:

'An Act to prohibit persons from having in their possession or custody dogs belonging to types bred for fighting; to impose restrictions in respect of such
j   dogs pending the coming into force of the prohibition; to enable restrictions to be imposed in relation to other types of dogs which prevent a serious danger to the public; to make further provision for securing that dogs are kept under proper control; and for connected purposes.'

The provisions of the 1991 Act which are relevant to this application are as follows:

'1. *Dogs bred for fighting.*—(1) This section applies to—(a) any dog of the
type known as the pit bull terrier ...

(2) No person shall ... (d) allow such a dog of which he is the owner or of
which he is for the time being in charge to be in a public place without being
muzzled and kept on a lead ...

(3) After such day as the Secretary of State may by order appoint for the
purposes of this subsection no person shall have any dog to which this
section applies in his possession or custody ... [The date appointed for the
purposes of this subsection was 30 November 1991: see SI 1991/1742] ...

(5) The Secretary of State may by order provide that the prohibition in
subsection (3) above shall not apply in such cases and subject to compliance
with such conditions as are specified in the order and any such provision may
take the form of a scheme of exemption containing such arrangements
(including provision for the payment of charges or fees) as he thinks
appropriate ...'

The order made under sub-s (1) by the Secretary of State provides that a
certificate of exemption may be issued in respect of a dog of the type known as
the pit bull terrier, or any other dog coming within s 1(1), whose owner satisfies
certain conditions in relation to the dog. Subsection (7) makes it an offence to
contravene the provisions of s 1.

The provisions continue:

4.—(1) Where a person is convicted of an offence under section 1 or 3(1)
or (3) above ... the court—(a) may order the destruction of any dog in respect
of which the offence was committed and shall do so in the case of an offence
under section 1 ...

5 ... (5) If in any proceedings it is alleged by the prosecution that a dog is
one to which section 1 ... applies, it shall be presumed that it is such a dog
unless the contrary is shown by the accused by such evidence as the court
considers sufficient ...'

It is agreed between counsel, in my view entirely correctly, that the burden
placed on the accused by this subsection is to prove the contrary on the balance
of probabilities.

The issues before the Crown Court

These were: (i) had the appellant proved, on the balance of probabilities, that
his dog was not of the type known as the pit bull terrier; (ii) if not, had the
prosecution proved that on 26 November 1991 the dog was not muzzled?

On 26 November 1991 Mr Dunne said that, in case his dog were to be found to
be of the type known as the pit bull terrier, he was about to take the necessary
steps to obtain a certificate of exemption for it. It is common ground that at that
date he had not done so.

We have a note of the judgment given by Judge Mendl in the Crown Court. It
starts by posing the two questions set out above. In considering the first
question, the judge properly started by deciding the proper interpretation of the
phrase 'any dog of the type known as the pit bull terrier'. He said:

'With regard to s 1(1)(a), if it were intended that it should refer to the
particular breed, there would have been no difficulty in defining the breed by
saying "any American pit bull terrier", even though that breed is not
accepted by the British Kennel Club. We therefore find that the meaning in
the *Concise Oxford English Dictionary* is appropriate—a general meaning not a

a technical one. The words mean that a dog "of the type known as a pit bull terrier" is an animal approximately amounting to, near to, having a substantial number of the characteristics of the pit bull terrier.'

Having so defined the phrase, the court went on to consider whether the evidence established that the applicant's dog was not of the type known as the pit bull terrier. The judge summarised the evidence of Dr Mugford, an expert b witness called on behalf of the applicant, and of witnesses called on behalf of the prosecution. He then said:

'Considering all the evidence that we have heard and the burden of proof, we conclude the appellant has not discharged the burden of proving that [the applicant's dog] is not a dog of the type known as the pit bull terrier.'

c The court however then concluded that the prosecution had not satisfied the burden of proving that at the relevant time the dog was unmuzzled. Thus the appeal was allowed.

The issue for this court
d The issue for us to decide is: did the Crown Court err in law in its interpretation of the phrase 'any dog of the type known as the pit bull terrier'? The submission of Mr Locke, for the applicant, is that the word 'type' in the 1991 Act has the same meaning as the word 'breed'.

Before expressing my conclusion on this application, I think it right to turn to e the appeal of Miss Brock, which raises wider issues.

Miss Brock's appeal
This is by way of case stated by the Crown Court at Wood Green which dismissed the appeal from justices for the petty sessional division of Barnet. On 4 August 1992 those justices convicted Miss Karen Brock of having in her f possession or custody a dog called 'Buster' to which s 1 of the 1991 Act applied, namely a dog of the type known as the pit bull terrier, contrary to s 1(3) of the Act. The Crown Court (Judge Zucker QC and magistrates) heard the appeal over three days and gave its judgment on 9 December 1992.

Facts admitted and proved
g The case stated as follows:

'3. The appellant admitted that—(a) she had the dog in her possession on 26th December 1991 (b) the dog had not been neutered, tattooed, implanted, insured nor registered. It was not therefore exempt on that ground from the h prohibition against possession or custody of a dog to which section 1 of the Act applied ...
5. We found the following facts:—(a) Pit bull terriers were first bred in England as fighting dogs. Some time in the middle of the last century they were imported into the United States of America. When dog fighting was banned and died out in England about the middle of the last century, pit bull j terriers were no longer bred here. The development of the breed however continued in the United States of America. In 1976 two female pit bull terriers were imported back into England, followed by a stud dog called "Al Capone". From that beginning pit bull terriers have been bred in England. (b) Dogs, generally, have breed standards which are laid down and recognised by different associations of dog breeders. The leading association in England is the Kennel Club. Because of the long period when pit bull terriers were

not bred in this country, The Kennel Club has no standard for pit bull
terriers, nor has any other association in this country. (c) Because pit bull
terriers have been bred over a long period in the United States of America
there are breed standards promulgated by associations of dog breeders in the
United States of America. (d) One of those associations is that of the
American Dog Breeders' Association (ADBA). ADBA was founded in 1909,
has always existed for pit bull terriers alone and has never registered any
other breed. It is the most detailed standard. It deals with physical
characteristics. It is widely used and accepted. The pit bull terriers originally
imported into this country were registered with ADBA. (e) A second, less
detailed standard is that of the United Kennel Club (UKC). (f) ADBA does
not recognise the standard of UKC and vice-versa.'

In para 6 the Crown Court summarised the evidence of Dr Mugford called on
behalf of the appellant. This mainly related to the behavioural characteristics of
Buster and of pit bull terriers generally.

The court recorded its conclusions as follows:

'9. We were of the opinion that:—(a) In determining whether a dog was
"of the type known as the pit bull terrier" the behaviour of the dog, whether
or not it had shown dangerous proclivities, was irrelevant. (b) Section 1(1) of
the said Act raises the questions: "Known to whom; and in accordance with
what criteria?" The answer is, known to those experienced in identifying pit
bull terriers and in accordance with a recognised and accepted standard. (c)
The ADBA's standard provides a criterion by which it can be determined
whether or not a dog is of the type known as the pit bull terrier. There may
be other such standards.

10. We accepted the evidence of the respondent's witnesses and did not
accept the evidence of the witnesses called on behalf of the appellant. We
found that the characteristics of the appellant's dog substantially conformed
to the ADBA's standard and was of the type known as the pit bull terrier.

11. The appellant therefore failed to adduce sufficient evidence to rebut
the presumption that her dog was of the type known as the pit bull terrier.

12. We therefore dismissed the appeal.

Questions

13. Questions for the opinion of the High Court are as follows:—(a) Were
we correct in deciding that in determining whether a dog was "of the type
known as the pit bull terrier", the behaviour of the dog such as whether or
not it had shown dangerous proclivities, was irrelevant? (b) Were we correct
in deciding that s 1(1) of the said Act raised the questions "Known to whom;
and in accordance with what criteria?" And that the answer was "Known to
those experienced in identifying pit bull terriers in accordance with a
recognised and accepted standard". (c) Were we correct that the ADBA
standard provided a criterion by which it could be determined whether or
not a dog is of the type known as the pit bull terrier?'

Conclusion

Interpreting the phrase 'of the type known as the pit bull terrier' in s 1(1) of the
statute simply by the normal canon of construction, ie by giving the words their
ordinary meaning, I entirely agree with the decision of the Crown Court in both
cases that the word 'type' is not synonymous with the word 'breed'. The
definition of a breed is normally that of some recognised body such as the Kennel

a Club in the United Kingdom. I agree with the Crown Court in both cases that the word 'type' in this context has a meaning different from and wider than the word 'breed'. I would so conclude by reading only s 1 of the 1991 Act. But that this is so is made even clearer by reference to a subsection to which I have not so far referred, namely s 2(4) of the 1991 Act. This provides:

b 'In determining whether to make an order under this section in relation to dogs of any type ... the Secretary of State shall consult with such persons or bodies as appear to him to have relevant knowledge or experience, including ... a body concerned with breeds of dogs.'

In that subsection the two words are being used in contradistinction to each other.

c We have been referred to two judgments of the High Court in Scotland on appeals by case stated from decisions of the Sheriff Court at Linlithgow in trials for offences against s 1(3) of the 1991 Act. Both judgments were given by the Lord Justice General (Hope) on 17 December 1992. In *Parker v Annan* 1993 SCCR 185, the first of the two judgments to be delivered, the question whether the word d 'type' in s 1 is synonymous with the word breed was considered. In his judgment, the Lord Justice General said (at 190–191):

'There is an absence of any precise criteria by which a pit bull terrier may be identified positively as a breed and by this means distinguished from all other dogs. One must of course be careful not to extend the application of e the section to dogs other than those which are described in it. A dog must be of the type known as the pit bull terrier if the section is to apply to it. But the phrase used by the statute enables a broad and practical approach to be taken, in a field in which it has been recognised that the pit bull terrier cannot, in this country at least, be precisely defined by breed or pedigree. For these reasons we do not think that the sheriff misdirected himself when f he regarded as highly significant Mr Hayworth's evidence that Kim resembled a pit bull terrier more than any other type of dog and declined to rely on Dr Peachey's opinion that although she resembled a pit bull terrier she was not in fact one but was a mongrel. He was right to approach the case on the basis that a dog could be of the type known as the pit bull terrier g although it was not purebred as such on both sides. We do not find anything in his use of words to suggest that he applied the wrong test in his approach to the evidence. The question whether the evidence as to Kim's characteristics was sufficient to show that she was not a dog of this type was a question of fact for him to decide.'

h I would respectfully agree with and adopt that passage.

Having decided that the word 'type' has a wider meaning than the word 'breed', a court then has to adopt some guide for determining the limits of the phrase 'any dog of the type known as the pit bull terrier'. What that guide should be, and where those limits lie, are questions of fact for the decision of the magistrates or the Crown Court, on the evidence. In these matters, the courts in j both cases heard evidence that the ADBA laid down a breed standard for pit bull terriers in the USA. The Crown Court in both cases was therefore entitled to use the ADBA standard as a guide. However, both courts were also entitled to find, on the evidence before them, that the fact that a dog does not meet that standard in every respect is not conclusive. Thus both courts could properly conclude that a dog was of the type known as the pit bull terrier if, as the Crown Court at Wood Green found, its characteristics substantially conformed to the ADBA's standard or, to use the words of the Crown Court at Knightsbridge, if the dog approximately amounted to, was near to, or had a substantial number of the *a* characteristics of the pit bull terrier as set out in the ADBA's standard.

This is sufficient to answer the question posed by Mr Dunne's application, and also to answer both questions (b) and (c) raised in Miss Brock's appeal in the affirmative.

It leaves the first question raised in Miss Brock's appeal, whether evidence as *b* to the behaviour of the dog in question was irrelevant. The transcripts of judgments given in the Crown Court in several cases show that different judges have differed about the proper answer to this question.

A copy of the ADBA's standard is exhibited to the case stated in Miss Brock's appeal. In somewhat colourful language, the standard does refer both to bodily characteristics of a dog and to its behavioural characteristics. It is true it contains *c* a long and detailed description of the bodily characteristics of an ideal pit bull terrier, but in another passage it is also said that the dog should have the following characteristics: (i) gameness, (ii) aggressiveness, (iii) stamina, (iv) wrestling ability, (v) biting ability.

No doubt the last three of these can be said to be functions of the dog's bodily *d* characteristics, but the first two are obviously aspects of behaviour. Moreover, the standard concludes that, in judging the American Pit Bull Terrier, up to 10 points, out of a maximum of 100, can be awarded for the dog's attitude. To an extent, therefore, the ADBA criteria include behavioural characteristics.

If, in framing the case stated, the Crown Court at Wood Green intended to say that evidence that the dog did not have some of the behavioural characteristics of *e* a pit bull terrier was not conclusive that it was not of the type of the pit bull terrier, I would entirely agree. But in my judgment it must follow, if the ADBA's standard is a proper starting point, that it is relevant to consider whether or not a dog exhibits the behavioural characteristics of a pit bull terrier, and evidence about the dog's behaviour cannot be irrelevant. *f*

I emphasise that such evidence is not conclusive. It is clear from the long title to the 1991 Act that its first purpose is 'to prohibit persons from having in their possession ... dogs belonging to types bred for fighting'. On appropriate evidence, a court would be entitled to express its conclusion in such words as: 'We find that this dog has most of the physical characteristics of a pit bull terrier. The fact that it appears not to be game or aggressive is not sufficient to prove, on *g* balance, that it is not a dog of the type of the pit bull terrier.'

Nevertheless in my judgment for the reasons I have sought to explain evidence on this subject is relevant and must be given some weight.

For these reasons I would refuse to grant a declaration in the terms sought by Mr Dunne. I would however answer the first question posed in the case stated on *h* Miss Brock's appeal in the negative. Thus I would allow her appeal. We will consider, after submissions from counsel, what results follow or should follow from our decisions in both these cases.

CRESSWELL J. I agree.   *j*

Declaration refused in Dunne's case. Appeal in Brock's case allowed; decision of Crown Court quashed; rehearing ordered.

                                                   Dilys Tausz   Barrister.

SECTION A

1. Who started the proceedings in *R. v. Crown Court at Knightsbridge, ex parte Dunne*?

2. Give a short statement of the issues raised by the *Dunne* case before the Divisional Court.

3. (a) In which courts were the cases of *R. v. Crown Court at Knightsbridge, ex parte Dunne* and *Brock v. Director of Public Prosecution* heard?

   (b) Were these criminal or civil proceedings?

   (c) What were the decisions in each of the cases at first instance?

   (d) Were the decisions of the first instance courts overturned on appeal?

   (e) Was either of the first instance decisions reported?

4. Are there any other reported cases on the Dangerous Dogs Act 1991?

SECTION B

5. Find alternative references to *R. v. Crown Court at Knightsbridge, ex parte Dunne* and *Brock v. Director of Public Prosecutions*.

6. Has *R. v. Crown Court at Knightsbridge, ex parte Dunne* and *Brock v. Director of Public Prosecutions* been cited in any subsequent case?

7. What use did Glidewell L.J. make of the case of *Parker v. Annan*?

8. What opinion did Glidewell L.J. express about the advice which had been given to Mr Dunne to the effect that he could not appeal against the Crown Court's conclusion that he had failed to prove that the dog was not of the type known as the pit bull terrier?

9. What are the characteristics of the procedure known as "case stated"?

10. Write a short statement giving the *ratio* of the case in relation to *Dunne*.

EXERCISE 4

Cases 2

a # R v Tower Hamlets London Borough Council, ex parte Begum
R v Tower Hamlets London Borough Council, ex parte Rahman

b
COURT OF APPEAL, CIVIL DIVISION
LORD DONALDSON OF LYMINGTON MR, BUTLER-SLOSS AND STAUGHTON LJJ
15, 20, 30 JULY 1992

Housing – Homeless person – Duty of housing authority to provide accommodation –
c *Application for priority need accommodation – Application by person suffering mental*
incapacity – Application made by another person on behalf of person suffering mental
incapacity – Housing authority rejecting application – Whether application for priority
need housing may be made on behalf of person unable to complete application form –
National Assistance Act 1948, s 21(1) – Housing Act 1985, ss 59(1)(c), 62.

d In two separate appeals concerning applications by homeless people for priority
need housing under s 62[a] of the Housing Act 1985 the question arose whether
the application could be made by a person acting on behalf of a potential applicant
who was unable, through lack of capacity, either to make or to consent to the
making of the application. In the first case the applicant, who was 24, had arrived
from Bangladesh with his family in 1991. He was moderately to severely mentally
e handicapped and was believed to have a mental age of between 10 and 13. At first
the family lived with relatives, but subsequently the applicant, assisted by an
organisation which assisted people with mental handicap living in the community,
applied to the local authority for accommodation under s 62 of the 1985 Act on
the basis that he fell within s 59(1)(c)[b] of that Act, which provided that a person
who was vulnerable as a result of, inter alia, 'mental illness or handicap or physical
f disability' was to be treated as a having a priority need for housing. However, the
local authority concluded that, given his mental condition and assessed mental
age, the applicant was not capable of making an application under s 62, nor could
he have acquiesced in any application and he was therefore to be treated as not
having made the application. The applicant applied for leave to move for judicial
g review but the judge refused the application. The applicant appealed and was
granted leave by the Court of Appeal, which then heard the substantive
application. In the second case, the appellant, who was 24, deaf and had limited
speech, had arrived from Bangladesh with her family in 1989. In July 1990 the
appellant and her father attended the homeless persons unit of the local authority
h and she signed an application under s 62 for priority housing in accordance with
s 59(1)(c). However, the local authority concluded that she lacked the necessary
capacity to make the application. The appellant applied for judicial review but
the judge dismissed the application on the basis that, for the purposes of an
application under s 62, prima facie there had to be knowledge on the part of the
applicant that an application was being made. The appellant appealed. In both
j cases the local authority contended that the structure of the 1985 Act presupposed
an applicant of sufficient comprehension to be able to make an application or to
consent to an application being made on his behalf and that persons under such
disability as not to understand that an application was being made were excluded

---

a Section 62, so far as material, is set out at p 451 *g h*, post
b Section 59(1) is set out at p 451 *e f*, post

from the mechanism of the 1985 Act and their needs, including the need to be
accommodated, had to be met by social services departments under the National   *a*
Assistance Act 1948, s 21(1)ᶜ of which authorised local authorities to provide
residential accommodation for persons aged 18 or over who 'by reason of . . .
infirmity or any other circumstances are in need of care and attention which is
not otherwise available to them'.

Held – An application for priority housing under s 62 of the 1985 Act could be   *b*
made by a person with capacity to make it, by another person with the consent of
the applicant or by someone acting on behalf of a person who was entitled to
make an application but who was unable through mental incapacity to make or
consent to the making of an application, provided the writer or maker of the
application on behalf of that person could demonstrate reasonable grounds for
making the application and that he was acting bona fide in the best interests of   *c*
the applicant, since on its true construction s 62 was procedural and provided no
barrier of mental capacity to the acceptance of an application. Furthermore, the
purpose of the legislation was to include within its framework those with mental
illness or handicap without reference to a definable cut-off point of mental
capacity and s 59(1)(c) of the 1985 Act clearly contemplated that applications   *d*
could be made by those under a disability or who were vulnerable. Moreover,
although the 1985 and 1948 Acts overlapped, they fulfilled different needs: the
1985 Act presupposed homelessness or the threat of it, whereas the 1948 Act
catered for those who were in need of care, albeit that they might be adequately
housed. It followed that the applicant and the appellant were clearly within the
ambit of the 1985 Act and had made valid applications for priority housing on   *e*
which the local authority was bound to act. Accordingly the decision of the local
authority in each case would be set aside (see p 454 *a* to *g*, p 455 *e f h* and p 456 *b*
c, post).

Notes
For accommodation for homeless persons and priority need for accommodation,   *f*
see 22 *Halsbury's Laws* (4th edn) paras 509–510, and for cases on the subject, see
26 *Digest* (Reissue) 797–801, 5325–5338.
    For the National Assistance Act 1948, s 21, see 40 *Halsbury's Statutes* (4th edn)
23.
    For the Housing Act 1985, ss 59, 62, see 21 *Halsbury's Statutes* (4th edn) (1990   *g*
reissue) 98, 101.

Cases referred to in judgments
Associated Provincial Picture Houses Ltd v Wednesbury Corp [1947] 2 All ER 680,
    [1948] 1 KB 223, CA.
Khawaja v Secretary of State for the Home Dept [1983] 1 All ER 765, [1984] 1 AC 74,   *h*
    [1983] 2 WLR 321, HL.
R v Oldham Metropolitan B C, ex p G (1992) Times, 20 April.

Cases also cited or referred to in skeleton arguments
Cocks v Thanet DC [1982] 3 All ER 1135, [1983] 2 AC 286, HL.
F v West Berkshire Health Authority (Mental Health Act Commission intervening) [1989]   *j*
    2 All ER 545, [1900] 2 AC 1, HL.
Lewis v North Devon DC [1981] 1 All ER 27, [1981] 1 WLR 328.
R v Bath City Council, ex p Sangermano (1984) 17 HLR 94.
R v Brent London BC, ex p Omar (1991) 23 HLR 446.

---

c   Section 21(1), so far as material, is set out at p 453 g, post

R v Chiltern DC, ex p Roberts (1990) 23 HLR 387.

a *R v Eastleigh BC, ex p Beattie* (1984) 17 HLR 168.

R v Fulham Hammersmith and Kensington Rent Tribunal, ex p Zerek [1951] 1 All ER 482, [1951] 2 KB 1, DC.

R v Lambeth London BC, ex p Ly (1986) 19 HLR 51.

Roberts v Dorset CC (1976) 75 LGR 462.

Zamir v Secretary of State for the Home Dept [1980] 2 All ER 768, [1980] AC 930,

b   HL.

Application for judicial review and appeal

R v Tower Hamlets London BC, ex p Begum

Ferdous Begum appealed from the order of Rose J made on 28 November 1991

c whereby he dismissed her motion for judicial review, brought with the leave of Popplewell J given on 2 September 1991, of the decision of the respondent, Tower Hamlets London Borough Council, communicated to the appellant's father by letter dated 11 July 1991 that the appellant had not made an application to the council pursuant to Pt III of the Housing Act 1985 as a homeless person and therefore the council was under no obligation to make inquiries into the

d appellant's homelessness pursuant to s 62 of that Act. The facts are set out in the judgment of Butler-Sloss LJ.

R v Tower Hamlets London BC, ex p Rahman

Lutfur Rahman applied by way of renewed application, with the leave of the Court of Appeal (Lord Donaldson MR, Stocker and Butler-Sloss LJJ) given on 23

e March 1992, for judicial review of the decision of the respondent, Tower Hamlets London Borough Council, given on 18 February 1992 that the applicant had not on 28 January 1992 made an application to the council pursuant to Pt III of the Housing Act 1985, the original application for such leave having been refused by Macpherson J on 13 March 1992. The court ordered that the substantive

f application be retained for hearing by the Court of Appeal. The relief sought was an order of certiorari to quash the council's decision, an order of mandamus requiring the council to consider and determine the application and a declaration that on 28 January 1992 the applicant had made a valid application to the council pursuant to Pt III of the 1985 Act. The facts are set out in the judgment of Butler-Sloss LJ.

g

Robert Carnwath QC and *Terence Gallivan* (instructed by *T V Edwards*) for the applicant Rahman.

David Watkinson and *Leslie Thomas* (instructed by *Hereward & Foster*) for the appellant Begum.

Ashley Underwood and *Lisa Giovannetti* (instructed by *J E Marlowe*) for the council.

h   council.

Cur adv vult

j 30 July 1992. The following judgments were delivered.

BUTLER-SLOSS LJ (giving the first judgment at the invitation of Lord Donaldson MR). The two matters before this court, one an appeal from the dismissal of judicial review and the second the retention by this court of a substantive application for judicial review after the granting of leave, raise the same issue under the Housing Act 1985 as to the right of people suffering from mental illness or mental handicap to apply for priority housing. The relevant facts of each appeal are as follows.

Lutfur Rahman

The applicant is 24. He and his family came to England from Bangladesh in 1991. His family consists of his mother and two sisters aged 16 and 11. They lived at first with relatives in Tower Hamlets and then approached the homeless persons unit. They have been housed in temporary accommodation pending inquiries. The housing authority decided that the mother was homeless, in priority need, and was intentionally homeless and that accommodation would not be provided beyond 3 February 1992. There has been no challenge to that decision.

The applicant came to the attention of the Community Team for People with Learning Difficulties (CTLD), which is part of the Royal London Trust and which assists people with mental handicap living in the community. The applicant was assessed by the same psychologist as Ferdous Begum (see post), who concluded that he had both moderate and in some respects severe mental handicap, that he had hearing difficulties and that he is functioning at a mental age of between 10 and 13.

The applicant, assisted by the CTLD, applied to the housing authority for accommodation under the provisions of s 59(1)(c) of the 1985 Act. A representative of the housing authority interviewed the family and the applicant and concluded that the applicant was not capable of making an application under s 62, and on 19 February 1992 another representative of the housing authority wrote to the applicant's mother setting out the applicant's mental condition and assessed mental age, and continued:

'I must therefore conclude that [Lutfur] is dependant on you. In all of these circumstances I conclude that he cannot have acquiesced in any application for housing and is not capable of making an application for rehousing. It follows that I must treat him as not having made an application and I therefore conclude that the purported application was merely a device by which you sought to get round the unchallenged finding of your intentional homelessness.'

On 13 March 1992 Macpherson J refused leave to move for judicial review, but leave was granted by a division of this court on 23 March 1992 and the hearing of the substantive application was retained to be heard by this court.

Ferdous Begum

The appellant is 24. She and her family arrived in England from Bangladesh on 17 December 1989. She has a father, mother, either two or three sisters and a brother. On arrival, after a night with relatives her father approached the homeless persons unit of the respondent housing authority, who housed the family in temporary accommodation pending inquiries. The housing authority found the father to be intentionally homeless and indicated that they would not provide accommodation for the family beyond 18 July 1990. The father took no steps to set aside that decision.

The appellant is profoundly deaf and has very limited speech. She communicates with her family by means of signs and words understood only by them. She has been assessed to a limited extent by a psychologist, who considered that she was functioning far below her potential level but did not come to a conclusion as to her mental age. Additional evidence has been accepted by this court which shows that she has an ability to function quite successfully within the family.

The appellant and her father attended the homeless persons unit on 17 July
a 1990 and she signed an application for priority housing in accordance with the
provisions of s 59(1)(*c*) of the 1985 Act. By letter dated 11 July 1991 a
representative of the housing authority notified the appellant's father that they
considered that she had not made an application. After setting out her disabilities
the letter concluded:

b   'Her only means of communication with us has been through you. In all
        of those circumstances I conclude not only that she could not have acquiesced
        in any act or omission by you rendering her homeless, I find that she cannot
        have acquiesced in any application for housing. It follows that I must treat
        her as not having made an application and I therefore conclude that the
        purported application was merely a device by which you sought to get
c   around the unchallenged finding of your intentional homelessness.'

The appellant was granted leave to move for judicial review by Popplewell J on
2 September 1991, but the application was dismissed by Rose J on 28 November
1991.
        The 1985 Act provides a framework in Pt III within which local housing
d authorities try to cope with the problems of homelessness within their local areas.
It consolidates earlier legislation dealing with the same problem. Section 58
defines homelessness and threatened homelessness. Section 59(1) sets out the
categories of priority need for accommodation, and para (*c*) is relied upon in both
cases before this court:

e   'The following have a priority need for accommodation—(*a*) a pregnant
        woman or a person with whom a pregnant woman resides or might
        reasonably be expected to reside; (*b*) a person with whom dependent children
        reside or might reasonably be expected to reside; (*c*) a person who is vulnerable
        as a result of old age, mental illness or handicap or physical disability or other
        special reason, or with whom such a person resides or might reasonably be
f   expected to reside; (*d*) a person who is homeless or threatened with
        homelessness as a result of an emergency such as flood, fire or other disaster.'

Section 60 defines intentional homelessness. Section 62 deals with the inquiry
into cases of possible homelessness or threatened homelessness and provides in
general terms for the application to be made:

g   '(1) If a person (an "applicant") applies to a local housing authority for
        accommodation, or for assistance in obtaining accommodation, and the
        authority have reason to believe that he may be homeless or threatened with
        homelessness, they shall make such inquiries as are necessary to satisfy
        themselves as to whether he is homeless or threatened with homelessness.
h   (2) If they are so satisfied, they shall make any further inquiries necessary
        to satisfy themselves as to—(*a*) whether he has a priority need, and (*b*) whether
        he became homeless or threatened with homelessness intentionally . . .'

Pending inquiries the housing authority have an interim duty under s 63 to
make accommodation available to the applicant. Notification of the decision and
the reasons for it is covered by s 64. Once a housing authority are—
i
        'satisfied that he has a priority need and are not satisfied that he became
        homeless intentionally, they shall . . . secure that accommodation becomes
        available for his occupation.' (See s 65(2).)

Sections 65 and 69 also lay other duties upon the housing authority to provide
accommodation for a limited period and to offer advice and assistance.

A local housing authority may refer an applicant to another housing authority and house him in the meantime (ss 67 and 68). False statements, withholding *a* information and failure to disclose change of circumstances are dealt with in s 74. Section 75 states:

> 'For the purposes of this Part accommodation shall be regarded as available for a person's occupation only if it is available for occupation both by him and by any other person who might reasonably be expected to reside with *b* him . . .'.

In discharge of their duties local housing authorities are assisted by the *Code of Guidance for Local Authorities on Homelessness*. The Secretary of State is empowered to issue such guidance by virtue of s 71(2) and a local housing authority is required to have regard to it. Paragraph 3.2 in ch 3 deals with 'What is an application?' and *c* continues:

> 'Under s. 62 of the Act an authority is required to take action whenever someone approaches it for help in obtaining housing and the authority has reason to believe that s/he may be homeless or threatened with homelessness. This duty exists regardless of which department of the local authority the applicant approaches or of the way in which the application is made. *d* Authorities should be aware of the need to recognise people who should be treated as homeless even if there is no formal application and they should monitor all applications.'

In paras 6.10 and 6.11 of ch 6 the code of guidance deals specifically with the groups within the community falling within s 59(1)(c) and in para 6.10 they are *e* advised in cases of vulnerability to have regard to medical advice and where appropriate to seek social services advice. Paragraph 6.11 refers in particular to liaison between the health authority and the housing authority. Section 72 of the Act sets out the duty of co-operation between local housing authorities and also by social service authorities when called on to render assistance to a local housing *f* authority.

The Act however does not state nor does the code of guidance assist as to the application itself—who may make it and in particular whether it can be made by someone acting on behalf of a potential applicant unable himself through lack of comprehension either to make or consent to the making of such an application for priority housing. This point has not previously been the subject of judicial *g* scrutiny and is by no means without difficulty.

The case for both the applicant and the appellant is that the Act provides a comprehensive set of rules for homelessness. Section 62, which alone deals with the threshold of the application, lays down no criteria nor rules for the making of the application. Section 59(1)(c) expressly recognises that the more vulnerable sections of society will be applicants and among them those who are old, with *h* mental illness or mental handicap. There is in the Act no restriction or limitation as to the degree of mental illness or mental handicap of a potential applicant and diminution in which will obviously reduce the cognitive ability of a person and in some cases may extinguish it. Indeed, the code of guidance recognises that an application may be informal, and local housing authorities are advised to have regard to medical advice and advice from social services. *j*

The primary argument of Mr Carnwath QC for the applicant and of Mr Watkinson for the appellant is that there is no line to be drawn between those with sufficient understanding to make their own applications or to consent to their applications being made by others on their behalf, and those with no comprehension whatsoever who none the less are homeless or threatened with *a* homelessness and whose plight ought to be considered and redressed within the framework of Pt III of the Act.

The secondary argument of both the applicant and the appellant is they have in fact sufficient understanding of the concept of homelessness and the need to seek help to come within the meaning of an applicant who knew he was making an application or consented to an application being made on his behalf. In *b* considering this argument, the letter of the housing officer in each case clearly demonstrates that he fell into error. For entirely understandable reasons, since in each case the parent had been declared intentionally homeless, the application under s 59(1)(c) was seen as a device to get round the refusal of housing on the previous application of the family. This approach, that it was a device, was subsequently abandoned by the housing authority. But it undoubtedly had an *c* effect on the thought processes of the housing officer and casts doubt on each decision. However, it is unnecessary to pursue this issue any further since Mr Underwood for the housing authority, with the advantage of further evidence as to the abilities of each of these young people, accepted that the housing authority would in any event have to reconsider their cases.

Mr Carnwath argued that the question 'Who is an applicant?' is not a matter *d* for the decision of the local housing authority to be challenged on the ground of *Wednesbury* unreasonableness (see *Associated Provincial Picture Houses Ltd v Wednesbury Corp* [1947] 2 All ER 680, [1948] 1 KB 223) but is a jurisdictional fact as to the point at which the duties laid upon the housing authority come into existence. Consequently, if the housing authority can be shown to have come to the wrong decision, this court may, if appropriate, substitute its own decision for *e* that of the housing authority.

Mr Underwood for the respondent local authority argued that the structure of the Act presupposes an applicant of sufficient comprehension to be able to make an application or consent to an application being made on his behalf. In these two cases the housing authority themselves involved a psychologist to assist in the *f* assessment of each of them. A line has to be drawn which excludes those under such a disability as not to understand that an application is being made. There is nothing in the Act to show that a person with no mental ability can none the less be treated as an applicant without his knowledge. He pointed to the sections of the Act which require notification by the applicant of change of circumstances and the provisions in respect of false statements. He invited our attention to *g* s 21(1) of the National Assistance Act 1948 part of which remains in force (with amendments) and authorises a local authority to make arrangements to provide—

'(a) residential accommodation for persons aged eighteen or over who by reason of age, infirmity or any other circumstances are in need of care and attention which is not otherwise available to them.'

h Section 21(1)(a) of the 1948 Act is however administered by the social services department and not the housing authority. The framework of the legislation therefore is that those incapable of understanding what they are doing or of making an application themselves do not come within the 1985 Act but their needs, including the need to be accommodated, are met by social services within *j* the structure of the 1948 Act.

Rose J asked himself the question in regard to Ferdous Begum: does the mind go with the application? and answered it on the basis that—

'the word "application" prima facie involves knowledge on the part of the applicant that an application is being made.'

Although I see the force of the argument, in the context of the 1985 Act I do not believe that it is correct. There is nothing in the Act to demonstrate that s 62 *a* is substantive rather than procedural and provides hurdles of mental capacity to surmount before an application can be accepted. On the contrary, s 59(1)(c) contemplates that applications will be made by those under a disability or who are vulnerable. Such legislation is in accord with the expressed policy of government departments to accept within the community those who might in former days have been shut away in long-stay institutions. I cannot construe from *b* the statute any indication that a line has to be drawn among those targeted by s 59(1)(c) according to degrees of mental capacity less than the normal capacity to make an application. The purpose of the framework of the overall legislation is to include those with mental illness or handicap without reference to a definable cut-off point of mental capacity. The argument that applicants are required to inform the housing authority of changes of circumstances would, in the context *c* of someone under a disability, be the obligation of the person who made or assisted in the making of the application. The offence of making a false statement is not restricted to the applicant alone.

In my view an application may be made under s 59(1)(c) by a person with capacity to make it, or by another with the consent of the applicant, or by *d* someone on behalf of a person who is entitled to make an application but is unable through mental incapacity to make or consent to the making of an application. In the latter case the writer or maker of the application on behalf of another must demonstrate reasonable grounds for making the application and for acting on behalf of the actual applicant and that he is acting bona fide in the interests of the person unable to act without such help. An application by a well- *e* meaning busybody would not be an acceptable application under s 62.

The 1985 Act and the 1948 Act undoubtedly overlap, and those administering each Act may from time to time have to consider the needs of the same person. There would be nothing surprising in that position since the wording of s 72(b) of the 1985 Act and of the code of guidance both contemplate the involvement of both services in housing the vulnerable homeless. However, the two Acts fulfil *f* different roles and meet different needs. The 1948 Act caters for those in need of care and attention who may none the less be adequately housed, with no question of homelessness or threat of homelessness. But their inability to manage their own affairs may require them nevertheless to be accommodated in sheltered housing and to leave their own homes. Part III of the 1985 Act presupposes either *g* homelessness or threat of homelessness; otherwise the application would not be made. Further, there is an important practical difference. Social services run residential accommodation for the person in need under the provisions of s 21(1) of the 1948 Act. They do not have a stock of housing as such and, without recourse to the local housing authority, would not be in a position to house the family of the person in need. The 1985 Act on the other hand specifically *h* recognises in s 75 an obligation to house not only the applicant with priority need but some at least of his family, if he lives with one or more of them. Section 75 does not however cast a duty upon the local housing authority to house all members of a large extended family but only those who come within the definition of 'any other person who might reasonably be expected to reside with him'. *j*

In problems which may arise both within the ambit of the 1985 Act and the 1948 Act the people involved will inevitably be within the most vulnerable group contemplated by the legislation and it is especially important that their needs are recognised and their problems addressed without passing them from one department to another.

a   The question whether a person is an applicant within the ambit of s 62 of the 1985 Act is not in my judgment a matter for the discretion of the local housing authority to be reviewed upon *Wednesbury* principles. It is a question whether the person comes within those contemplated by Pt III of the 1985 Act as applicants for priority housing, the receipt of whose applications will be the threshold for the assumption by the local housing authority of their various duties under the Act. Henry J in *R v Oldham Metropolitan BC, ex p G* (1992) Times, 20 April decided

b that dependent children could not be applicants in their own right under the provisions of Pt III of the 1985 Act. I do not wish to comment upon the issue raised in that decision, but the judge made general observations about applicants under s 62 which included the proposition that a person can only be considered as an applicant if he can establish a priority need. I do not agree. In my view the housing authority has to accept genuine applications and consider, on the facts

c revealed in the application and after any necessary inquiries, whether a duty arises under Pt III of the 1985 Act. The housing authority has to establish the precedent fact, as it was described by Lord Fraser in *Khawaja v Secretary of State for the Home Dept* [1983] 1 All ER 765 at 771, [1984] 1 AC 74 at 97, that an application for housing, in however informal terms, has been made. The question whether an

d application has been made and whether the housing authority have erred in their approach to this issue is a collateral question preceding the main decision-making process. Consequently I agree with Mr Carnwath that, if he can demonstrate that the housing authority wrongly excluded an application, this court has the jurisdiction to substitute its own decision. For the reasons which I have set out earlier I consider that both the appellant and the applicant made applications

e which the housing authority was bound to receive and to act upon and consequently they were not justified in rejecting them. It would seem to me unlikely that the housing authority would be able to reject applications made in similar circumstances although, of course, in carrying out their duties they may have a variety of options in responding to the applications.

    In each case I would set aside the decision of the local housing authority.

f

STAUGHTON LJ. I agree with the orders proposed by Butler-Sloss LJ and Lord Donaldson MR for the reasons which they have given. In particular, I agree that a decision whether a person has made an application under s 62(1) of the Housing Act 1985 is not one which Parliament has entrusted to the local housing authority.

g If the authority has concluded that no application was made, it will be for the courts to decide whether the authority was right. But I prefer to express no opinion on the other requirement in s 62(1), that 'the authority have reason to believe that he may be homeless or threatened with homelessness...' That was not in issue in these cases.

h **LORD DONALDSON OF LYMINGTON MR.** I too would set aside the decisions of the local housing authority for the reasons given by Butler-Sloss LJ.

    This appeal and application are concerned with a human problem affecting the least advantaged citizens. I appreciate that what may be compendiously described as 'social services' and 'housing' are often, as a matter of administrative convenience, dealt with by separate departments in a single local authority and

i may, where there is multi-tiered local government, be dealt with by different authorities. This should be of no concern to the person who is homeless or threatened with homelessness (the 'homeless person'). Whether he applies to the right or the wrong department or authority should not matter. That department or authority should either itself deal with the application or pass it on to what it considers to be the correct department or authority *and* should tell the homeless person what it has done. It should not tell that person to apply elsewhere. The game of 'pass the parcel' has no place in this field. And, if disputes arise between *a* departments or authorities as to whether this is a 'social services' or a 'housing' problem, that should be sorted out between them and should not directly involve the homeless person.

I agree that reading s 59(1)(c) with s 62 makes it clear that no 'application' in the ordinary sense of the word is required of a homeless person as otherwise it would be quite impossible for some people who are 'vulnerable as a result of old *b* age, mental illness or handicap' to attract the protection which it is the clearly intended duty of housing authorities to provide under Pt III of the 1985 Act. Accordingly s 62 must be construed as contemplating only that the homeless person and his circumstances will be brought to the attention of the housing authority by an application by him, by someone else on his behalf and with his authority or by someone else on his behalf and in his interests, such person having *c* a bona fide concern with those interests.

In my judgment s 62(1) of the 1985 Act contains a double-barrelled threshold or precedent question of fact which has to be answered in the affirmative if the local housing authority's duties under Pt III of the Act are to come into force. The first part of this question is whether a person has applied to it for accommodation *d* in the sense which I have indicated. The second part is whether the authority has reason to believe that he *may* be homeless or threatened with homelessness. This is to be distinguished from the Pt III duty which follows immediately afterwards in the same sentence, namely, to make such inquiries as are necessary to satisfy itself as to whether he *is* homeless or threatened with homelessness. I cannot believe that Parliament intended that whether or not a local housing authority *e* became subject to the duties set out in Pt III of the Act should depend upon whether it happened to be credulous or incredulous, myopic or far-sighted. The intention must have been that an objective test should be applied. The authority's decision on both aspects of this threshold question therefore falls to be reviewed not on *Wednesbury* (see *Associated Provincial Picture Houses Ltd v Wednesbury Corp* [1947] 2 All ER 680, [1948] 1 KB 223) but on *Khawaja* principles—does the *f* evidence justify the conclusion (see *Khawaja v Secretary of State for the Home Dept* [1983] 1 All ER 765 at 777, [1984] AC 74 at 105 per Lord Wilberforce).

We have not had to consider whether an application can be made under s 62 by or on behalf or in the interests of a child. This was considered by Henry J in *R v Oldham Metropolitan BC, ex p G* (1992) Times, 20 April. I express no view on the *g* basis of that decision, save to say that children who do not come within s 59(1)(c) or (d) are not within the priority need category. Although 'dependent children' feature in para (b) they do so as a qualification of a different applicant, namely one with whom they reside or might reasonably be expected to reside. They do not feature in that paragraph in their own right.

h

Application granted and appeal allowed. Leave to appeal to the House of Lords refused.

18 January 1993. The Appeal Committee of the House of Lords gave leave to appeal.

                                                    Frances Rustin   Barrister.

a
Garlick v Oldham Metropolitan Borough Council
and related appeals

HOUSE OF LORDS

b LORD GRIFFITHS, LORD BRIDGE OF HARWICH, LORD ACKNER, LORD SLYNN OF HADLEY
AND LORD WOOLF

18, 19 JANUARY, 18 MARCH 1993

*Housing – Homeless person – Duty of housing authority to provide accommodation –
Application for priority need accommodation – Application by person suffering from
c incapacity – Application made by another person on behalf of person suffering mental
incapacity – Application made on behalf of four-year-old child – Housing authorities
rejecting applications – Whether application for priority need housing may be made on
behalf of person suffering from incapacity – Whether dependent child having priority
need for accommodation as result of 'special reason' making them vulnerable – Whether
d decision of local authority that applicant for accommodation lacks capacity to make
application by reason of lack of understanding susceptible to judicial review – Housing
Act 1985, ss 59(1)(c), 62.*

In three separate appeals concerning applications by homeless people for priority
need housing under s 62[a] of the Housing Act 1985 the question arose whether
e the application could be made by a person acting on behalf of a potential applicant
who was unable, through lack of capacity such as mental handicap or being a
dependent child, either to make or to consent to the making of the application.

In the first two appeals the parents of four-year-old children had become
homeless because in the one case the family home had been repossessed following
the parents' failure to keep up mortgage repayments and in the other the child's
f mother had been evicted for failure to pay rent. In each case the parents'
application for accommodation under the 1985 Act had been refused by the local
authority on the grounds that the parents had become homeless intentionally due
to the failure to pay the mortgage and rent respectively. The parents then
submitted applications for accommodation under the 1985 Act on behalf of their
four-year-old children, claiming that the children were homeless and in priority
g need under s 59(1)(c)[b] by reason of each being 'a person who is vulnerable as a
result of . . . [a] special reason', namely their age. In each case the local authority
refused to entertain the application on the ground that the application by the
children was a device to get round the provisions of the 1985 Act. Applications
were then made on behalf of the children for judicial review of the local
h authorities' decisions. The judge dismissed the applications and on appeal the
Court of Appeal upheld his decision. The applicants appealed to the House of
Lords.

---

a   Section 62, so far as material, provides:
j   '(1) If a person (an "applicant") applies to a local housing authority for accommodation . . . and
    the authority have reason to believe that he may be homeless or threatened with homelessness,
    they shall make such inquiries as are necessary to satisfy themselves as to whether he is homeless
    or threatened with homelessness.
        (2) If they are so satisfied, they shall make any further inquiries necessary to satisfy themselves
    as to—(a) whether he has a priority need, and (b) whether he became homeless or threatened with
    homelessness intentionally . . .'
b   Section 59(1) is set out at p 69 e, post

In the third appeal the appellant, who was 25, deaf and had limited speech, had
arrived from Bangladesh with her family in 1989. In July 1990 the appellant and *a*
her father attended the homeless persons unit of the local authority and she signed
an application under s 62 for priority housing in accordance with the provisions
of s 59(1)(c). However, the local authority concluded that she lacked the necessary
capacity to make the application and refused to entertain it. The appellant applied
for judicial review of the local authority's decision but the judge dismissed the
application on the basis that, for the purposes of an application under s 62, prima *b*
facie there had to be knowledge on the part of the applicant that an application
was being made. The appellant appealed to the Court of Appeal, which allowed
the appeal on the ground that an application for priority housing under s 62 could
be made on behalf of a person who was entitled to make an application but who
was unable through mental incapacity to make or consent to the making of an
application, provided the writer or maker of the application on behalf of that *c*
person could demonstrate reasonable grounds for making the application and
that he was acting bona fide in the best interests of the applicant. The local
authority appealed to the House of Lords.

Held – (1) Section 59(1)(c) of the 1985 Act was not intended to confer any rights *d*
to priority need housing under s 62 of that Act on dependent children since it was
the intention of the Act that a child's accommodation would be provided by his
parents or those looking after him and it was to those people that the offer of
accommodation had to be made, not to the dependent child. Dependent children
were not amongst those classified as in priority need as a result of a 'special reason'
making them vulnerable as they depended on their parents or those looking after *e*
them to decide where they were to live and any offer of accommodation could
only sensibly be made to those in charge of them. Furthermore, a dependent
child suffering from some disability did not thereby acquire an independent
priority right to accommodation since healthy four-year-old children were just as
vulnerable as disabled four-year-old children from a housing point of view;
neither were capable of looking after themselves let alone deciding whether to *f*
accept an offer of accommodation. It followed that the appeals in the first two
cases would be dismissed (see p 69 *f* to p 70 *b d*, p 72 *j* to p 73 *b* and p 74 *j*, post).

(2) Similarly (Lord Slynn dissenting), no duty was owed under the 1985 Act to
persons so disabled that they had neither the capacity to make an application
themselves nor to authorise an agent to make it on their behalf. It was implicit in
the provisions of the 1985 Act that a local authority's duty to make an offer of *g*
permanent accommodation was only owed to those who had the capacity to
understand and respond to such an offer and if they accepted it to undertake the
responsibilities that would be involved. If a person caring for a person who was
vulnerable by reason of mental incapacity became homeless s 59(1)(c) gave him
the status of priority need and, provided his homelessness was not intentional, he *h*
would qualify for an offer of accommodation which would enable him to
continue to look after the vulnerable person. The local authority's appeal in the
third case would therefore be allowed (see p 71 *e h* to p 72 *a j* to p 73 *b* and p 74 *j*,
post).

Per Lord Griffiths, Lord Bridge, Lord Ackner and Lord Woolf. A decision by a
local housing authority that a particular applicant lacks the capacity to make an *j*
application because he cannot understand or act upon an offer of accommodation
can only be challenged on judicial review if it can be shown to be unreasonable
(see p 72 *h* to p 73 *b* and p 74 *g* to *j*, post).

Decision of the Court of Appeal in *R v Tower Hamlets London BC, ex p Begum*
[1993] 1 All ER 447 reversed.

Notes

a For accommodation for homeless persons and priority need for accommodation, see 22 *Halsbury's Laws* (4th edn) paras 509–510, and for cases on the subject, see 26 *Digest* (Reissue) 797–801, 5325–5338.

For the Housing Act 1985, ss 59, 62, see 21 *Halsbury's Statutes* (4th edn) (1990 reissue) 98, 101.

b **Cases referred to in opinions**

Associated Provincial Picture Houses Ltd v Wednesbury Corp [1947] 2 All ER 680, [1948] 1 KB 223, CA.
Kelly v Monklands DC 1986 SLT 169, Ct of Sess.
R v Tower Hamlets London BC, ex p Monaf (1988) 86 LGR 709, CA.

c **Appeal**

Garlick v Oldham Metropolitan BC

Graham Anthony Garlick, a minor suing by his mother and guardian Sharon Garlick, appealed with leave of the Court of Appeal from the decision of that court (Ralph Gibson, Nolan and Scott LJJ) on 6 August 1992 dismissing his appeal *d* from the decision of Henry J on 13 April 1992 dismissing his application for judicial review of the decision of the respondent, Oldham Metropolitan Borough Council (Oldham), refusing to consider the application made on behalf of the appellant for accommodation under Pt III of the Housing Act 1985. The facts are set out in the opinion of Lord Griffiths.

e *Bentum v Bexley London BC*

Moses Bentum, a minor suing by his next friend and father, appealed with leave of the Court of Appeal from the decision of that court (Ralph Gibson, Nolan and Scott LJJ) on 6 August 1992 dismissing his appeal from the decision of Henry J on 13 April 1992 dismissing his application for judicial review of the decision of the respondent, Bexley London Borough Council (Bexley), refusing to consider the *f* application made on behalf of the appellant for accommodation under Pt III of the Housing Act 1985. The facts are set out in the opinion of Lord Griffiths.

Tower Hamlets London BC v Begum

Tower Hamlets London Borough Council (Tower Hamlets) appealed with the *g* leave of the Appeal Committee of the House of Lords Lord Mustill given on 18 January 1993 from the decision of the Court of Appeal (Lord Donaldson MR, Butler-Sloss and Staughton LJJ) ([1993] 1 All ER 447, [1993] 2 WLR 9) on 30 July 1992 allowing the appeal of the respondent, Ferdous Begum, from the order of Rose J (24 HLR 115) made on 28 November 1991 whereby he dismissed the respondent's motion for judicial review of Tower Hamlet's decision, communi-*h* cated to the respondent's father by letter dated 11 July 1991 that the respondent had not made an application to Tower Hamlets pursuant to Pt III of the 1985 Act as a homeless person and therefore Tower Hamlets was under no obligation to make inquiries into the respondent's homelessness pursuant to s 62 of that Act. The facts are set out in the opinion of Lord Griffiths.

j Andrew Arden QC and *George Warr* (instructed by *Moon Beever*) for the applicant Garlick.
Timothy Straker (instructed by *Sharpe Pritchard*, agents for *David Shipp*, Oldham) for Oldham.
Patrick Elias QC and *David Watkinson* (instructed by *Norton & Co*) for the applicant Bentum.

James Goudie QC and *Brenda Morris* (instructed by *L J Birch*, Bexleyheath) for
    Bexley.   a
Ashley Underwood and *Lisa Giovannetti* (instructed by *J E Marlowe*) for Tower
    Hamlets.
Derek Wood QC, *David Watkinson* and *Leslie Thomas* (instructed by *Hereward &*
    Foster) for the respondent Begum.

LORD GRIFFITHS. My Lords, your Lordships heard these three appeals b
together because they all concern the nature of the duties owed by local housing
authorities to homeless persons under Pt III of the Housing Act 1985 which re-
enacts the provisions first contained in the Housing (Homeless Persons) Act 1977.
The first two appeals raise the question of what if any duty is owed under the
1985 Act to dependent children of four years of age who are living with their
parents.   c

    I take the facts of the first two appeals from the judgment of Henry J:

    'The facts of the two cases are these. In the first, that involving Bexley
    London Borough Council, Mr and Mrs B are political refugees from Ghana.
    They had been here for a number of years with their youngest child, the
    applicant. They had purchased their own property. They mortgaged it and d
    remortgaged it. They got into financial difficulties and were unable to keep
    up the mortgage payments. The property was repossessed and on 15 August
    1990 they presented themselves to Bexley council as homeless, applying for
    accommodation under s 62 of the 1985 Act. On 2 February 1991 their three
    other children, born respectively in 1966, 1974 [and] 1980, together with the
    young daughter of the eldest then just three months old, arrived in the e
    United Kingdom from Ghana. On 4 February 1991 their housing application
    was amended to add those recently arrived persons. In February 1991 the
    family was placed by the [council] in temporary accommodation while their
    claim was considered. On 23 September 1991 the council found that Mr and
    Mrs B were homeless, that they were considered to be in priority need, but f
    they were considered to have become homeless intentionally on the basis
    that the loss of their accommodation was caused by a deliberate omission to
    make the mortgage repayments due. Accordingly they gave Mr and Mrs B
    28 days to find alternative accommodation. There was no legal challenge to
    that decision. Instead, on 17 October 1991 a fresh application was made,
    physically by Mr B but in the name of his youngest son, who was then aged g
    four. By letter of 24 October that application was not accepted as an
    application but, in the alternative if it were to be considered to be a valid
    application, it was rejected on the basis that the four-year-old applicant was
    not considered to be in priority need. It is that decision that the applicants
    here apply to quash. Meanwhile the council have been providing
    accommodation pending the outcome of this hearing. The other application h
    concerns Oldham Metropolitan Borough Council. Again the applicant was
    four at the date of his application. In January 1991 his mother was evicted
    for failure to pay rent. She applied to the local housing authority claiming
    homelessness. After investigation the local authority found her to be
    homeless, found her to have priority need but to have become homeless
    intentionally due to her failure to make any payment towards her rent. j
    Again she was temporarily accommodated for a short period under the
    provisions of the 1985 Act and before that period had expired on 19 March
    1991 an application for accommodation was made on behalf of the applicant.
    On 4 April 1991 the [council] refused to entertain the application on the basis

a   that it was a "transparent device to get round the provisions of the Housing
      Act". It is to quash that decision that the second set of proceedings are
      brought.'

Henry J and the Court of Appeal dismissed these applications and in my opinion
they were right to do so.

It is of the first importance to understand the nature of the duty imposed upon
b local housing authorities by Parliament. It is not a duty to take the homeless off
the streets and to place them physically in accommodation. The duty is to give
them and their families the first priority in the housing queue. The duty is
expressed in s 65(2) as a duty to 'secure that accommodation becomes available
for his occupation'. It is a duty to offer a homeless person who applies to them for
assistance suitable permanent accommodation to house him and his family (see
c s 75). It is then up to the applicant to decide whether or not he will accept the
accommodation. The local housing authority cannot force the applicant to accept
it but they will have discharged their duty under the 1985 Act by finding and
offering suitable permanent accommodation.

The persons to whom this duty is owed are those who are homeless and in
      priority need and have not disqualified themselves by becoming homeless
d intentionally. Those in priority need are classified in s 59(1):

            'The following have a priority need for accommodation—(a) a pregnant
      woman or a person with whom a pregnant woman resides or might
      reasonably be expected to reside; (b) a person with whom dependent children
      reside or might reasonably be expected to reside; (c) a person who is vulnerable
e   as a result of old age, mental illness or handicap or physical disability or other
      special reason, or with whom such a person resides or might reasonably be
      expected to reside; (d) a person who is homeless or threatened with
      homelessness as a result of an emergency such as flood, fire or other disaster.'

Dependent children are not amongst those classified as in priority need. This is
f not surprising. Dependent children depend on their parents or those looking
after them to decide where they are to live and the offer of accommodation can
only sensibly be made to those in charge of them. There is no definition of a
dependent child in the 1985 Act but the *Homelessness Code of Guidance for Local
Authorities* (3rd edn, 1991), to which local authorities must have regard for
guidance (see s 71), suggests in para 6.3 that authorities should normally include
g as dependent all children under 16 and all children aged 16 to 18 who are in, or
about to begin, full-time education or training or who for other reasons are unable
to support themselves and who live at home. This seems to me to be sensible
guidance and likely to result in families being housed together until the children
are reasonably mature. There will obviously be the case from time to time when
h a child leaves home under the age of 16 and ceases to be dependent on the parents
or those with whom he or she was living and such a child may be vulnerable and
in priority need by virtue of s 59(1)(c): see *Kelly v Monklands DC* 1986 SLT 169.
But however that may be, it cannot possibly be argued that a healthy four-year-
old living with parents is other than a dependent child. Such a child is in my
opinion owed no duty under this Act for it is the intention of the Act that the
j child's accommodation will be provided by the parents or those looking after him
and it is to those people that the offer of accommodation must be made, not to
the dependent child.

I cannot accept the argument that extreme youth is a 'special reason' making
the child vulnerable and thus giving it a priority need under s 59(1)(c). 'Old age'
is mentioned as a cause of vulnerability but 'young age' is not. The reason of

course is that already stated. Parliament has provided for dependent children by giving a priority right to accommodation to their parents or those looking after *a* them. Nor can I accept the argument that if a dependent child suffers from some disability it thereby acquires an independent priority right to accommodation. A healthy four-year-old is just as vulnerable as a disabled four-year-old from a housing point of view; neither is capable of looking after himself let alone deciding whether to accept an offer of accommodation. I am satisfied that s 59(1)(*c*) was not intended to confer any rights upon dependent children.   *b*

It is also to be observed that the Act imposes a duty on the authority to give written advice to the applicant and makes it a criminal offence for an applicant not to notify an authority of a change in his circumstances (see ss 64 and 74). This is all part of a pattern that supports the view that the intention of this Act was to create a duty to offer accommodation to those homeless persons in priority need *c* who can decide whether or not to accept the offer and that this does not include dependent children.

If a family has lost its right to priority treatment through intentional homelessness the parent cannot achieve the same result through the back door by an application in the name of a dependent child; if he could it would mean that the disqualification of intentional homelessness had no application to families *d* with dependent children. If this had been the intention of Parliament it would surely have said so.

For these reasons I would dismiss the first two appeals. I wish however to point out that there are other provisions of our social welfare legislation that provide for the accommodation and care of children and of the duty of cooperation between authorities in the discharge of their duties. Section 20(1) of the Children *e* Act 1989 provides:

.

'Every local authority shall provide accommodation for any child in need within their area who appears to them to require accommodation as a result of—(*a*) there being no person who has parental responsibility for him; (*b*) his being lost or having been abandoned; or (*c*) the person who has been caring *f* for him being prevented (whether or not permanently, and for whatever reason) from providing him with suitable accommodation or care.'

And I also draw attention to s 27, which deals particularly with co-operation between authorities.

The third appeal concerns the duty owed to a vulnerable adult. The facts are as *g* follows. The respondent, the applicant, is a 25-year-old Bangladeshi woman who lacks hearing, speech and education. Communication with her is very difficult and within the family takes place by a unique form of sign language. She arrived in the United Kingdom in December 1989 with her parents, sisters and a brother. On 18 December 1989 her father applied to the local authority's homeless persons unit. He was interviewed several times in early 1990. By letter of 1 June 1990 to *h* the father the authority communicated their decision that the family had been rendered homeless and were in priority need because of the dependent children but that the family were intentionally homeless, having left accommodation in Bangladesh which it was reasonable for them to continue to occupy. Temporary accommodation was offered the family until 18 July 1990. On 17 July the respondent attended with her father at the local authority's offices bringing a *j* letter dated 15 July from the solicitors who had been acting on behalf of the father. This letter said that the solicitors were now acting on behalf of the daughter and submitted that the authority had a duty to provide her together with the other members of her family with accommodation. The letter contained the following paragraph:

a   'If, which is not admitted, you were correct in your finding that Mr Ali [the father] is intentionally homeless, we submit that Ferdous Begum [the daughter] is not intentionally homeless because given her abilities and level of understanding, she could not have acquiesced in any act or omission by her father rendering her homeless.'

b   On 11 July 1991 the authority wrote the decision letter refusing the application which contained the following paragraph:

c   'I have carried out a number of inquiries and I do indeed conclude that Ferdous's abilities and level of understanding are very low. She suffers from a double disability in that she has neither speech nor hearing. She uses a form of sign language apparently unique to her. She is under-stimulated and educationally undeveloped. Her only means of communication with us has been through you [the father]. In all these circumstances I conclude not only that she could not have acquiesced in any act or omission by you rendering her homeless, I find that she cannot have acquiesced in any application for housing. It follows that I must treat her as not having made an application and I therefore conclude that the purported application was merely a device *d*   by which you sought to get around the unchallenged finding of your intentional homelessness.'

The judge dismissed the applicant's challenge to the local authority's decision but the Court of Appeal reversed his decision and the local housing authority now appeal to your Lordships.

e   The first question to be considered is whether any duty is owed under the 1985 Act to persons so disabled that they have neither the capacity to make an application themselves nor to authorise an agent to make it on their behalf. The judge answered this question in the negative, the Court of Appeal in the affirmative. I agree with the judge.

I have already pointed out that the duty under this Act is a duty to make an *f*   offer of permanent accommodation. As Purchas LJ pointed out in *R v Tower Hamlets London BC, ex p Monaf* (1988) 86 LGR 709 at 732, the Act is primarily to do with the provision of bricks and mortar and not with care and attention for the gravely disabled, which is provided for in other legislation.

The priority need of the disabled is dealt with in s 59(1)(c), which I will set out *g*   again:

'... a person who is vulnerable as a result of old age, mental illness or handicap or physical disability or other special reason, or with whom such a person resides or might reasonably be expected to reside ...'

Many vulnerable people are cared for in the community by their relatives or *h*   other good-hearted people with whom they live. If such a 'carer' should have the misfortune to become homeless then s 59(1)(c) gives him the status of priority need, and provided his homelessness was not intentional, he will qualify for an offer of accommodation which will enable him to continue to look after the vulnerable person.

Other people although vulnerable are nevertheless able to lead an independent *j*   existence, albeit sometimes in sheltered accommodation; these people also have the status of priority need and can apply for assistance if they are homeless but not intentionally so. When they are made the offer of accommodation they can decide whether or not to accept it.

But I can see no purpose in making an offer of accommodation to a person so disabled that he is unable to comprehend or evaluate the offer. In my view it is

implicit in the provisions of the Act that the duty to make an offer is only owed
to those who have the capacity to understand and respond to such an offer and if   *a*
they accept it to undertake the responsibilities that will be involved. If a person is
so disabled that he cannot do this he is not left destitute but is protected by the
National Assistance Act 1948, which by s 21(1) provides:

> 'It shall be the duty of every local authority, subject to and in accordance
> with the provisions of this Part of this Act, to provide—(a) residential   *b*
> accommodation for persons who by reason of age, infirmity or any other
> circumstances are in need of care and attention which is not otherwise
> available to them; (b) temporary accommodation for persons who are in
> urgent need thereof, being need arising in circumstances which could not
> reasonably have been foreseen or in such other circumstances as the authority
> may in any particular case determine.'   *c*

In the present appeal the authority regarded the applicant as so disabled that
she lacked the capacity to be regarded as an applicant and that they thus owed her
no duty under the Act. At the hearing before the Court of Appeal further evidence
of the mental capacity of the applicant was admitted. The authority wish to
evaluate this evidence and have undertaken to reconsider their decision that the   *d*
applicant lacks capacity to make an application. But if they decide that the
applicant does lack capacity to make an application the question arises whether
that decision is one which Parliament entrusted to the authority and so can only
be reviewed on *Wednesbury* grounds (see *Associated Provincial Picture Houses Ltd v
Wednesbury Corp* [1947] 2 All ER 680, [1948] 1 KB 223) or whether it is to be
regarded as a question of precedent fact going to the jurisdiction and so to be   *e*
decided by the court.

If, as the Court of Appeal decided, an application can be made on behalf of a
totally mentally incapacitated person because a duty is owed to him or her under
the Act it is understandable to regard the question of whether or not an application
has been made to be a question of fact to be decided by the court. But if, on the   *f*
true construction of the Act, Parliament only imposes the duty in respect of
applicants of sufficient mental capacity to act upon the offer of accommodation
then it seems to me it must have intended the local housing authority to evaluate
the capacity of the applicant. In this field of social welfare all those concerned
with the welfare of the victims must necessarily work closely together. When an
application is made by or on behalf of a homeless person an immediate   *g*
investigation must be started and if it is decided that the homeless person is so
disabled as to be incapable of looking after himself and there is no one to care for
him then the social services must be alerted immediately so that they may look
after him. All these very immediate investigations and decisions are necessary to
make the system work and they can only be carried out by the authorities
concerned. I therefore conclude that a decision by a local housing authority that   *h*
a particular applicant lacks the capacity to make an application because he cannot
understand or act upon an offer of accommodation can only be challenged on
judicial review if it can be shown to be *Wednesbury* unreasonable. As the local
housing authority is in any event going to review its decision there is no purpose
in entering upon a *Wednesbury* review at this stage. But on the material before
the learned judge he was in my view right to dismiss the application and I would   *j*
allow this appeal.

LORD BRIDGE OF HARWICH. My Lords, I have had the advantage of
reading in draft the speech prepared by my noble and learned friend Lord Griffiths.

a I agree with it and, for the reasons he gives I would dismiss the first two appeals and allow the third.

b **LORD ACKNER.** My Lords, I have had the advantage of reading in draft the speech prepared by my noble and learned friend Lord Griffiths. For the reasons he gives I too would dismiss the first two appeals and allow the third appeal.

LORD SLYNN OF HADLEY. My Lords, I have had the advantage of reading in draft the speech prepared by my noble and learned friend Lord Griffiths. I agree that, for the reasons he gives, the first two appeals should be dismissed.

c I have more difficulty with the third appeal. The cases are prima facie different in that 'a person who is vulnerable as a result of old age, mental illness or handicap or physical disability or other special reasons', unlike a dependent child, has a priority need for accommodation in his or her own right (s 59(1)(c) of the Housing Act 1985).

By s 62(1) of the Act, if a person (an 'applicant') applies to a local housing authority for accommodation or for assistance in obtaining accommodation, the

d local authority must first ask if he is homeless or threatened with homelessness. If they are satisfied that he is they must then ask if (a) he has a priority need and (b) whether he is homeless intentionally.

I do not think it right to define the phrase 'a person (an "applicant")' who 'applies to a local housing authority for accommodation' as meaning a person who has a priority need and who is capable both of being offered and accepting

e accommodation if he establishes that he is homeless and has a priority need. I agree with Nolan LJ in the Court of Appeal when dealing with the first two appeals that that is putting the cart before the horse. Any person can be an applicant. The local authority must then consider, step by step, the three matters referred to in s 62 of the Act.

By s 65 of the Act, if the local authority are satisfied that a person is homeless

f (other than intentionally) and that he has a priority need, they must 'secure that accommodation becomes available' for his occupation either—

> 'by making available suitable accommodation held by them, or by securing that he obtains suitable accommodation from some other person, or . . . by giving him such advice and assistance as will secure that he obtains suitable
g accommodation from some other person . . .' (See s 69(1) as substituted by s 14(3) of the Housing and Planning Act 1986.)

There is thus not simply a duty to provide accommodation from the housing stock of the local authority itself. However, this section must be read subject to s 75 since accommodation is to be regarded as available for a person's occupation

h 'only if it is available for occupation both by him and by any other person who might reasonably be expected to reside with him'.

If a person is so disabled, mentally or physically, that he cannot make the application himself then someone else may, in my view, do it on his behalf. Section 74 of the Act impliedly recognises this as a possibility since it makes it an offence for a person to make a false statement, with intent to induce a local

j housing authority to believe, in connection with the exercise of their functions under this part, *that he or another person is homeless*, has a priority need or did not become homeless intentionally.

I do not consider that the person making the application is to be excluded from the class of vulnerable persons who can establish a priority need because he or she is not capable of understanding the nature or details of a lease or a contract. Nor do I consider that the fact that such a person, physically or mentally handicapped, *a* is incapable of doing everything for himself means that he is excluded. Persons who are physically or mentally disabled may be able to do much for themselves. In any event the accommodation must by virtue of s 69 of the Act be 'suitable' accommodation. If the vulnerable person is alone with no existing carer, he may need special accommodation under s 69(1)(*b*) of the Act. If he is not alone but has an existing carer or family 'who might reasonably be expected to reside with him' *b* then the accommodation must be available for their occupation also.

Section 74 of the Act is said to create difficulties for this approach. Section 74(1) does not do so because of the words already referred to. Section 74(2) must be read as meaning that if a person makes an application on behalf of another, the former must notify the authority of any material change of fact and the local *c* authority must make the explanation required to that person on behalf of the applicant. A person incapable of understanding has a reasonable excuse for non-compliance with s 74(2) within the meaning of s 74(3). Whether the person making the application is covered by s 74(3) (as I tend to think) it is not necessary in this case to decide.

I fully accept that the provisions of other Acts (eg the National Assistance Act *d* 1948) may also cover a person in the position of the present applicant. It may be that facilities for care and accommodation can be provided more appropriately under other legislation. Like Butler-Sloss LJ in the Court of Appeal ([1993] 1 All ER 447 at 453, [1993] 2 WLR 9 at 16), however, I do not consider that this is conclusive against the applicant's argument in the present case. The question still has to be asked whether relief is available under this statute. I also accept that as *e* the legislation stands, this may mean that a parent or carer who has himself become intentionally homeless may obtain accommodation as being a person who might reasonably be expected to reside with the person having a priority need. That a person should have been admitted to the country without any accommodation being available, or being likely to be available, for them, obviously raises a different question. *f*

At the end of the day, however, and with considerable diffidence in view of the forceful reasoning of my noble and learned friend Lord Griffiths, I would not read into the statute a requirement of capacity which is not spelled out there but would give the provisions their ordinary meaning. I consider, like all the members of the Court of Appeal, that the present appellant was 'an applicant' and *g* her case must be considered under s 62 of the Act.

It follows in my view that the local authority were wrong in law as a matter of the interpretation of s 62 of the Act to refuse to consider her as an applicant. Their subsequent decision as to whether she was homeless, has a priority need, was homeless intentionally and as to what is suitable and available accommodation, can only be reviewed by the courts on *Wednesbury* principles (see *Associated* *h* *Provincial Picture Houses Ltd v Wednesbury Corp* [1947] 2 All ER 680, [1948] 1 KB 223). These are not matters to be decided de novo by the courts.

In the circumstances I would dismiss the third appeal.

LORD WOOLF. My Lords, I have had the advantage of reading in draft the speech prepared by my noble and learned friend Lord Griffiths. For the reasons *i* he gives I too would dismiss the first two appeals and allow the third appeal.

First and second appeals dismissed ; third appeal allowed.

Mary Rose Plummer   Barrister.

SECTION A

1. Which of the cases heard by the Court of Appeal and reported at [1993] 1 All ER 447 came before the House of Lords?

2. On what dates did Court hearings take place, and before which judges, after the Tower Hamlets LBC had made its decision in relation to Ferdous Begum?

3. Who were counsel for Ferdous Begum in the House of Lords?

4. How many cases were referred to in the Opinions delivered by the Law Lords in the case of *Garlick v. Oldham Metropolitan Borough Council and related appeals*?

5. Did all of the judges agree as to the outcomes of the various appeals in *Garlick v. Oldham Metropolitan Borough Council and related appeals*?

SECTION B

6. What is meant by:
   (i) an "order of certiorari";
   (ii) an "order of mandamus";
   (iii) a "declaration".

7. Where in the report does it tell you where you would find out more about the law relating to accommodation for homeless persons and priority need for accommodation?

8. A dissenting judgment is one which, by definition, is not, in the majority view, the correct analysis of the law. Nevertheless you will be expected to read dissenting judgments. There is an example of a partial dissent in the Opinions delivered by in *Garlick v. Oldham Metropolitan Borough Council and related appeals*. What example is this and why is it necessary to read it?

9. For what reasons does Lord Slynn take a different view in relation to "the third appeal" from that expressed by Lord Griffiths?

10. Since Lords Bridge, Ackner and Woolf merely agreed with and adopted the reasoning developed by Lord Griffiths in *Garlick v. Oldham Metropolitan Borough Council and related appeals*, what purpose, if any, was served by their sitting on the case?

EXERCISE 5

Reading research materials

Reading and understanding research materials does not just involve seeing what conclusion the author has reached. Understanding the evidence the author has for the conclusion drawn is as important as understanding the conclusion itself. This section is intended to improve your critical awareness of the materials that you are reading. Reading something critically means reading it to see what weaknesses there are in it. The fewer the weaknesses, the stronger the conclusion. When reading something remember that there are flaws in all articles and books. As a reader your task is to assess the merit of a particular argument by being aware of its weaknesses as well as its strengths. With practice critical reading will become an unconscious habit which you will bring to all your reading.

Start by reading "Equal Opportunities in Policing: a Comparative Examination of Anti-Discrimination Policy and Practice in British Policing" by Ian McKenzie, the article reprinted below. When you have read the article once go back and read it again making detailed notes. When doing this, concentrate on trying to identify the strand of argument that McKenzie is trying to develop, paying close attention to the evidence that he presents for the various points that he makes. Your notes should tell you both what the author has written and what you think the possible objections to the various details of his argument are.

When you think you understand McKenzie's article, and have made your notes, try to answer the questions set out in Section A below. Refer to the original article when your notes give you insufficient information to answer the question. After you have finished the questions in Section A compare your answers with those that we have given at the back of this book. If your answers differ from our you may need to go back and reread the article in order to get a better understanding of it. Once you are sure you understand the answers to Section A go on and complete the questions in Section B.

EQUAL OPPORTUNITIES IN POLICING: A COMPARATIVE EXAMINATION OF ANTI-DISCRIMINATION POLICY AND PRACTICE IN BRITISH POLICING

IAN K. McKENZIE
Centre for Police and Criminal Justice Studies, University of Exeter, UK

Introduction

This paper addresses equal opportunities issues as they impinge upon law enforcement, particularly police, activities and is a comparative examination of legislative and other attempts to integrate and to allow access to policing of three specific groups: women, members of minority ethnic groups and homosexuals. In the main, the comparative aspects will use Britain as the primary source but will employ American and other examples to amplify particular points.

Comparative studies are both beneficial and at the same time problematic. The beneficial aspects of comparative studies are that they may show alternative approaches and strategies to similar problems and that such alternatives may consequently provoke debate about previously unconsidered options. The problematic elements lie in the very societal elements that have bred the strategic approaches in the first place. As Bayley (1977) pointed out it is an error to consider the nature of policing in any country without considering the societal forces which mould it. Bayley notes that, "If it is a mistake to assume that police institutions operate independently of their social environment, it is equally mistaken to assume that they are shaped entirely by forces outside them." Thus the internal structures of the subjects of comparison must also be considered.

Therefore, before commencing an examination of hiring and employment policy/practices for the three groups noted above, it will first be necessary to sketch, very briefly, the nature of policing in Britain and the USA.

The administration of police activity differs in the three units which make up the United Kingdom; England and Wales, Scotland and Northern Ireland (Ulster).

Although once centred in villages, towns, boroughs, cities and counties the nature of policing in Scotland and in England and Wales, is such that police activity is currently administered and controlled through eight regional forces in Scotland and 43 constabularies in England and Wales. There are a number of commonalities between these three elements of British policing. Each of the forces is supervised by a chief constable (called a Commissioner in the two London forces), each of whom has independent authority over the police force he commands. Although there is some central resourcing of policing and despite the fact that slightly more than half the necessary funding comes from central government, each chief constable is autonomous and is, in theory, through interpretation of British constitutional law, free from political interference, particularly in "operational matters" (see McKenzie & Gallagher 1989 for a more complete discussion of these factors). Chief Constables have considerable security of tenure, many serving for 10 years or more. Central government supervision of police activity is undertaken by the Home Office and through the holder of the British Cabinet office of Home Secretary. In Ulster there is one single, effectively national, police force, the RUC.

There are differences between the law and the administration of it in each of the three major geographical areas, and the RUC, the regional police forces in Scotland and the 43 forces in England and Wales are for all practical purposes considered separate entities. For that reason, although much of what follows is to some extent applicable to the others, there will hereafter be a concentration on EO issues as they apply to England and Wales, and no reference will be made to the other parts of the UK.

Only one police force in England and Wales has less than 1000 officers and the mean establishment is approximately 3500 "sworn" staff.

Police officers, in England and Wales, regardless of the police force within which they serve have (since 1964) jurisdiction anywhere in those two parts of the UK. Through central resourcing facilities, training and some other elements are standardized across the country. However, the constitutional autonomy of the chief constable means in practice that the Home Office do not seek to impose direction of either policy or practice upon individual chief constables. Rather, it is the case that the Home Office issues "memoranda" which each chief can accept, adapt or (in theory) ignore. In many areas this has the effect of producing disparate policy (and sometimes practice) and in some cases, despite the small size of the country, makes the comparison of like with like an impossibility. Even in the EO area this autonomy has an impact, for Chief Officers may decide the nature of their initiatives and the extent of their intervention with total freedom.

Overall "supervision" of police efficiency is carried out by Her Majesty's Inspectors of Constabulary (HMIC) whose task it is to inspect forces and certify their capability. In the face of a failure to achieve the necessary "efficiency" rating (a rare occurrence) HMIC may advise the government to withhold the 51% of financial support provided by them.

In the USA, the 17,613 police departments (McKenzie & Gallagher 1989: table 1.1 p. 7) may be seen as a complex multifaceted, multi-tiered edifice in which jurisdictional problems, direct (and convert) political involvement including involvement in operational matters, is commonplace. Departments can range in size from less than 10 officers to some thousands, although 98.1% of PDs have less than 200 sworn staff (McKenzie & Gallagher 1989: table 1.2, p. 8). Security of tenure for chiefs is problematic, particularly where election to a post is a consideration. Save for a controversial "accreditation" programme, centralised supervision is non-existent and funding is entirely locally based.

In Britain, access to work is, in theory, controlled by the provisions of the Race Relations Act 1975, the Sex Discrimination Act 1975 and the Equal Pay Act 1970. This legislation was framed in an effort to encourage employers to "toe-the-line" in hiring and reten-tion practice and broadly, sets out to prevent overt discrimination whilst at the same time addressing the troublesome matter of ensuring that the "majority society" does not perceive that an unfair advantage accrues to the minority.

This *notionally* legalistic approach to equality is supported by two government funded bodies, the Commission for Racial equality (CRE) and the Equal Opportunities Commission (EOC) who seek to examine complaints of discrimination, mediate and very occasionally to prosecute.

Following street disorder in Brixton, south London in 1981 a report (Scarman 1981) suggested that steps should be taken (a) to eliminate or control overt racist behaviour by police officers against minority-group citizens, and (b) to increase the number of minority ethnic police officers.

It was argued in later reports (eg Home Office 1982) that in an effort to motivate minority ethnic recruiting it is of critical importance to ensure that, "all officers understand that . . . the effect of months of hard work by officers at all levels can be destroyed by an isolated act of rudeness or insensitivity."

In addition the report pointed to the need to

"make it clear that black and Asian[2] officers are treated the same as white officers by their colleagues and [by their] supervis[ors]."

Thus, in the Police and Criminal Evidence Act 1984, an offence was added to the (national) discipline regulations; that of "racially discriminatory behaviour". Although this disciplinary offence is seemingly addressed at police-citizen encounters, it might equally well be used as a sanction with regard to police-police encounters.

In the USA, as in Britain, much of the activity seeking to enhance minority (particularly black) representation in policing was predicted on street disorder. As Holdaway (1990 pp. 5–6) puts it,

"Civil disturbances acted as a catalyst to a public consciousness of civil rights and a protest movement among black Americans. Legal change followed, first within a framework of equal opportunities, affirmative action then developed as a prelude to the acceptance of positive discrimination and the setting of formal hiring quotas"

Title VII of the Civil Rights Act 1964 prohibited preferential treatment of minorities but, as time has passed the declared intention of the Department of Justice to demonstrate its intention to vigorously use "litigation and the threat of litigation to achieve the hiring rights of minorities and women" (Raphey 1979) has nullified these limitations and produced a system that attempts to ensure that selection and retention criteria are "job related" and thus, in theory, not discriminatory in *any* direction.

This reliance on litigation and its associated developments (eg the US Civil Service Reform Act, 1978 and the Equal Opportunities Commission's requirements to avoid unfairness in selection, and equality and job relatedness in on-the-job evaluation) has had a powerful effect in addressing behaviourally, if not attitudinally, discrimination in hiring and retention practices.

There has been a marked difference of approach in the UK. Resort to litigation has been the exception rather than the rule and the observation that "positive discrimination is degrading and insulting" to serving minority officers (Taylor *et al* 1990) is used as a lever to ensure that both positive discrimination and quotas are avoided. (See also Scarman 1981.) In addition, litigation in the UK is confined to hearings before tribunals and not criminal or civil hearings, which, as they do in the USA, seek to assess financial liability through jury deliberations.

One critical distinction between Britain and North America (including Canada) is that, in the former, no legislation exists that is similar in import or content to the Canadian Employment Equity Act or to the requirement in American law for "Contract Compliance"; (ie the restriction of Federal funding to public and private organisations who fail to meet "formal hiring quota" objectives which are set as part of the funding contract). Consequently, the mediate, mollify and minimise policies of the British approach, fail to address the critically important elements of minority ethnic representations in policing through any *centrally generated government initiatives*. In addition, although many Americans and non-Americans alike are critical of it, litigation leading to substantial financial liability (or the threat of it) is a powerfully force toward compliance. As a general rule, since awards are, by and large, "capped" in the UK[3], no such fiscal levers operate.

It has been suggested, somewhat tendentiously, by Pettigrew (1989) that the single best predictor of a riot is the number of minority police officers in a police department, a conclusion that must be deeply insulting to law abiding minority group members who nevertheless feel under represented in the policing of their community. Under representation in British Policing is a critical problem and one to which the Home Office, in 1986, committed itself to resolve. However, this commitment was a fudging exercise of the first order.

Despite a declared intention of achieving (a) clarity in policy objectives and, (b) a demonstration by chief police officers of viable and effective race relations policy, the Home Office removed themselves from direct intervention, choosing instead to adopt a supportive role. This supportive role, as noted above, allows each chief officer (as it must do under British Constitutional Law) to develop his own programme of recruiting and monitoring and retention. In the absence of a clear, centrally directed (and if necessary, imposed) strategy, many critics of this approach (*cf.* Holdaway 1990, Luthra 1986) see such developments as beyond the abilities of individual police organisations, particularly in the case of promotion and appraisal, and with regard to the contentious issue of the management of organisational change. However in a recent report by the HMIC (HMIC 1993) it has been suggested that any inertia in this respect is as much the consequence of police culture as it is of management inactivity.

One of the anomalies in the British system is the existence of two "supervisory" bodies; the Equal Opportunities Commission and the Commission for Racial Equality, each of which is charged with the supervision, in broad terms, of the application of grievance procedures and to mediate if necessary. Such a division clearly defines "race" as a separate problem from equality, a view supported by Fairmanner (1992) who cites the vice-chairman of EOC as maintaining that there remains "a clear delineation . . . between the duties of the CRE and those of the EIC." The particular anomaly here lies in noting that recently, the Home Office (Home Office 1989) expressed the view that minority ethnic recruitment should be removed from beneath the umbrellas of "discrimination" (of the racial kind) and placed under a more general policy umbrella of "equal opportunities."

At a national police seminar on "equal opportunities," introducing and explaining this strategy, Skitt (1991) pointed out that the notion of equal opportunities "represented both individual and organizational change" and that the "hierarchical and militaristic structure of policing" had led to a belief that any group which did not conform to required behaviours could be labelled as trouble makers and dealt with. Thus, one may infer, complaints of discrimination by both minority ethnic officers and by women had, for some time been crushed and/or dismissed as mendacious. The view that it is litigation not mediation that produces change is supported by considering that only the previous year, one of the very few cases in which tribunal-type litigation had been undertaken by the CRE (*Nottinghamshire Constabulary v Constable S. Singh*, 1990, in which an Asian officer claimed that selection procedures for detective work were of an institutionally discriminatory nature) had resulted in a finding in favour of the plaintiff. In addition, the court had noted that the Home Office, Her Majesty's Inspectors of Constabulary and the Association of Chief Police Officers had accepted that the problem did not solely relate to the force named in the case, nor solely to the selection of detectives. To which one might add, neither solely to the *selection* of nonwhite officers.

Formal allegations of racism, by police officers against their nonwhite colleagues are not common, but this may not be reflective of the true situation; it may merely be the surface of a problem. The Police Studies Institute Report (PSI, 1983, p. 151) cited the use of racist language and of racist "jokes" as a major source of concern.

"Racialism within the force causes considerable embar-
rassment, distress and difficulty to black and brown police
officers. A relief that [a researcher] worked with contained
both a black and an Asian officer. There was a group of three
experienced officers on the relief who engaged in quite extreme
racialist talk when they were in the threesome or with members
of the relief other than the black and Asian officer. When these
two officers were present the racialist talk and jokes continued,
but were considerably moderated. The white members of the
relief thought that the Asian and black officers didn't mind
the racialist talk too much . . . They were quite mistaken about
this."

It is the case that many nonwhite officers are affected by the nature
of the "banter" which takes place about them. however, because,
particularly in the early stages of socialisation into the service, they
are reticent to speak-up, they make no complaint, formal or
otherwise.

Equal opportunities is not only a non-racist notion, it is a non-
sexist philosophy. The lot of women in policing, despite an earlier
entry than minority ethnic group members has been and continues
to be problematic.

Although a literature search reveals no cases of riots being brought
about as a consequence of under representation of women in
policing, it remains the case that many women feel that access, and
once access is achieved, promotion and unbiased appraisal are a
problem.

As a general rule, although a form of institutional racism can be
inferred from the minimum height requirement for British police
forces, which was recently abandoned, there is a distinction between
the overtly discriminatory grounds on which women, as opposed
to minority ethnic group members, are rejected. Rejection on racial
grounds had tended in the worst case to be based on stereotypical
images like intellectual capacity, motivation to work, and
acceptability to the public. Rejection on grounds of gender has been
in the main based on negative assessments of physical competency,
leadership ability, motivation to become a police officer, reasons
for continuing to serve and stress proneness (Coffey *et al.* 1992).
Of these, physical competency is seen as being a critical variable
by many policemen towards their female colleagues. In many cases,
with minimal justification the stereotype of the "little woman,"
who is "only fit for two things and the other one's making coffee,"
still has tremendous power.

Studies in both the UK and the USA have repeatedly shown, despite a belief to the contrary, that there is little difference between females and males on the measure of physical competency, leadership ability, motivation to become a police officer, reasons for continuing to serve and stress proneness and, in any case, the first of these may well be based on an excessive over valuing of the role of physical strength in patrol tasks. Furthermore, Balkin (1988) in an overview of a number of American studies, found that female officers perform as well as male officers in a wide range of assignments. However Steel & Loverich (1987) pointed out that many female officers are not deployed on equivalent tasks to their male colleagues and that thus, although no deleterious effects appeared to accrue to the presence of women officers, it is too early to make a final judgement. Such a judgement must be delayed until full access is achieved[4].

Nevertheless, it is the alleged physical danger of police work that predisposes male officers to use the "protect the little woman" gambit in seeking to exclude women from policing. First, it is suggested that women should not be exposed to the unpleasant nature of physical injury and death and second, that in the event of a threat to life or some such happening, a male officer would feel obliged to perform the ultimate act of "good breeding" and lay his life on the line. Such an attitude is at the core of male attitudes to female officers. Females cannot according to research on both sides of the Atlantic, expect to achieve either the full confidence of supervising officers or of their working colleagues. Neither can they expect, whilst such attitudes exist, to achieve the full range of duties available to male officers (Martin 1979, Jones 1987).

Despite the fact that past research (eg Martin 1979) suggested that some women in policing lack career ambition, avoid promotion and seek only to fulfil a feminine role in police work, the position now seems to have changed. Coffey et al. (1992) have demonstrated, using the surprisingly unusual technique of asking women in their own right about their experiences rather than comparing them with their male colleagues,

> "that serving police women do aspire to specialist duties but are often inhibited from . . . applying in the first instance or believe that they are thwarted from being appointed because of perceived prejudice"

Similar trends have been noted in Scotland (CPS 1989). Although Americans can point to Chiefs Elizabeth M. Watson (Austin PD,

Tx.), Cathleen Manchester (Norway, Maine), Mary Ann Viverette (Gaithersburg, MA), Joan M. Henderson (Decatur, Michigan), Linda K. Wait (Union City, Michigan) and Linda L. Weaver (Johnstown, PA) as exemplars of freedom of access, the same is not true in the UK (including in this case Scotland and Northern Ireland). Writing in 1988, McKenzie & Gallagher (1989) pointed out that it was safe to refer to Chief Officers in the UK as "him" for at that time they wrote, "there are no female chiefs—yet." Nothing has changed.

However, it may well be that litigation will have its effect. The early months of 1992 saw a blood-letting in equality circles, the like of which, at least in policing circles, had never before been seen. Alison Halford, an assistant chief constable (ACC) in the Merseyside Police, took action through the Equal Opportunities Commission, against her chief constable, against one of Her Majesty's Inspectors of Constabulary (HMI), against the Northamptonshire police authority (roughly the equivalent of a Public Safety Commission) to whom she had applied for a post as deputy chief constable and against the Home Office. The case was brought on the grounds that she had been denied access to higher rank (viz, Deputy Chief Constable) on the grounds of her sex. Ms Halford had been the first (there are now three) female officer to rise to the ACC level. She claimed that the nine applications she had made for higher posts had been denied to her and that the posts had been, in the end, awarded to officers of lesser merit and experience. The respondents countered with allegations of homosexuality, excessive alcohol consumption and unprofessional conduct.

Halford's problems began, by her own admission, when she responded to a publication by Lock (1987) in which that author posed a question about the likelihood of the appointment of female chief officer by asking, "How long must she wait." Halford's (1987) cynical reply, "Until the twelfth of never" was the start of the troubles she then encountered. In that article, Halford spoke of the "inability of some very senior men to cope with a woman of comparable rank," of "strong but covert resentment or mistrust of the competence of a woman," and of the male perception of the "oddness" of a woman wanting to progress in her career at the expense of a man with whom she would be in competition, "who after all has a family to support."

The Halford case highlighted many embarrassing elements of the macho side of policing, even at high level. Following weeks of "sensational allegations [of] systematic drunkenness and gross and sexist behaviour" (*Independent* 20 July 1992) all made, and carefully reported in lascivious detail, the blinding glare of massive publicity proved too much and an out of court settlement was reached. This conclusion, a kind of cop's cop-out, was to say the least unfortunate. It is clear that in the interests of the public and because the case did not achieve a final conclusion within a judicial or even quasi-judicial process, the question of women's rights inside the British police is still moot. Women in British policing were poorly served. Bevins (1992) wrote that a Labour member of parliament had "facts and figures given by the Home Office [which] showed that concern was more than justified."

In 1992 about 15% of all officers in the UK were women and, in accordance with quota thinking, if fair promotion practices were operating one would expect to see that 15% reflected in other grades. However, Home Office figures (July 1992) showed that 14 of the 43 forces had no female officer at higher rank than inspector (roughly equivalent to lieutenant or other second level supervisor), and that two of those forces had no female officer higher than sergeant. Of the remaining 29 forces, three women held the rank of Assistant Chief Constable, there were 11 Chief Superintendents and 29 Superintendents (Bevins 1992). It is likely therefore, as is the case with minority ethnic selection, retention and promotion practices, that behind the scenes, the Home Office, Her Majesty's Inspectors of Constabulary and the association of Chief Police Officers have accepted that the problem does not solely relate to the force named in the case, nor solely to promotion to the highest levels of the organization. As Commander Sally Hubbard as Assistant HMI put it (*Independent* 26 July 1992), "[The Halford case] has made police forces around the country realise that their policies and procedures are not as equitable as they thought."

Data showing the most recent figures for minority ethnic and female recruiting in England and Wales are shown in Table 1.

Equal opportunities is not only non-racist and non-sexist philosophy, it is also a non-sexual orientation notion. The lot of both male and female police officers who happen to be homosexual and whose sexual orientation is declared is, in one respect at least, like that of independent heterosexual women: the homosexual officer and the emancipated female officer are a threat (real or imagined) to the notion of "family": husband, wife and 2.3 children.

There are other shared features. For those who may wish so to do, the emancipated woman and the homosexual may both be denigrated on the basis of religious dicta. According to Anthony (1992), in the context of police hiring, retention and promotion practices, homophobia and misogyny also share the confounding effect of

Table 1 **Minority ethnic and female members of all 43 police forces in England and Wales 1985 to 1991**

Year	Minority ethnic	Women officers	National strength
1985	761 (0.67%)	11,304 (9.38%)	120,707
1986	898 (0.74%)	11,707 (9.63%)	121,550
1987	1108 (0.89%)	12,613 (10.16%)	124,102
1988	1197 (0.96%)	12,192 (10.52%)	124,759
1989	1306 (1.04%)	13,829 (10.97%)	126,110
1990	1418 (1.12%)	14,513 (11.42%)	126,790
1991	1592 (1.25%)	15,061 (11.85%)	127,127

(Source: EO monitoring, F1 Division, Home Office and Home Office memorandum 104/91).

lack of clear and unambiguous guidance from the top of the organisation.

This is a complex area beset with ethical, moral and legal difficulty. Even recent presidential candidates took different sides in a debate on the employment of homosexuals in the armed forces of the USA. It still remains to be seen if President Clinton will (as in many things) take the promised action, although a recent article (22 November 1992) in the *Washington Post* pointed out that there were only four reported cases of sexual misconduct of a homosexual nature (by both men and women) among nearly 200,000 American Troops deployed in the Gulf War by contrast to six courts martial for rape and 16 official complaints of sexual harassment " . . . on top of many unfiled incidents" of similar behaviour. Perhaps, if as President Clinton suggested, it is conduct, not sexual orientation that is important, homosexuality is less of a problem than heterosexual men preying on women.

Because homosexuals of either gender do not conform to the expected gender-roles, that is, because they are, in the mind of the opposer, not macho "real men," they are, it is sometimes alleged, unsuited to the work. Anthony's (1992) recent research demonstrates that there is a reliance on an unfounded assertion about "public opinion" which is used to denigrate the role of women in policing (eg "members of the public seeking emergency assistance expect a police*man*, not a police woman") which with minor variation is invoked to support an anti-gay position (eg "The public wouldn't like it").

Jones (1987) and Whittacker (1979) have suggested that male

officers resent women who are capable of undertaking police work without the need to resort to stereotyped "masculine" behaviours. It may equally be argued that such apprehensions exist when, in the absence of fully stereotyped male behaviours (including those in private life, which are, in fact, irrelevant) homosexual officers are found to be quite capable of "doing the job". In support of this contention one may cite the observation made by Darryl Gates, former Chief of LAPD, who suggested that female homosexual officers were to be admired because of their "well developed upper body strength" (Interview 20/20 NBC TV, April 1990) and the consequent veiled inference that such would not be found in homosexual male officers.

Resistance to the notion of openly homosexual police officers is based on a number of separate but interlinked factors: ignorance; fear of "corruption;" an alleged instability and "the law." First ignorance. There is in general society a commonly held negative stereotype of the homosexual as a "camp," limp wristed, transvestite, wannabe transsexual, child abuser. Transvestism and transsexualism are commonly seen as a chosen, deviant way of life and as is the way with stereotyping, all homosexuals are so labelled. There is, as we know considerable ignorance about the nature and transmission mechanisms of HIV. The link between the suggestion of freely chosen (particularly male) homosexuality, HIV/AIDS and the police may be clearly seen in the declaration made by a chief constable in the UK (now retired) who asserted that people carrying the HIV, and consequently potential AIDS patients, are "swirling around in a cesspit of their own making." As is regrettably common, and is again the norm in stereotyping, HIV in the heterosexual community is conveniently ignored. Associated with this stereotypical view of the homosexual is a belief that, as with drug abuse, a person can be turned: that the hetero can become the homo through association, through the "teaching" of homosexuality as an "alternative lifestyle" and consequently, coupled with this there is a fear of homosexual assault. Although the likelihood of such assault is low, there is an anomaly here. Fear of harassment by male officers and the potential for sexist abuse are common currency amongst female officers and as a consequence, equal opportunities statements seek to develop mechanisms of redress. In the event that an officer of either sex sought to use the mechanism to "deal with" a homosexual harassment problem, one wonders about the response of the "authorities" in question. On the other hand the male officer's fear of harassment by a homosexual colleague is beset with difficulty, in part because of the apprehension that the allegation might result in the assailant using the same defence as that commonly used in indecent assault and rape case brought by or on behalf of females—consent. Furthermore, as noted above, the sexual threat posed by homosexuality in the workplace may be grossly over blown. Munyard (1988) suggests for example that,

> "Because of the social prejudice that exists, lesbians and gay men are, in fact, generally much more reticent than heterosexuals and would usually be very cautious about doing anything which could be misconstrued as a sexual advance."

The key here seems to lie in the observation by Smith (1988) that it is personality integration, maturity and the acceptance of societal homophobia that are the critical issues. In other words as in all other spheres, sexuality is not important. What is important is the extent to which the individual has come to terms with his or her own sexual identity. And it is here, as will be considered below, that the American approach has the potential to provide a solution.

In Britain, beyond a certain patchy application of IQ testing, no psychological screening of applicants for the police service takes place (see McKenzie & Gallagher 1989). In the USA, the requirement that applicants to police departments shall be psychologically evaluated means that amongst other evaluations of psychological health, the investigation should, where an acknowledgement of homosexuality is made, be considered with an assessment of the extent to which psychological integration has taken place. Although homosexuality *per se* has, quite properly, been removed from the diagnostic categories of DSM III-(R) (1987), lack of integration can be assessed and classified on the basis of existent DSM III-(R) (302.90. Sexual Disorder NOS) criteria. No such judgemental opportunity is provided in the British selection process.

Of course, many patrol officers, supervisors and chiefs, and certainly too many psychologists would deny employment on the basis of homosexuality, integrated or otherwise, but, as with the notion of quotas in hiring of minority ethnic officers and females, exposure of the majority to the minority is of critical importance. Despite the existence of some US police departments, such as San Francisco PD, that openly acknowledge the existence of homosexual officers in their midst, the problem, in part, remains one of the law. Many sworn officers in the USA, because of their oath of office to "uphold the law," have difficulty in coming to terms with the potentially illegal acts of sodomy implied by overt male homosexual orientation. It is hard to see how such an attitude can be applied to female homosexuality.

It is possible to accept, without reservation, that gender, racial or ethnic background and sexual orientation are complicated and divisive issues. Equally, there is little doubt that in both the UK and the USA (and indeed in all countries of the world) homophobia, racism, misogyny and misandry, will be a long time in dying. There are, therefore two aims, long and short term. In the long term elimination of unacceptable values and attitudes must be sought. In the short term it is the control of these attitudes and values for which we must aim. The strength of the police culture cannot be underestimated. Resistance to change is strong and conservative attitudes prevail. There is little evidence to support the view that people who become police officers are in some way similar and likely to manifest prejudiced behaviour *because of* personality variables which pre-determine their desire to become cops. Indeed, the most commonly held view is that the vast majority of recruits come from "unexceptional" (Bradley *et al.* 1986) backgrounds which hardly set them apart from the population as a whole.

However, it is suggested (Bradley *et al.* 1986) that in common with others who, from similar backgrounds, move into non-manual work, they suffer status anxiety: in experiencing upward social mobility they become marginalised, belonging to neither one group nor the other. Having moved into the middle class, but still feeling alienated from it, the police officer, as with many that have been proselytized in other settings, becomes more fervent than the existent members. The marginality of such a position, it is suggested, leads police officers to embrace middle-class values more readily than the middle class. Furthermore, since the new officer moves into an area in which such strongly held middle-class (and possibly authoritarian views) are already standard, he or she rapidly learns to accept those views. Finally, as the Coleman & Gorman (1982) study suggests the longer a person is a police officer, the more likely he or she is to show conservative attitudes. The corrosive effects of "continued police service" seem to produce increasingly illiberal and intolerant attitudes (Coleman & Gorman 1982; Brown & Willis 1985); attitudes that feed upon and are reinforced by stereotypical thinking, macho posturing and covert discriminatory behaviour.

However, perhaps the most important dimension in the EO debate is that which deals with the extent to which policy initiatives, and value statements are translated into practice. The power of the police culture to "subsume and subvert attempts to change" (Brown 1992) remain a real problem. There are those who argue that it is impossible to produce legislation that will alter attitudes. One can but agree. However, there is little legislation that can achieve, in any area of human behaviour, such a long term objective. In the short-term-aim of control of attitudes, however, things may be different.

Although in one sense, an attitude of mind can be said to be an internal and personal collection of ideas, it is the case that a person's attitude may only be inferred from that person's behaviour. Psychologists, particularly those of a behaviourist orientation have long argued that the modification of attitudes is obtained through the modification of behaviour. Thus, the power of EO legislation is that it does aim to modify behaviour. Although, for the psychologist, punishment *per se* is viewed as an inadequate method of changing behaviour, the opposite is true of reinforcement—both positive and negative. Negative reinforcement, often confused with punishment, is best described as that which produces "avoidance behaviour:" behaviour which, when it is produced, successfully avoids a noxious stimulus. By the rules of reinforcement, successful avoidance, since it is a positive event, is likely to lead to an increase in the frequency with which such behaviour is produced. When, according to Social Learning theory (Bandura 1977), a person sees another punished, that individual will, if the punishment is seen as sufficient, actively avoid the behaviour for which the punishment was administered. Thus, where people are seen to be punished for espousing discriminatory practices, there is, provided the punishment is seen as "sufficient," an effect on others. Thus the power of EO legislation, supported by powerful sanctions, is of paramount importance for it serves as a negative-reinforcer, increasing the likelihood of non-discriminatory behaviour. But where, as is the case in the UK EO legislation offers mediation and, even at the end of the day, only minimal financial liability for non-compliance, the attitude changing ability of the legislation is slight. Where mediation is the norm, mendacity is the standard; behavioural change is considerably less likely.

In the USA, financial liability and withdrawal of Government approval are present, and the likelihood of behaviour change is increased. The dynamic American "litigation-approach," which in the broad area of law enforcement has had a marked pro-fessionalising effect (see McKenzie & Gallagher 1989; Gallagher 1992) leads to specific activity; *viz*, avoidance behaviour. For example, where civil service promotion regulations are breached by Chiefs of Police or hiring practices are found to be discriminatory, substantial financial penalties may be imposed, both to punish the malefactor and "to encourage the others."

The overall effect of this is that although racism, sexism and homophobia continue to be seen in USA policing (and in society generally), powerful figures from the Supreme Court, through the Senate Judicial Committee and on down, can be seen to be actively involved, even if we do not like all that they say or do. In the UK, by contrast, although government figures may publicly disparage such behaviour, for all practical purposes the control and limitation of the unacceptable face of human nature, is left in the hands of a faceless and tiny minority, albeit well intentioned; members of the CRE and the EOC. And, on top of that, the penalties for non-compliance with the legislation are derisory.

At the final count, however, a shift to a litigation based model in the UK is unlikely. Nevertheless, within a disciplined service the opportunity for imposing sanctions exists and may be used in much the same way. Brown (1992, p. 320) in an examination of change in the police service concludes that "the present emphasis [on producing policies] should move away from progress towards change to making it happen." However, this begs the question of whether sufficient numbers of police managers at all levels are able, or indeed, willing, to "make it happen,": to invoke the discipline code, to serve as substantial role-models and to translate policy into practice. For it does seem that such a translation does require more than exhortation programmes seeking simply to encourage people through appeals to their better nature. "Thou shalt not discriminate" can only be effective if overt and sufficient punishment for failure so to do is attached. It may even be that a form of "contact compliance" could be applied by Her Majesty's Inspectorate of Constabulary, through the definition of inactivity on EO issues being designated as a form of inefficiency.

Notes

1 This paper is an amended version of a paper on a similar theme read at The Academy of Criminal Justice Sciences Conference, Kansas City, Mo. 16–20 March 1992.
2 In British parlance, the expression Asian refers to those who come from the Indian sub-continent. Those from China, Vietnam etc. are referred to as Oriental.
3 The maximum financial redress provided through such tribunals is £10,000 plus costs. A paltry sum by comparison with the multi-thousand and sometimes multi-million dollar awards in similar cases in the USA.
4 During a recent field trip to the State Penitentiary (Parchman Prison) Mississippi, the Deputy Superintendent informed the author that the staff men to women ratio was 50/50. He added that in an all male prison, many of the female correction officers stood to one side and waited for fights between inmates to end. The remark was intended to carry a pejorative connotation. However, such an action may simply be the most effective way of dealing with these events.

References

Anthony, R. (1992) An investigation of the requirement for the Metropolitan Police Service to include the words "sexual orientation" in its statement of equal opportunities policy. MA Dissertation: University of Exeter, England.

Balkin, J. (1988) Why policemen do not like police women. *Journal of Police Science and Administration*, **16**, 29–38.

Bandura, A. (1977) *Social Learning Theory*. Englewood, NJ: Prentice Hall.

Bayley, D. H. (1977) The limits of police reform. In *Policy and Society* (Bayley, D. H. ed.). London: Sage.

Bevins, A. (1992) Labour MP says police are sexist. *Independent*, Saturday, 18 July 1992.

Bradley, D., Walker, N. & Wilkie, R. (1986) *Managing the Police*. Brighton: Harvester Wheatsheaf.

Brown, J. (1992) Changing the police culture. *Policing*, **8**, 307–322.

Brown, L. & Willis, A. (1985) Authoritarianism in British police recruits: importation, socialisation or myth. *Journal of Occupational Psychology*, **57**, 97–108.

Coffey, S., Brown, J. & Savage, S. (1992). Policewomen's career aspirations: Some reflections on the role and capabilities of women in policing in Britain. *Police Studies*, 13–19.

Coleman, A. M. & Gorman, P. L. (1982) Conservatism, dogmatism and authoritarianism in British police officers. *Sociology*, **161**, 1–11.

CPS. (1989) *The Effect of the Sex Discrimination Act on the Scottish Police Service*. University of Strathclyde: Centre for Police Studies.

DSM III-(R) (1987) *American Diagnostic and Statistical Manual III-R*. American Psychiatric Association: Washington DC.

Fairmanner, S. (1992) Equal opportunities in two countries. MA Dissertation: University of Exeter, England.

Gallagher, G. P. (1992) *Risk Management Behind the Blue curtain: A Primer on Law Enforcement Liability*. Arlington VA: Public Risk Management Association.

Halford, A. (1987) Until the twelfth of never. *Police Review*, 4933, p. 2019.

HMIC (1993). *Equal Opportunities in the Police Service*. London: HMIC.

Holdaway, S. (1990) *Recruiting a Multi-racial Police Force*. London: HMSO.

Home Office (1982) Report of a study group: Recruitment into the police service of members of ethnic minorities. London: HMSO.

Home Office (1989) *Equal Opportunities Policies for the Police Service*. Home Office Circular 87/89. London: HMSO.

Jones, S. (1987) *Policewomen and Equality*. London: Macmillan.

Lock, J. (1987) How long must she wait. *Police Review*, **95**, 4929, pp. 1810–1811.

Luthra, M. (1986) Increasing the black and blue line: Some key questions on recruitment of black officers and equal opportunities in the Police. Unpublished paper cited in Fairmanner (1992).

Martin, S. E. (1979) *Police*men and police*women*: occupational role dilemmas and choices of female officers. *Journal of Police Science and Administration*, 7, 314–323.

McKenzie, I. K. & Gallagher, G. P. (1989) *Behind the uniform: Policing in Britain and America*. New York: St Martins Press.

Munyard, T. (1988) Homophobia at work and how to manage it. *Personnel Management*, June, 48.

Pettigrew, T. F. (1989) Police and ethnic minorities. Paper presented to a conference on "Police organizations and minority groups". Noordwijk, Netherlands: January 1989.

Raphey, D. M. (1979) Racial discrimination in urban police departments. Cited in Winship, P. J. (1982). Towards a multi-racial police service. 19th Senior Command Course, Police Staff College: Bramshill, Hants.

Scarman LJ. (1981) *The Briston Disorders: 10–12 April 1981*. (Cmnd, 8427). London: HMSO.

Skitt, B. (1991) The implementation of equal opportunities in the police service. Unpublished papers, The Police Staff College, Bramshill, Hampshire.

Smith, J. (1988) *Psychology, Homosexuality and Homophobia*. New York: Haworth Press.

Steel, B. S. & Loverich, N. (1987) Equality and efficiency trade-offs in affirmative action; real or imagined? The case of women in policing. *Social Science Research Journal,* **24,** 53–70.
Taylor, S., Ainsworth, N. & Gallan, P. (1990) *The Metropolitan Police seminars on recruiting and retention of black and Asian officers: Analysis of data from Seminar, July 1990.* London: Metropolitan Police.
Whittacker, B. (1979) *The Police in Society.* London: Methuen.

SECTION A

1. What issue is the author intending to discuss?

2. How are police forces organised in England and Wales?

3. Why is it important to know how police forces are organised when considering issues about equal opportunities?

4. What arguments could be put to counter McKenzie's own view of the percentage of women police officers that should be found in senior ranks?

5. McKenzie sees the United States system as being more effective in countering illegitimate discrimination. To what extent does he produce convincing arguments to prove his case?

6. Do you agree with McKenzie's reasons for seeing litigation as a useful strategy in equal opportunities cases?

SECTION B

7. What legislation effects the hiring of workers in police forces
   (a) in England and Wales?
   (b) in the USA?

8. Do you think McKenzie has explored all the possible reasons for discrimination against homosexuals in police forces? If not, what other reasons can you give?

9. At page 178 McKenzie criticises the use of the Equal Opportunities Commission and the Commission for Racial Equality as a way of implementing equal opportunities policy. You may think his criticisms are just. However, can you think of any advantages in having the two bodies exercise the role that they do?

10. Equal opportunities, McKenzie writes at page 173 is "not only a non-racist and non-sexist philosophy, it is also a non-sexual orientation notion." Can you think of any other forms of discriminatory behaviour which would normally be

perceived as being illegitimate? Would it be illegitimate for police forces to let such beliefs effect them when deciding who to hire as police officers or who to promote?

11. What criticisms might be made of McKenzie's argument that police officers suffer status anxiety because they move from manual to non-manual occupations when they become police officers?

12. McKenzie's article offers much interesting material for reflection. Equally, however, it leaves many questions to be answered. What questions do you think need further investigation? How would you go about investigating them?

EXERCISE 6

Study skills

These exercises have a different format to those which have preceded them.

1. Take brief notes of the first two pages of the case report of *R v Terry* which you will find in chapter 5 of this book. Before you start, re-read the suggestions about taking notes in the section of chapter 7 entitled "Lectures—Listening and Notetaking". When you have finished take a break of one hour. After your break assess your notes against the following criteria.

   Presentation—use of paragraphs, headings, underlining.
   Clarity—how easy are they to read?
   Use of abbreviations—can you remember what your abbreviations mean? Are there any words you are likely to come across frequently, for which you could make up your own standard abbreviation?
   Content—have you included all the important information? Do you have a full reference, so that you could consult the original text at a later date if necessary?

   You can do this by yourself, or you can work with another student and compare each other's work.

2. In this exercise, you are asked to evaluate written work. In each case, you are given the plan for an essay, and then the essay which was written, using the plan. In each case you are asked to carry out a number of tasks. Again, you can do this on your own, or with another student.

a) Read the plans below. Write down any comments you have on good or bad features of each plan.

b) Now read the two essays as if you were the tutor. Decide which one is better, and why. In each case, write down a list of the reasons for your decision.

c) Draw up a list of criteria for judging the essays. Read the two answers again, and decide whether the two students have performed well or badly on each item in your list. If you wish, you can award each essay a mark, in the same way as a tutor would.

d) Imagine you are the tutor handing back the essays to the students who wrote the essays. What was good about the answers? How are you going to tell them about the less good points? Make sure you are able to explain clearly how the students might improve their weaker points.

e) Is there any similarity between these answers and your own, in terms of approach, style, strengths and weaknesses? Imagine you are the student who has written the answer. How would you feel about the comments of the tutor? What are you going to do about them?

ESSAY EVALUATION

Essay title:

"Small claims are, by their very nature, unimportant; the current system for dealing with them is entirely adequate." Discuss.

Essay Plan 1:

*Small claims not unimportant—small amount of money (£1,000 or less under County Court Rules, Ord. 19, r.3)—but not unimportant:
a) ?large amount for person involved
b) ?only contact with legal system—very important
c) everyone should have access to justice
*Current system = CCR 019.

*Under r.3, amounts under £1,000 automatically referred to arbitration
Idea of arbitration = cheap, simple—litigants in person
Lawyers discouraged—"No costs" rule = r.4.2

*019 amended in 1992 cf The County Court (Amendment No. 2) Rules 1992 S.I. 1992 No. 1965. Improvements made, e.g.

r.6.4 preliminary hearings only if necessary, r.7.4 overturns effect of CA case

*However, still things to be done e.g. r.7.2 (hearings in different venues) must be implemented, staff training is important.

Essay 1

Small claims are in fact a very important aspect of the English legal system. Under Order 19 rule 3(1) of the County Court Rules a small claim is defined as "Any proceedings in which . . . the amount involved does not exceed £1,000 . . . ". Consequently, the sums of money involved are unimportant, when compared to the massive sums which may be involved in High Court litigation. However, the relatively low monetary value does not relegate a small claim to the realm of the unimportant. An amount of money which is less than £1,000 may be a very large sum for the individual concerned, especially if they are living on a fixed income. The piece of litigation involved may be an individual's first contact with the legal system. In a country where the rule of law is an integral part of parliamentary democracy, it is very important that everyone should feel fairly treated by the legal system, however small their claim is in financial terms. It is also a basic tenet that everyone has the right to access to justice, whatever the size of their claim.

The current system for dealing with small claims can be found in Order 19 of the County Court Rules. Under Order 19 rule 3(1) any claim where the amount in dispute does not exceed £1,000 is referred automatically to arbitration, rather than going to a formal County Court hearing. The idea of arbitration is that it should be approachable, cheap and simple, so that people can take their claims to arbitration without using a lawyer. The use of lawyers is discouraged by rule 4(2), which provides that even if a person wins their case, they will not be able to claim the cost of using a lawyer. The idea is that small claims should be brought by litigants in person, since the financial amounts involved are so small that using a lawyer would not make economic sense; the cost of a lawyer would usually be more than a successful litigant could recover, even if they won their case.

Order 19 was amended in 1992 by the County Court (Amendment No. 2) Rules 1992 (S.I. 1992 No. 1965) and improvements were introduced (largely as a result of the Civil Justice Review) which made the system for dealing with small claims much better for litigants in person. One improvement was that Rule 6(4) makes it clear that preliminary hearings should not be held as a matter of course, but only if there is a good reason for them. This is a sensible provision, in the light of the findings of George Appleby in his research project, published in 1978, Small Claims in England and Wales. *Appleby found that litigants in person did not understand the purpose of preliminary hearings and that they were very inconvenienced by the need to appear at court to attend them, since this often necessitated taking time off work and losing pay. Another improvement introduced by Rule 7(4) is that the effect of the Court of Appeal decision in Chilton v. Saga Holidays [1986] 1 All ER 841 is overcome. This decision prevented arbitrators from assisting unrepresented parties who were opposed by a party represented by a lawyer, and was out of sympathy with the small claims system.*

However, although the reforms have improved the situation for small claimants, the system is still not entirely adequate. We have yet to see to what extent District Judges will take advantage of the new provisions in Order 19. For instance, Rule 7(2) provides for the arbitration to take place at the court or any other place convenient to the parties—but this will only be of use to small claimants if it is used in practice. Equally, the whole system will not be user-friendly unless the court staff are trained to deal with litigants in person, as the Consumer Council have long advocated (see chapter 10 of Ordinary Justice, *1989). The current system is much improved, but more progress is needed before we can say that it is entirely adequate.*

Essay title:

"Small claims are, by their very nature, unimportant; the current system for dealing with them is entirely adequate." Discuss.

Essay Plan 2:

Small claims—a lot of research since the 1970s
Small claims are usually about consumer issues
In small claims, usually have a repeat-player and a one-shotter

A small claim is under £1,000

It is referred to arbitration
No lawyers costs
Have to fill in forms—can be difficult
The Civil Justice Review introduced improvements
Also Courts and Legal Services Act

Now—difficult to say

Essay 2

There has been a lot of research carried out about small claims since the 1970s, much of it by researchers at Birmingham University. The research has shown that there is a lot wrong with the system for dealing with small claims.

Small claims are usually about consumer issues, often involving a dispute about faulty goods or services. In a small claim, you usually have a one-shotter on one side and a repeat-player on the other side; these terms were invented by an American researcher called Marc Galanter. Small claims are about small amounts of money, so they tend to be rather unimportant in financial terms, although even £10 is a lot of money to some people. It is therefore a matter of dispute whether small claims are unimportant or not.

A small claim is any claim which is worth less than £1,000, as stated in the County Court Rules. Small claims are automatically referred to arbitration, which is a special kind of informal hearing. This is very helpful for people bringing small claims, as it means they do not have to use a lawyer. Lawyers can be used, but they are very expensive, and in a small claims arbitration, there is a "no costs" rule.

The small claims system was improved in 1992. The Civil Justice Review introduced a lot of improvements. There was also an important statute, called The Courts and Legal Services Act 1990. A statutory instrument introduced a system of lay representatives to the small claims system. This was a major improvement, as it means that a small claimant, who is a litigant in person, can take a person with them to assist them at the hearing. This person can be a friend, or an advice worker—anyone except a qualified lawyer. The idea is that this will help to redress the imbalance which otherwise exists between repeat-players and one-shotters. The reforms also included a provision that the hearing could be at the court or at any other place *which is convenient to the parties. It is likely that this will prove very popular with litigants in person. There used to be some voluntary small claims schemes which had a similar provision, and hearings were often held "on site" and this was very successful. It meant, for example, that if the matter in dispute was a sofa which was alleged to be faulty, the hearing could take place in the front room where the sofa was situated.*

Now that these reforms have been introduced, you could argue that we have an ideal system for dealing with small claims. However, we do not know how the reforms will work out in practice, so perhaps all we can conclude is that time will tell.

PART 4

CHAPTER 8

Where Next?

This chapter introduces students to questions they should consider when applying to read law as a degree subject and outlines the career options open to students wishing to qualify as lawyers.

LAW COURSES

Law may be studied at degree level at a range of universities and colleges. Law may be studied as a single subject, or in combination with another discipline, such as economics, politics or a foreign language. Thus, a student wishing to study law has two different decisions to make, "Do I want to study law on its own" and "Where do I want to study"? There are currently over eighty institutions offering law degree courses on either a full or part-time basis.

Before making these decisions, it is wise to obtain a wide selection of law prospectuses from universities and colleges. After looking at these, it will quickly become clear that law courses differ radically from institution to institution. There is a wide variety of legal subjects which can be studied, different balances of optional to compulsory subjects, and varying views about the purpose of studying for a law degree.

Begin by asking:

—why do I want to study law? Is it my intention to qualify as a lawyer or am I studying law for other reasons? Do I principally want a good professional training or do I principally want to study law as an academic subject (in which case what is my specific reason for studying law).

—do I want to combine the study of law with the study of

some other subject? What other subjects am I interested in? Which combination would suit my interests?

—if I want to qualify as a solicitor or barrister is the degree course which I am interested in approved by the Law Society/Bar?

—what useful information and guidance can I obtain from my school, teachers, family or friends?

Bearing in mind the answers to these questions, read the prospectuses you have obtained and ask:

—what reputation has the course, law school and institution got? Why does it have that reputation and is it one which I find attractive? Some universities have a good overall reputation, but an indifferent law school, some universities have a good law school, but a poor overall reputation. You will need to consider what criteria are of most importance to you. Some factors to consider will be highly subjective (e.g. geographic location). Universities and colleges are submitting themselves increasingly to public scrutiny and assessment of their standards. A quality assessment report on teaching in individual law schools was published in 1994 by the Quality Assessment .Division, HEFCE, Northavon House, Coldharbour Lane, Bristol BS16 1QD. These ratings are reproduced at the end of this chapter.

—how much choice does the course offer me and is the law school of sufficient size to offer a wide variety of optional subjects? (Be suspicious of small law schools which claim to offer a wide variety of subjects. Only a few may actually be on offer in any one year).

—what connections has the law school got with the legal profession and the wider world and what are the career opportunities it considers open to its students?

—what guidance does it offer to students on optional choices and careers? Does it offer to help in selecting courses best suited for my intended career?

—how much flexibility does the course give if my motivations or interests change during my three years at college?

—what type of teaching methods are used and what is the mode of assessment?

Eventually, you will have to decide to which university or college to apply. With a few exceptions, applications to full-time courses of higher education are made through a central "clearing house" called UCAS (Universities and Colleges Admission Service). An applicant completes one form only but can make applications to up to eight choices of institution/course: the form is reproduced and copied to the admissions tutor of each course selected. Application forms and UCAS Handbooks, which detail application procedures, and universities, colleges and courses, are available free of charge via schools and colleges, and local careers offices also have stocks. Completed forms should be received at UCAS by 15 December (15 October if Oxford and Cambridge Universities are included). The address of UCAS is Fulton House, Jessop Avenue, Cheltenham, Gloucestershire GL50 3SH. Tel. 01242 222444, 01242 227788 for applicant enquiries.

In deciding where to apply you should bear in mind the examination grades which the institution may expect you to get if you are given an offer of a place (can you realistically hope to get the required grades?). Do not judge an institution's reputation purely by the grades it demands. Obtain guidance on admission policies and examination grade requirements from your school or college.

Some law schools will want to interview selected candidates before deciding whether or not to give them a place. An interview is not only a chance for the law school to find out about the candidate. It is also a chance for the candidate to find out about the law school. Be prepared to ask questions about the aims of the law degree, the range and nature of the optional subjects available, and the research interests of the staff. Never ask a question that can be easily answered by reference to material that has already been sent to you or which you should already have obtained. Do not, for example, ask what subjects are taught if this is in a faculty brochure which you have been given. Do ask if the brochure does not tell you, the philosophy behind a particular course and, for example, its emphasis on traditional legal study or on the study of law in its social context. Asking no questions at all shows that you have not prepared for the interview and perhaps have little interest in the institution. Asking questions that can be answered from available information shows the same thing. Use the information that you have been sent as a basis for asking further, more detailed questions.

In many degree courses contract, tort, criminal law, land law, equity and trusts and constitutional and administrative law will be studied as compulsory subjects, in either the first or second year. One reason for this is that many academics see these subjects as being basic to the study of English law. Either they contain principles or concepts that are of importance in a wide range of legal subjects or they are about matters which are themselves of general significance. There is also a pragmatic justification for making these subjects compulsory. Students wishing to qualify as barristers or solicitors must normally study these subjects at degree level in order to be exempt from having to take them in professional examinations. The subjects are sometimes referred to as *core subjects*. As from 1 September 1995, students commencing law degree courses are likely to have to study European community law in order to qualify as barristers or solicitors.

In addition to the six subjects above, a normal law degree would involve a student in studying another seven or eight subjects. A list of typical subjects might include:

> English Legal System, European Union Law, Labour Law, Commercial Law, Public International Law, Family Law, Jurisprudence, Sociology of Law, Revenue Law, Company Law, Law and Medicine, and Private International Law.

There may be scope for a student to write a dissertation (an extended essay) on a subject of their choice under the supervision of a member of staff as an alternative to study of one of the optional subjects. Prospectuses should be read so as to get an idea of the context of the courses and the different individual emphases and approaches adopted. Choice of course options is dictated by many factors. The student's own interests, career intentions, the way in which the subject is taught and the folk-lore surrounding it within the institution where a student is studying all play their part. Subjects vary both in content and the style in which they are taught. For example, international law in one institution may involve different material and be taught in a different way from another course labelled international law in another.

Many optional subjects, with the notable exceptions of subjects such as the sociology of law and philosophy of law, have as their starting points principles, concepts and techniques which are acquired in studying the core legal subjects. The core subjects studied tend to place an emphasis on common law rather than statute law, on private law rather than public law and on applying legal principles without considering their origins and social effects in any detail. Some law degree courses seek to redress this balance as there is an argument that the core subjects, with their emphasis on individuals' property and other private rights perpetuate a narrow vision of English law.

No law school can guarantee that it will still be offering the same subjects in its syllabus three years hence. Lecturers may leave, or may lose interest in something which they have taught. Thus, be wary of deciding to go to a particular institution just because of one course, particularly if it is unusual, and particularly if it is taught in the third year. It may not be there when you reach the third year.

LAW AS A PROFESSION

When looking and deciding on your future career, it is vital to make a realistic assessment of the range of career opportunities open to you. This means deciding what are your own aptitudes, preferences and interests, as well as what are the actual jobs on offer. Vacation or other temporary work experience of any sort can be a very useful way in which to test out your prejudices and instincts about different types of work and to help you make an informed choice about them. Such experience will also help you in job applications and interviews for other, more permanent, jobs. Never be afraid to ask teachers and friends about their jobs and career decisions. Use every opportunity to take advantage of careers advice that is available in your school, college or university. Consider whether participating in a placement scheme would help. When you have made a tentative decision and apply for a job, take time in preparing your letter of application, application form and/or curriculum vitae (resumé of your career to date). Get friends and your tutor to read through your applications and ensure that you present yourself in as interesting and as favourable a light as possible. Never hesitate to take advice. Never be diffident about applying for a particular job.

There is a wide variety of jobs with some legal content. The level and kind of prior legal knowledge which they demand (if any) varies from job to job. You will find an extensive list of such jobs, together with addresses to write for more information about them, in the appendix to this book. In the remainder of this chapter we will concentrate on the legal profession—by this we mean solicitors and barristers.

SOLICITORS AND BARRISTERS

The legal profession in England and Wales is divided into two branches (solicitors and barristers) which have their own entry and training schemes. The majority of lawyers are solicitors. There are over 50,000 solicitors in England and Wales. Firms of solicitors exist in all large towns, although there is a high concentration in the South East, particularly in London. It has been said that solicitors are generalists. They advise clients from all walks of life on a wide variety of legal matters, with a traditional emphasis on conveyancing and other property related matters. The Law Society reports that in a recent survey 100 solicitors were asked how they spent their time. It worked out as follows:

- Business Affairs   20.6%
- Commercial Property   18%
- Residential Conveyancing   18.5%
- Family   10.6%
- Probate, Wills etc.   7.2%
- Personal Injury   7.1%
- Crime   6.7%
- Other   11.3%

The majority of solicitors work in private practice, in partnerships employing fewer than 50 people. There are, however, around 6,000 solicitors employed in commerce and industry, local government, law centres and other occupations. Their work can be summarised in the following way:

Category of Employment	Total
Local government	2,234
Commerce/Industry	2,177
Crown Prosecution Service	1,100
National undertaking	227
Clerk/Assistant clerk to Justices	201
Law Centre/Citizens Advice Bureau	86
Government service	54
Agent CPS	30
Total	6,109

. . . .

(Source: Law Society)

The majority of the 7,000 plus practising barristers work in central London. They have restricted access to clients. They can normally only represent a client when instructed by a solicitor. They have a near-exclusive right to act as paid advocates in the High Court, Court of Appeal and House of Lords. Barristers work as individual fee-earners on their own account, sharing overheads with other barristers who are members of a set of chambers. They have few of the protections which are afforded to employees and partners in firms of solicitors. Their success or failure is linked directly to their own ability, flair, preparedness to work, luck and connections.

Historically, comparisons have been drawn between the legal and medical professions. Solicitors, in common with general practitioners, are generalists. Barristers, in common with consultants, are specialists. This comparison still has some validity, although it does not give nearly enough emphasis to the highly specialist and intellectually demanding work undertaken by many firms of solicitors covering such areas as commercial, company and tax law. It also is the case that a considerable number of solicitors act as advocates before tribunals, magistrates' courts and other courts. Many barristers spend much of their time out of court, advising solicitors and their clients on points of law and drafting pleadings during the initial stages of litigation. It is only a small proportion of barristers who are able to specialise in the area of law in which they wish to work. The majority are involved in general court work (advocacy).

Those primarily interested in advocacy should normally consider becoming barristers. Court work done by solicitors has tended to involve less important cases, even for those solicitors who specialise in the area. However, the enhanced "rights of audience" granted to solicitors to appear in the higher courts may, over time, change the position. In making a career decision, thought should be given to the relative opportunities at the Bar and in practice as a solicitor. Practice as a solicitor, in the early stages of a person's career, has the attraction of providing some element of predictability and financial security. It is often the case, at the Bar, that it is only the extremely able who have the opportunity to specialise. Newly qualified barristers must be prepared to put up with career uncertainties and fairly modest incomes in their first years of practice, compared with newly qualified solicitors, particularly in City of London practices.

Choosing between the two branches of the profession in extremely difficult, especially at the present time, when the legal profession is in a state of transition. Changing attitudes towards the function and conduct of the legal profession, the advent of professional advertising, and greater competition between the two branches of the profession, will all change the nature of legal practice and career opportunities within it. The debate as to whether or not the legal profession is overstaffed is likely to continue and the effects of the existing age profile of the profession have yet to be fully evaluated. Lawyers have less job security than in the past, and their range of work and differences in their terms and conditions of employment have grown in recent years. Qualification as a lawyer is no longer (if it has ever been) an automatic passport to a high standard of living or permanent employment.

EDUCATION AND TRAINING OF SOLICITORS

The Law Society's Careers and Recruitment Service, 227/228 Strand, London WC2R 1BA issues a series of helpful guidance notes covering: becoming a solicitor, and careers as a solicitor in local government and commerce and industry. Guidance is also given on financial support for students, together with a list of institutions which offer "qualifying" law degrees, postgraduate diplomas in law, the legal practice course and the common professional examination.

This section reproduces and summarises guidance supplied by the Law Society in June 1994. You should check this summary as against material which you yourself obtain from the Law Society. The Law Society prescribes the legal education and training required to qualify as a solicitor of England and Wales. The main routes to become a solicitor of England and Wales are the law degree route, the non-law degree route and the non-graduate route.

Law Degree Route:

This is the quickest and most common way to qualify as a solicitor in England and Wales.

If you decide to take a law degree, you will need to have a good academic record, as competition for places is very intense. You should aim for three "A" levels or equivalent. You may study any academic subject. It is important that you try to obtain high grades. Science "A" levels are as acceptable as arts subjects and no one subject is essential for admission to a Law Degree course.

You should study for a qualifying law degree, which covers the six core subjects required by both the Law Society and the Bar Council to complete the Academic Stage of Training. The subjects include Constitutional & Administrative Law, Contract, Tort, Criminal, Land Law and Equity and Trusts. At the time of writing, European Union Law is being considered for inclusion as a seventh core subject. A list of approved degrees is available from the Law Society. You should check that your degree is approved by the Law Society.

Non-Law Degree Route:

This is the second most common way to qualify as a solicitor, and is growing in popularity.

If you have a degree in a subject other than law, you are required to undertake a one year full-time or two year part-time course leading to the Common Professional Examination, which covers the six core subjects which constitute the Academic Stage of Training. The course is offered at around thirty academic institutions across the country and a full list can be obtained from the Law Society. A current alternative to the Common Professional Examination course is the course leading to the post-graduate Diploma in Law, which also covers the six core subjects, and will enable you, for Law Society purposes, to complete the Academic Stage of Training. A full list of these courses, which are offered at ten institutions, can be obtained from the Law Society. Courses start in Autumn of each year and application is by means of a clearing house for most institutions. The closing date for applications is normally in the spring of the year in which the course commences, e.g. Spring 1995 for the 1995–6 course. Completion for places is extremely strong and students who have not obtained a II (i) degree or better may find it difficult to gain a place on a course.

Many people ask if they will have problems obtaining employment if they do not have a law degree. Most employers are keen to recruit law and non-law students and progression in the profession is not affected by degree subject.

Before starting the Common Professional Examination course, you will require from the Law Society a Certificate of Eligibility. An application form must be completed and submitted to the Law Society, together with a certified true copy of your degree, the appropriate fee and a letter from a recognised institution confirming that you have been granted a place on their Common Professional Examination Course.

Student Membership:

Upon completion of the Academic Stage of Training, by the Common Professional Examination, Diploma in Law, or a qualifying law degree, you must apply for student membership of the Law Society in order to proceed to the next stage of training. Application forms must be submitted to the Law Society no later than 31 March of the year in which you wish to undertake professional training. You will be asked a number of questions on the form about such matters as criminal convictions. Particular care must be taken in filling in the forms and making certain that you are eligible for membership.

Vocational Stage of Training:

Professional training for solicitors is by means of the Legal Practice Course. The purpose of the course is to ensure that trainee solicitors entering training contracts have the necessary knowledge and practical skills to undertake appropriate tasks under proper supervision during the contract. A full-time Legal Practice Course will run for one academic year; a part-time course for two years. The introduction of part-time courses will increase the flexibility of the training scheme and access to the profession. A list of courses, which are offered at twenty-four institutions is available from the Law Society.

The course will cover Conveyancing; Wills Probate and Administration; Business Law and Practice; Litigation and Advocacy; plus two optional legal topics, Professional Conduct; Investment Business; European Community Law and Revenue Law will be assessed through the compulsory subjects. Further information about the course can be obtained from the providing institutions. Application forms for the Legal Practice Course can be obtained from the Central Applications Room, Admail 44, London SW1P 3YL.

Practical Stage of Training:

After successful completion of the Legal Practice Course, you have to undertake a two-year training contract (Articles) with a firm of solicitors or other authorised organisation. This involves working in paid employment under the supervision of an authorised firm and undertaking your own work. Finding a training contract is up to you, but help can be obtained from a variety of sources. Competition for training contracts is strong at present and many employers recruit two–three years in advance.

During your training contract you will be required to complete the *Professional Skills Course*, which will cover the areas of Accounts, Investment Business; Personal Work Management; Professional Conduct and Advocacy. The course will last for twenty days if taken full-time. However, it is likely that it will be possible to take the five sections individually.

The Non-Graduate Route (Legal Executive Route):

If you have four GCSEs (waived for those over twenty-five), you can become qualified through the Institute of Legal Executive route.

You should gain employment in a legal office, join the Institute of Legal Executives and over the first one to two years undertake the Institute's Part I Examination. Over the next one to two years undertake the Institute's Part II Examinations. The choice of law subjects is optional, but you should, if possible, study for three of the six core subjects that constitute the Academic Stage of Training to become a solicitor of England and Wales.

After passing the Part II Examination, you will become a member of the Institute of Legal Executives. You must have served five years (two after membership) in a legal office before you become eligible to be a Fellow of the Institute of Legal Executives. During this time you should undertake the remaining core subjects as Diploma examinations within the Institute.

As a Fellow of the Institute of Legal Executives and having passed the six core subjects, you may then enrol as a Student member of the Law Society and attend the Legal Practice course. Where a FILEX has been in continuous legal employment, the requirement to serve Articles of Training may be waived. All FILEX will be required to complete a Professional Skills Course.

The above career routes can be summarised as follows:

Trainee solicitors

a) Private Practice

Most training contracts (articles) are served with private firms of solicitors. Firms vary considerably in size and type of work; therefore the trainee solicitor's range of experience and salary may also vary considerably. An overview of individual law firms can be obtained from Roset (the register of solicitors employing trainees), John Pritchard's Legal 500 and Chambers Directory of Law Firms. Many large law firms now produce their own recruitment brochures, which should be obtained as they give a good indication of opportunities. Before making an application you need to think of the sort of training you are seeking.

(i) In rural areas, firms will tend to consist of five or six partners at the most, with total staffs often not exceeding fifteen people. Most such firms will be "general practitioners," which means that they will mostly do conveyancing, landlord and tenant, trusts, wills and probate, small-scale commercial and company work, family law, civil and criminal litigation.

(ii) In large towns most firms will also do the kinds of work listed above though there will tend to be some degree of specialisation, (*e.g.* towards property work and conveyancing, or crime). The larger firms do more commercial work. Some of these firms may have around twenty partners (with some specialising in certain types of work) and staffs of one hundred or more. Generally, in inner city areas, the higher the percentage of legal aid work done and the greater the emphasis of welfare law, (*e.g.* family employment, social security and housing law). Such firms have been affected by reductions in the availability of legal aid for many people.

(iii) In London and other major cities, there is the greatest degree of specialisation, with the large firms in the City of London concentrating very heavily on company, financial, commercial and shipping work. Such firms are very large with over one hundred partners and staffs of seven hundred and fifty or more and with offices around the world. Smaller specialist firms have developed significantly with "niche", specialist practices covering such areas as intellectual property law, employment and media law.

b) Public Service

Legal work in local government covers many aspects of conveyancing and planning and commercial work. Local authorities do a certain amount of prosecuting work both in those areas where they have special law enforcement responsibilities, (*e.g.* weights and measures or public health legislation) and also sometimes, on behalf of the public. Some local authorities are involved in child care law.

There are also substantial opportunities for legal careers in Central Government and the Crown Prosecution Service (for relevant addresses see the Appendix).

c) Industry and commerce

A number of companies and other organisations, both in the private and public sectors have their own legal departments, with qualified solicitors who occasionally take on trainee solicitors.

While the work tends to be specialised, large commercial organisations can offer valuable experience in property and commercial work and in areas such as employment, insurance and pension law. Considerable opportunities exist to work in commerce once a person has qualified with a large City of London firm. Limited opportunities also exist to work as a lawyer for a range of trade and employer associations, trade unions, pressure groups and charities.

d) Law Centres

In the inner areas of a number of cities there are Law Centres, offering occasional opportunities for trainee solicitors seeking to specialise in welfare law. There are opportunities for solicitors to work for Law Centres and similar agencies, especially where they have had an all-round experience of litigation during articles. The development and continuance of many Law Centres have been affected by public spending restraints.

EDUCATION AND TRAINING OF BARRISTERS

The academic stage of training for solicitors and barristers (the Bar) is to all intents and purposes the same. The Bar is predominantly a graduate profession. Full details of the entrance requirements can be obtained from The Council of Legal Education, 39 Eagle Street, London WCiR 4AJ. More general information is available from The General Council of the Bar, 3 Bedford Row, London WC1R 4DB.

The academic stage

The academic stage for law graduates will normally be covered in their degree course, provided that they study the six core subjects at institutions and on courses approved by the Bar. Non-law graduates must establish that they have obtained a certain standard of education at degree and "A" level. They must then normally attend the Common Professional Examination course at one of a number of institutions and take the Common Professional Examination. Special provisions exist for mature students over the age of twenty-five who are not graduates but have shown exceptional ability in other fields.

The vocational stage

Intending barristers must be admitted to one of the four Inns of

Court (*Students' Officer, The Honourable Society of Middle Temple, Treasury Office, London EC4Y 9AT (Tel: 071–353 4355); Students' Officer, The Honourable Society of Inner Temple, Treasury Office, London EC4Y 7HL (Tel: 071–797 8208); Students' Officer, The Honourable Society of Lincoln's Inn, Treasury Office, London WC2A 3TL (Tel: 071–405 0138); Students' Officer, The Honourable Society of Gray's Inn, 8 South Square, Gray's Inn, London WC1R 5EU (Tel: 071–405 8164)*). They must comply with certain requirements of the Inn. The most noteworthy of these is the need, prior to qualification, to "keep term," which means eating a certain number of dinners in the Inn of Court during set periods. This requirement is said to enable judges, barristers and intending barristers to meet and get to know each other. Advice should be taken from careers tutors as to the appropriate Inn to join. Much will depend on your career intentions, scholarship opportunities, your likely pupillage arrangements and the contacts which exist between your law department and particular Inns.

The vocational stage can take the form of the year's compulsory Vocational Course at the Inns of Court School of Law or, in the future, at an approved university, for students intending to practice at the Bar, or the Bar examination for intending non-practitioners in the UK, for which there are no compulsory courses.

The Bar vocational course covers practical skills, the rules of procedure, sentencing and evidence, professional conduct and a degree of specialisation (*e.g.* General Practice, Chancery Practice and Commercial Practice). Examination is by a combination of multi-choice and in-course and final assessment. The Bar examination contains certain compulsory elements (General Papers covering common law and criminal law, equity and trusts and papers on civil and criminal procedure and evidence) and two options from a wide list of subjects.

Students who pass the Bar examination are "called to the Bar." They are barristers. In contrast to the solicitor's qualification, the Bar qualification does not entail the successful completion of a period of apprenticeship training. However, barristers intending to practise, rather than teach law or to go on to some other career, must complete a period of apprenticeship ("a pupillage") which is normally for a period of one year, during the last six months of which the pupil barrister can undertake work for a fee. The regulations governing training at the Bar are currently under review. Students should check the up-to-date position with the Council of Legal Education or the General Council of the Bar.

Pupillage

In selecting pupillage a student must have regard not only to the range of training on offer but also to the future prospects in the set of chambers which offers a pupillage. Students should not only consider pupillage in London, but also in sets of chambers in cities such as Manchester or Birmingham. Regard must also be had to the number and amount of pupillage awards and scholarships given by the chambers, to help off-set the living expenses for pupils. Many chambers, particularly those in the provinces, do a mixture of litigation work covering crime, personal injury litigation and other common law areas. Students wishing to obtain pupillage and to earn a reasonable living at an early stage at the Bar will often choose such chambers. In London, particularly, there is a large number of specialist chambers covering such fields as commercial law, chancery, patents, tax, libel, planning, employment law and so on. Competition is very fierce for places in such sets of chambers. A very good academic record is required and even those students who are offered places are not assured of making a career at the specialist Bar. Even if offered a place for pupillage there is no guarantee that the student will subsequently be offered a position in the chambers ("a tenancy") after its completion.

PRACTICAL POINTS: SOLICITORS AND BARRISTERS

The following points may be of assistance to those considering entering the legal profession:

• consider when applications need to be made for the various professional examination courses, obtain advice from your tutor and from the Law Society and Bar Council and the growing number of institutions offering the professional courses.
• intending solicitors should give thought to the advantages and disadvantages of choosing either the College of Law or one of the other appropriate institutions for the solicitors' final course. Some local education authorities are willing to give discretionary grants to cover the costs of such courses, only when a student chooses the institution nearest to his home address. Some firms of solicitors will help their prospective trainee solicitors with the course fees and living expenses.
• intending entrants to the legal profession should assess the total costs of entry, (*e.g.* tuition and living costs, membership fees and other expenses), the possibility or not of obtaining a discretionary local authority grant, a bank loan, the availability of scholarships

from the various Inns, chambers and law firms and the conditions attached to such awards.

• the desirability of obtaining work experience in a solicitor's office or attached to a barrister's set of chambers during student vacations. Many firms of solicitors and barristers' chambers now organise student placement schemes.

• advice should be sought to ensure that you obtain a satisfactory apprentice training which reflects your career and subject interests either as a trainee solicitor or as a pupil barrister and that the articles or pupillage is arranged at the appropriate time.

• an assessment should be made of prospects in either branch of the profession and the overall treatment of trainees and new recruits.

• read regularly the legal recruitment/jobs pages in *The Times* and other national newspapers, the *Law Society Gazette* and *The Lawyer*. These publications provide an accurate barometer of vacancies, salaries and employment trends in the legal profession.

Students should make every effort possible to explore career opportunities which are open to them and find out "first-hand" what work as a solicitor or barrister is like whilst they are at university. Do not assume that your interest in the law as a degree subject automatically means that you will enjoy working as a lawyer, or that your disinterest in law as a degree subject means that you will not enjoy working as a lawyer. Appendix I summarises other career opportunities open to students who have studied law or have an interest in a career with a legal content.

[HEFC QUALITY ASSESSMENTS]
[(August 1994)]

Institution	Assessment Outcome	Quality Assessment Report
Anglia Polytechnic University	Satisfactory	
University of Birmingham	Satisfactory	*
Bournemouth University	Satisfactory	Q2/93
University of Bristol	Excellent	Q21/94
Brunel University	Satisfactory	
University of Cambridge	Excellent	Q6/94
University of Central England in Birmingham	Satisfactory	
University of Central Lancashire	Satisfactory	
City University	Satisfactory	
Coventry University	Satisfactory	
Croydon Institute	Satisfactory	
De Montfort University	Satisfactory	Q1/94
University of Derby†	Unsatisfactory	Q145/94
University of Durham	Excellent	Q46/94
University of East Anglia	Excellent	Q111/94
University of East London	Satisfactory	
University of Essex	Excellent	Q5/93
University of Exeter	Satisfactory	*
University of Greenwich	Satisfactory	
University of Hertfordshire	Satisfactory	*
University of Huddersfield	Satisfactory	
University of Hull	Satisfactory	Q24/93
University of Humberside	Satisfactory	
University of Keele	Satisfactory	
University of Kent at Canterbury	Satisfactory	
Kingston University	Satisfactory	
University of Lancaster	Satisfactory	
University of Leeds	Satisfactory	Q16/93
Leeds Metropolitan University	Satisfactory	
University of Leicester	Excellent	Q48/94
University of Liverpool	Excellent	Q20/94
Liverpool John Moores University	Satisfactory	
University of London		
Birkbeck College	Satisfactory	
King's College London	Excellent	Q4/93
London School of Economics and Political Science	Excellent	Q83/94
Queen Mary and Westfield College	Satisfactory	*
University College London	Excellent	Q19/94
School of Oriental and African Studies	Excellent	Q138/94
London Guildhall University	Satisfactory	
Luton University	Satisfactory	

Institution	Assessment Outcome	Quality Assessment Report
University of Manchester	Excellent	Q36/94
Manchester Metropolitan University	Satisfactory	
Middlesex University	Satisfactory	Q49/94
Nene College	Satisfactory	Q70/94
University of Newcastle Upon Tyne	Satisfactory	
University of North London	Satisfactory	Q137/94
University of Northumbria at Newcastle	Excellent	Q22/94
University of Nottingham	Excellent	Q56/94
The Nottingham Trent University	Satisfactory	
University of Oxford	Excellent	Q153/94
Oxford Brookes University	Excellent	Q65/94
University of Plymouth	Satisfactory	
University of Reading	Satisfactory	
Salford College of Technology	Satisfactory	
University of Sheffield	Excellent	Q37/94
Sheffield Hallam University	Satisfactory	
University of Southampton	Satisfactory	
Southampton Institute of Higher Education	Satisfactory	Q13/93
South Bank University	Satisfactory	Q26/93
Staffordshire University	Satisfactory	
University of Sussex	Satisfactory	Q84/94
University of Teesside	Satisfactory	
Thames Valley University	Satisfactory	
University of Warwick	Excellent	Q85/94
University of Westminster	Satisfactory	Q9/94
University of the West of England, Bristol	Excellent	Q14/93
University of Wolverhampton	Satisfactory	Q41/94

* Quality Assessment Report in the Process of publication.
† A subsequent assessment of the University of Derby gave it a rating of satisfactory.

(Reproduced from HEFCE 'Subject Overview Report "Quality Assessment of Law 1993–94")

APPENDIX 1

Careers directory

This alphabetical list of career opportunities is an attempt to summarise a selection of those careers which have some legal content or contact with the legal profession. The materials contained in this book are designed to be of assistance to trainees for the vast majority of these occupations. Students who have studied law will sometimes find that they can negotiate exemptions from law examinations in professional courses. In some cases they will automatically have such exemption. The fifty or so organisations mentioned in the directory were all written to in June 1994, and their amendments to previous entries have been included, where relevant. We are extremely grateful to them for their comments. Most academic institutions and professional bodies now consider a wide variety of qualifications such as BTEC, GNVQ, Scottish Highers, and SCOTVEC.

ACCOUNTANCY

Accountants are usually thought of in association with companies. Working both as the employees of the company and as independent advisers they are involved in the day-to-day financial control of businesses as well as larger-scale matters such as the creation of new businesses and the restructuring of established ones. Companies must appoint independent accountants to audit (check) their accounts. In recent years their work as liquidators and receivers, dealing with the closing down of businesses, has expanded. The accountancy profession has shown itself to be very adaptable and enterprising. Its work has developed over the past decades. They have also expanded their activities into the more general area of management consultants. They are also heavily involved in tax planning both for individuals and companies. They often have to work closely with solicitors and, in recent years, have expanded their business into areas traditionally the prerogative of solicitors.

Many accountants work in industry or local authorities. Some firms of accountants employ lawyers and take on law graduates as trainees. There are a number of different kinds of accountants, *e.g.* Chartered, Certified, Management.

Academic and other entry requirements and training periods vary as between the different types of accountants.

Further information:

> Institute of Chartered Accountants in England and Wales, PO Box 433, Chartered Accountants' Hall, Moorgate Place, London EC2P 2BJ
> The Chartered Association of Certified Accountants, 29 Lincoln's Inn, London WC2A 3EE
> The Chartered Institute of Management Accountants, 63 Portland Place, London W1M 4AB
> The Chartered Institute of Public Finance and Accountancy, 3 Robert Street, London WC2N 6BH.

ACTUARY

Most actuaries work for insurance and pension fund companies. They calculate matters such as the life expectancies of certain occupational groups and assess a wide range of insurance risks.

Minimum entry standard:	2 "A" levels (one being at B in Maths or C in further Maths) and 3 "GCSE" levels. (Mostly a Maths graduate profession).
Training period:	5–6 years for graduates.

Further information:

> Institute of Actuaries, Napier House, 4 Worcester Street, Oxford OX1 2AW.

ADVERTISING

There is a wide range of job opportunities for graduates in the advertising industry.

Further information:

The Advertising Association, Abford House, 15 Wilton Road, London SW1V 1NJ
Institute of Practitioners in Advertising, 44 Belgrave Square, London SW1X 8QS.

BANKING

The High Street Banks have expanded the range of services they offer to corporate and personal customers. Advice is given on a wide range of services including investments, taxation, securities, loans and leasing schemes. The Banks have substantial trust and probate departments. Merchant banks give specialist advice, manage clients' investments, and advise on company acquisitions, flotations and mergers. They employ a number of lawyers.

Qualifications and training periods depend on the Bank and the relevant traineeship.

Further information:

Banking Information Service, 6th Floor, 10 Lombard Street, London EC3V 9AT
British Merchant Banking and Securities Houses Association, 6 Frederick's Place, London EC2R 8BT
The Chartered Institute of Bankers, First Floor, 10 Lombard Street, London EC3V 9AS.

BARRISTER

See Chapter 8.

BUILDING SOCIETY MANAGEMENT

At present Building Societies have to deal with solicitors over the granting and drawing up of mortgages. They employ a number of lawyers. It is likely that the scope of Building Societies operations will grow in the future to include more commercial initiatives and the provision of a wider range of legal services for their clients. No mandatory qualification exists but there is provision to obtain a "building society" qualification from The Chartered Institute of Bankers.

Training period: Variable.

Further information:

>The Chartered Institute of Bankers, 10 Lombard Street, London EC3V 9AS
>Building Societies Association, 3 Savile Row, London W1X 1AF.

CHARTERED SECRETARY

Chartered Secretaries are professional administrators with training in finance, law, personnel and information systems. The work will vary depending on the size and function of the organisation. It may include looking after pension schemes, insurance, premises management, liaison between directors and shareholders, company law, committee management and office management.

No academic qualifications are needed for entry but exemptions from professional examinations may be granted for degrees, Higher National Awards and some professional qualifications.

>Training period: Variable.

Further information:

>Careers Department, Institute of Chartered Secretaries and Administrators, 16 Park Crescent, London W1N 4AH.

CIVIL SERVICE

The range of jobs in the civil service is enormous; from prison warder to Permanent Secretary. Many have a legal content. The civil service employs a large number of solicitors and barristers. For details of the various openings in the civil service write to:

>Civil Service Commission, Civil Service Department, Alencon Link, Basingstoke, Hampshire RG21 1JB
>Government Legal Services, Recruitment Team, Queen Anne's Chambers, 28 Broadway, London SW1H 9JS.

CUSTOMS AND EXCISE

HM Customs are responsible for collecting excise duties, import restrictions and, very importantly, for VAT.

Further information:

Customs and Excise, New Kings Beam House, 22 Upper Ground, London SE1 9PJ.

ENGINEERING

Most professional engineers study aspects of law during some part of their training; generally this will relate to matters such as contract, employment and building law.

Further information:

Engineering Careers Information Service, 41 Clarendon Road, Watford WD1 1HS
The Engineering Council, 10 Maltravers Street, London WC2R 3ER
Women into Science and Engineering (c/o The Engineering Council).

ENVIRONMENTAL HEALTH OFFICERS

Environmental Health Officers work in both the public and private sectors. The work includes responsibility for ensuring that certain food, hygiene, housing and other regulatory provisions are complied with. The job includes some involvement with lawyers and the courts and requires detailed knowledge of a number of Acts of Parliament and related statutory instruments.

Minimum entry standard:	2 "A" levels and 5 "GCSE" levels (including English, Maths and 2 science subjects). (Provision for graduate entry).
Training period:	4 year sandwich course leading to BSc (Hons) Environmental Health. 2 year MSc in Environmental Health for science graduates. Some courses offered on a part-time basis.

Further information:

The Institute of Environmental Health Officers, Chadwick Court, 15 Hatfields, London SE1 8DJ.

FACTORY INSPECTOR

Much of a factory inspector's time is spent visiting appropriate premises advising on safety requirements and ensuring that a variety of statutes are complied with. The job involves some contact with courts and lawyers.

Minimum entry standards:	Graduate entry plus further experience normally required.
Training period:	2 years

Further information:

The Health and Safety Executive, Room 321, St Hughs House, Bootle, Liverpool L20
Civil Service Commission, Alencon Link, Basingstoke, Hampshire RG21 1JB.

HEALTH SERVICES MANAGEMENT

Health service managers play a key role in the organisation, staffing, equipping and functioning of hospitals. Moves towards privatising some services, (*e.g.* catering and laundering), industrial relations problems, and intricate commercial decisions which have to be taken by hospital trusts have all increased the legal content of the work done.

Minimum entry standards:	No set pattern.
Training period:	Variable. It is possible to take the Institute of Health Services Management courses but other qualifications such as those in law, accountancy or personnel management may be adequate.

Further information:

Institute of Health Services Management, 39 Chalton Street, London NW1 1JD.

HOUSING

Housing professionals work to develop, supply or manage housing and related services. People who work in housing tend to work for a local authority, housing association or a commercial landlord. The work varies according to the particular functions of the housing organisation, its size and location, however, much of the work has a legal content due to the statutory framework surrounding the field of housing management.

Minimum entry standards: 1 "A" level and 3 GCSE or equivalent.

Training period: 4 years (less for Graduates).

Further information:

Chartered Institute of Housing, Octavia House, Westwood Way, Coventry CV4 8JP. Tel: 01203 694433.

INSURANCE

The insurance field offers a wide range of different employment opportunities. The precise nature of insurance contracts and the wide range of specialist legal rules means there are many openings for lawyers in this area.

Further information:

Careers Information Officer, The Chartered Insurance Institute, The Hall, 20 Aldermanbury, London EC2V 7HY.

JOURNALISM AND BROADCASTING

This is a wide field offering opportunities not just as a broadcaster or journalist, but also behind the scenes in the administration and management of business. Many media companies have "in house" legal departments. The BBC's is probably the largest.

Further information:

Newspaper Society, Bloomsbury House, Bloomsbury Square, London WC1B 3DA
BBC Recruitment Service, White City, 201 Wood Lane, London W12 7TS
ITV Network Centre, 200 Gray's Inn Road, London WC1 8XS
Independent Television Commission, 33 Foley Street, London W1P 7LB

National Council for the Training of Journalists, Latton Bush Centre, Southern Way, Harlow, Essex CM18 7BL

Periodical Publishers' Association, Imperial House, 15–19 Kingsway, London WC2B 6UN

Radio Authority, Holbrook House, 14 Great Queen Street, Holborn, London WC2B 5DG.

LEGAL CAREER OPPORTUNITIES

Solicitors and Barristers are covered in Chapter 8. This entry reproduces material supplied by the Law Society in June 1994 on other careers in the legal profession.

(a) Legal Executives

Legal Executives work as assistants to solicitors, predominantly in the area of private practice. They must take the examinations of the Institute of Legal Executives (ILEX). To qualify as a Fellow of the Institute they must also have at least 5 years experience in legal work. They do a wide range of legal work and often develop their own individual specialisations (particularly in the field of conveyancing, accounts, trusts, wills and litigation). It is possible to move from being a legal executive to qualifying as a solicitor. Some people are employed by solicitors to do the same work as legal executives although they are not qualified as such.

Entry qualifications: 4 GCSE levels in approved subjects or the ILEX preliminary certificate in legal studied or the ILEX para legal training qualification.

Further information:

The Institute of Legal Executives, Kempston Manor, Kempston, Bedford MK42 7AB.

(b) Outdoor Clerks

Many large firms of solicitors employ school leavers as Clerks who deliver Writs and Summonses or attend Court to pay fees and have documents stamped. There is a booklet called "Duties of an Outdoor Clerk" available from The Law Society Bookshop, 227–228 The Strand, London WC2R 1BA.

(c) Barristers' Clerks

Barristers' Clerks manage the diaries, Court lists and fees of barristers in practice.

Further information:

Institute of Barristers' Clerks, 45 Essex Street, London WC2B 3JF.

(d) Legal Secretaries

Legal Secretaries provide the secretarial and clerical backup for solicitors, barristers, law courts, civil service, and banks. They deal with large amounts of correspondence and the preparation of documents such as wills, divorce petitions and witness statements.

Further information:

Association of Legal Secretaries, The Mill, Clymping Street, Clymping, Littlehampton, West Sussex BN17 5RN.

(e) Legal Cashiers

Legal Cashiers are usually employed in solicitors' practices, and their main duties are to keep solicitors up to date with the financial position of the firm and to maintain records. A cashier often deals with the payment of salaries, pensions, National Insurance contributions and Income Tax. Cashiers are increasingly using computerised accounting systems.

Further information:

The Institute of Legal Cashiers, 1st Floor, 136 Well Hall Road, Eltham, London SE9 6SN.

Law Costs Draftsmen

Law Costs Draftsmen ensure that the firm's clients are properly charged for the work that has been done on their behalf. They are concerned with all areas of law and deal with every type of legal matter that passes through solicitors' hands. They are not therefore restricted to one narrow area of law but must acquire a knowledge of law to enable them to deal with the files. A knowledge of legal procedure is vital.

Further information:

Association of Law Costs Draftsmen, 16 St Saigh's Lane, Norwich, Norfolk NR1 1NN.

(g) Licensed Conveyancers

Licensed Conveyancers are involved in the preparation of transfers, conveyances, contracts and other documents in connection with the selling and buying of property or land. To become a Licensed Conveyancer you need a minimum of four GCSEs including English Language, and must be prepared to sit and pass further examinations and undergo further practical training.

Further information:

The Council for Licensed Conveyancers, 16 Glebe Road, Chelmsford, Essex CM1 1QG.

(h) Justices' Clerks

Justices' Clerks are barristers or solicitors who manage the magistrates' courts service and are responsible for providing legal advice to lay magistrates. They also train newly appointed magistrates and act as secretary to management and selection committees and are widely involved in liaison with other professionals in the criminal justice system.

Further information:

A. R. Heath, Honorary Secretary, The Justices' Clerks' Society, The Court House, Homer Road, Solihull B91 3RD.

(i) Court Clerks

Court Clerks work in Justices' Clerks' offices and advise lay magistrates on law and procedure in court. They are also responsible for the Licensing and Betting and Gaming Committees which involves visiting premises with a Magistrate. Court Clerks often have to be on standby at weekends just in case it is necessary to set up an emergency court.

Further information:

> The Association of Magisterial Officers, 35 High Street, Crawley, West Sussex RH10 1BQ.

(j) Crown Prosecution Service

The Crown Prosecution Service prosecutes offenders on behalf of the police. The Crown Prosecutors are qualified solicitors or barristers. The Crown Prosecution Service is itself part of the Civil Service, and all Prosecutors are Civil Servants. Prosecutors have a support staff of executive officers and administrative officers and assistants to prepare papers for hearings in Court.

Further information:

> The Crown Prosecution Service, 50 Ludgate Hill, London EC4M 7GG.

(k) The Lord Chancellor's Department

This office, part of the Civil Service, employs civil servants, some of whom are lawyers, to deal with matters relating to the administration of the Courts. The Department also deals with policy matters concerning the legal profession.

Further information:

> Lord Chancellor's Department, Trevelyan House, Great Peter Street, London SW1P 2BY.

(l) Armed Forces

There are a number of vacancies for lawyers in the armed forces.

Further information:

> Directorate of Armed Legal Services, MoD, Lillie Road, London SW6 1TR.

LIBRARY, INFORMATION AND TRAINING SERVICES

An increasing number of the larger firms of solicitors have specialist departments covering legal information and practice developments, library services, precedents, education and training programmes, research and publications.

These departments are often staffed by lawyers.

Further information:

Library Association, 7 Ridgmont Street, London WC1W 7AE.

LOCAL GOVERNMENT

Some specific careers in local government are listed in this appendix under the appropriate headings. There are a wide range of careers in local government either as a lawyer or in management. For information about them you should consult the appropriate department of the Town Hall or Council Office in the area in which you wish to work.

MANAGEMENT

Most companies in industry, commerce and the financial sectors have graduate recruitment programmes. A good law degree will often be considered a suitable background to a career in management. Please consult your own careers' service on particular opportunities, when to apply, and to obtain an overview of a career in management. Some companies will actually come to your university or college to interview prospective trainees and employees.

PATENT OFFICE

Patent agents advise on all aspects of the protection of ideas through patents, copyright and trade marks. Registration of a patent or industrial design is a way of preventing anyone copying your invention without them first paying an appropriate fee. The job involves a knowledge of both science and law and is particularly suitable for a science or engineering student with an interest in the law.

Minimum entry standard: Science or engineering degree.

Training period: 3–4 years.

Further information:

Chartered Institute of Patent Agents, Staple Inn Buildings, London WC1V 7PU.

PERSONNEL MANAGEMENT

The continual development of employment law and health and safety legislation over the past decades has resulted in an increased need for some personnel managers to have a specialist knowledge of law so that they can advise their companies on such matters and, if necessary, represent them in Industrial Tribunals.

Minimum entry standard: Varies (provision for graduate entry).

Training period: Variable.

Further information:

Institute of Personnel Management, 35 Camp Road, London SW19 4UX.

POLICE

For details of entry schemes write to your local police force or to:

The Police Recruiting Department, The Home Office, Queen Anne's Gate, London SW1H 9AT.

PUBLIC RELATIONS

Many of the largest firms of solicitors now employ external or internal public relations advisers to help them with their overall "image" and relations with the media, clients and prospective clients.

Further information:

Institute of Public Relations, 15 Northburgh Street, London EC1V 0PR.

PUBLISHING

Some law publishers are interested in employing law graduates and newly qualified lawyers in their editorial and marketing departments. If you are interested in working for a particular publisher you should contact them directly. Your law tutor should be able to advise you about which law publishers you should approach.

Further information:

Publishers' Association, 19 Bedford Square, London WC1B 3HJ.

RECRUITMENT CONSULTANTS

There is some scope for law graduates and lawyers to work for the recruitment consultants for the legal profession. To obtain an idea of the "market leaders," read the legal job vacancy pages of the national newspapers, the *Law Society Gazette* and the *Lawyer*.

SOCIAL WORK AND PROBATION

Social work

The majority of social workers are employed by local authorities. They provide a social work service to families, children, the elderly, the sick, those with disabilities and the community at large. They are employed in a variety of settings; hospitals, residential homes and in the community. Some are specialists working in such areas as mental health or child care where a good knowledge of the relevant area of law is particularly important. Other elements of social work include providing advice and support where a general awareness of the law is frequently required.

Probation

Probation officers are social workers with special responsibility for offenders. They prepare social inquiry reports to assist the courts in determining sentences, supervise probation orders and community service orders and provide an aftercare service for former prisoners. Through the Divorce Court Welfare Service probation officers also provide services for families involved in marriage breakdown. They assist with conciliation of parties and prepare welfare reports for use in resolving custody disputes. A legal background in this work is helpful though not essential.

Minimum entry standard: A Diploma in Social Work is needed to practice as a qualified social worker. The entry standard for this varies.

Training period: For graduates and non-graduates 2 years.

Further information:

CCETSW, Derbyshire House, St Chad's Street, London WC1H 8AD
Probation Service, Home Office, Queen Anne's Gate, London SW1H 9AT.

For graduates and non-graduates:

Social Work Admissions Systems (SWAS), Fulton House, Jessop Avenue, Cheltenham, Gloucestershire GL50 3SH.

SOLICITORS

See Chapter 8.

STOCK EXCHANGE

Graduates with either law or law-related degrees may find jobs in firms of stockbrokers working in their research and investment analysis departments. There is no formal training for these positions.

The London Stock Exchange organises and regulates the activities of its 400 plus member firms which range from large international securities houses to small two-partner firms of brokers.

It is the member firms, rather than the Exchange, which employ stockbrokers. You should contact the firms directly as recruiting requirements vary. Most reference sections of business libraries hold the London Stock Exchange Member Firms Book, which gives the names and addresses of stockbroking firms.

The London Stock Exchange itself runs a Youth Trainee and Graduate Training Scheme. If you are interested in either of these, please write to Human Resources at the Stock Exchange, London EC2N 1HP.

There are also a number of securities industry courses and exams. For more information, write to:

The Securities Institute, Centurion House, 24 Monument Street, London EC3R 8AJ.

SURVEYING AND AUCTIONEERING

Membership of the Royal Institute of Chartered Surveyors (12 Great George Street, London SW1P 3AD) and the Incorporated Society of Valuers and Auctioneers (3 Cadogan Gate, London SW1X 0AS) requires study of a number of subjects which have a legal content covering such topics as contract, agency and land law.

TAX INSPECTOR

Those who are interested in tax law or the tax system and who have a good degree or an accountancy qualification may be interested in this career option. Progress in the tax inspectorate depends on both the ability to pass internal Revenue examinations and the willingness to be mobile. Some tax inspectors later leave the service in order to start work as tax consultants with firms of accountants.

Minimum entry standard:	First or Second class honours degree or equivalent.
Training period:	3 years.

Further information:

Inland Revenue, Government House, Strand, London WC2R 1LB
Civil Service Commission, Alencon Link, Basingstoke, Hampshire RG21 1JB.

TEACHING AND POST-GRADUATE OPPORTUNITIES

If you are interested in either of the above options you should consult your law tutor or your careers tutor. The majority of university law faculties have facilities for post-graduate research and/or run taught post-graduate courses. You normally need a second class honours degree to obtain a place on such a course. Most of these courses can either be studied full-time or part-time. Some are run on a "distance learning" basis. It is very difficult to obtain scholarships or state grants for such courses. Some universities are able to offer scholarships or other forms of assistance. A post-graduate degree is of some assistance to anyone wishing to teach law. The majority of university law lecturers have an upper second class honours degree or better. Many also have a professional qualification or further degree or both. Although opportunities to lecture in law are limited there are more openings than in many other disciplines.

It is possible to pursue post-graduate research in foreign countries, particularly in the United States and Canada and, increasingly, with the European Union.

Further information:

For further degrees and diplomas by examination and research write direct to a range of law faculties. Diplomas and higher degrees can be obtained in a vast array or legal and law related subjects on a part-time or full-time basis at a wide range of institutions.

Study in the United Kingdom:

Grants Information: British Academy (Post-Graduate Student Office), Block One, Spur 15, Government Buildings, Honey Pot Lane, Stanmore, Middlesex HA7 1AZ. The Department for Education, Room 1/27, Elizabeth House, York Road, London SE1 7PH. Law Commission, Conquest House, 38–00 John Street, London WC1N 2BQ (for research assistant positions). The Economic and Social Science Research Council, Polaris House, Swindon SN2 1ET.

Registry of Post-Graduate Research Topics in Law: The Institute of Advanced Legal Studies, 17 Russell Square, London WC1B 5DR (contact P. Norman).

Overseas Opportunities:

Association of Commonwealth Universities, John Foster House, 36 Gordon Square, London WC1H 0PF. British Council, 65 Davis Street, London W1Y 2AA.

For the USA:

The United States–United Kingdom Educational Advisory Service, 62 Doughty Street, London WC1N 2LS.

TRADING STANDARDS OFFICER

Trading standards officers are responsible for the enforcement of a wide range of legislation including the Trade Descriptions Act 1968, the Consumer Credit Act 1974, the Consumer Protection Act 1987 and other regulatory provisions covering food and drugs and weights and measures. They are also often involved in the provision of advice and assistance to traders and to consumers. They are employed by local authorities.

Minimum entry standard:	2 "A" level and 3 "GCSE" levels (including English, Maths and a science subject). (Provision for graduate entry).
Training period:	3 years.

Further information:

Institute of Trading Standards Administration, Estate House, 319D London Road, Hadleigh, Benfleet, Essex SS7 2BN.

APPENDIX II

Abbreviations

The short list below contains some of the standard abbreviations that you will find most frequently referred to in books and case reports. It is not exhaustive. It will help you whilst you are beginning your study of law but, if you intend to acquire a more detailed knowledge of law, you will need to consult one of the detailed lists found in the books mentioned in the section, "General Reference," in Appendix III.

A.C.	Appeal Cases (Law Reports).
All E.R.	All England Law Reports.
C.L.J.	Cambridge Law Journal.
Ch.D.	Chancery Division (Law Reports).
C.M.L.R.	Common Market Law Reports.
Conv.(n.s.)	Conveyancer and Property Lawyer (New Series).
Crim.L.R.	Criminal Law Review.
D.L.R.	Dominion Law Reports.
E.L.R.	European Law Reports.
E.L.Rev.	European Law Review.
E.R.	English Reports.
Fam.	Family Division (Law Reports).
Fam.Law	Family Law (A journal which also contains notes about cases).
H. of C. or H.C.	House of Commons.
H. of L. or H.L.	House of Lords.
I.L.J.	Industrial Law Journal.
K.B.	King's Bench (Law Reports).
L.Q.R.	Law Quarterly Review.
L.S.Gaz.	Law Society Gazette.
M.L.R.	Modern Law Review.
N.I.L.Q.	Northern Ireland Legal Quarterly.
N.L.J.	New Law Journal.

P.L.	Public Law.
O.J.	Official Journal of the European Communities.
Q.B.D.	Queen's Bench Division.
R.T.R.	Road Traffic Reports.
S.I.	Statutory Instrument.
S.J. or Sol.Jo.	Solicitors' Journal.
W.L.R.	Weekly Law Reports.

APPENDIX III

Further reading

The number of books about law and legal rules increases each day. They range from simple guides, written for the GCSE student, to thousand-page, closely argued texts, written for the academic. Some are encyclopedias; others are exhaustive surveys of a very small area of law. This short list of further reading is intended to be of use to those readers who want to take further specific themes raised in this book. The list is not a guide to legal literature as a whole. Readers who have specific interests should consult their library catalogues for books in their area.

INTRODUCTORY BOOKS

Atiyah, P. *Law and Modern Society* (1983) Oxford University Press. Intended for the law reader, rather than the student already studying for a law degree, this is an introduction both to the legal system and ideas about law. It is written in an accessible style and is suitable for those contemplating studying law at degree level as well as anyone with a general interest in law.

Waldron, J. *The Law* (1990) Routledge. Another general introduction to law. The author is a political scientist and philosopher. The book is particularly concerned with questions about the relationship of politics and law in the United Kingdom.

BOOKS ON THE ENGLISH LEGAL SYSTEM

White, R. *The Administration of Justice* (2nd ed., 1991) Basil Blackwell. This is primarily a textbook for law degree students studying an English Legal System course. It gives the reader a basic background in the institutions and rules of the system but concentrates on how the system actually works in practice. The book is written in a more accessible style than many other similar books. It presumes no previous knowledge of law.

Cross, R. *Precedent in English Law* (4th ed., 1991) Oxford University Press.

Cross, R. *Statutory Interpretation* (2nd ed., 1987) Butterworths. These are standard textbooks on traditional doctrinal theory (the theory of the way in which judges use previous judgments and statutory material) for students and practitioners.

Farrar, J. H. and Dugdale, A. M. *Introduction to Legal Method* (3rd ed., 1990) Sweet and Maxwell. This is both concerned with the nature of law and the way in which it functions within the English legal system. The book draws on sociological literature as well as traditional doctrinal and legal theory.

Goodrich, P. *Reading the Law* (1986) Basil Blackwell. Like Farrar and Dugdale, above, this book is concerned with the nature of law and legal reasoning. However, it takes its inspiration from studies of literature and theology. It is the best introduction to the newest and most innovative analyses of legal reasoning.

BIBLIOGRAPHICAL TECHNIQUES AND DICTIONARIES

Dane, J. and Thomas, P. *How to Use a Law Library* (3rd ed., 1994) Sweet and Maxwell. A very detailed account of the different techniques used in finding and updating legal material. The title is somewhat misleading since the book also gives guidance in how to find material outside the confines of the law section of a library. Useful for those interested in advanced study.

Osborn's Concise Law Dictionary (7th ed., 1983) Sweet and Maxwell. A good pocket guide.

APPENDIX IV

Exercise Answers

EXERCISE 1

1. The Act creates criminal liability for failure to provide a notice of the right to cancel a timeshare agreement. Note that section 2(3) states: "a person who contravenes this section is guilty of an offence." Details of the enforcement process and prosecution authority are in the schedule. However, the Act also affects civil liability because it provides the offeree with a statutory right to cancel a timeshare agreement to which it applies, see s.5(1), and to recover any payment made (s.5(8)). There are similar, but more complex provisions relating to credit purchases.

2. Section 1(7) states that the Act applies to any agreement (a) . . . "governed by the law of the United Kingdom or (b) . . . entered into in the United Kingdom." The United Kingdom means England, Wales, Scotland and Northern Ireland. S.13(3) also makes clear that the Act extends to Northern Ireland.

3. The normal rule is that an Act comes into force on the day it receives the Royal Assent. However s.13(2) makes it clear that this is not the case and s.12(6)(8) gives the Secretary of State the power to make a statutory instrument which will bring the Act into force. This is called a *commencement order*. Details of the commencement order and other Statutory instruments made under an Act will be found in the Current Law Statute Citator. The order is on page 120.

4. No, because any rights to accommodation which John acquires will be for a period of less than three years, see s.11(1)(b). The term periods are also not "of short duration" under s.1(1)(a) because they presumably last more than 1

month (see s.1(2)(b)). One might also query whether student accommodation could be said to be "wholly or partly for leisure purposes" within s.1(1)(a).

5. The agreement is entered into by two people in Spain so it does not come within s.1(7)(b). It is possible, but unlikely, that Ina has specified that the contract is governed by English law. If so, it would come within 1(7)(a).

6. Sunhols plc is in the United Kingdom its agreements are within s.1(7)(b) even if they are stated to be governed by French Law and signed by Stella in France. s.12(4) prevents the exclusion of the provisions of the Act so Stella may exercise her right to cancel under ss.5(1) or 5(2).

EXERCISE 2

1. Section 8 of the Act came into force on the date of the Royal Assent. The remainder of the Act, except s.1(3), came into force on 12 August. Section 1(3) came into force on 30 November. See the entry in the Current Law Statute Citator which refers to SI 91/1742.

2. The Act applies in England, Wales and Scotland. Section 8 provides for an Order in Council to be made under the Northern Ireland Act 1974. Such an order would make comparable provision for Northern Ireland.

3. There is no definition of "dangerous dog" in the Act although s.1(1) lists types of dogs the possession of which becomes an offence. Under s.2(1) the Secretary of State may extend s.1(2) to other types of dog; such an order has been made (see S.I. 1991/1743). Other offences are created by s.3 for all types of dog which are "dangerously out of control."

4. Possession of a pit bull terrier only became illegal under s.1(3) on 30 November 1991. If Darren complies with the order made under s.1(5) he can gain exemption from s.1(3). If Darren was unable to comply with these conditions he would need to ensure the dog went to a country where pit bull terriers are legal.

5. If Sally can be said to be "dangerously out of control" Rosemary has committed an offence under s.3(1)(a) because the park is a public place, see s.10(2). It is immaterial that Sally bit the ice cream and not the children (see s.3(5)(a)) but there must be grounds for reasonable apprehension that Sally would injure someone (see s.10(3)).

(a) Possession of a pit bull terrier is not illegal on 1 October 1991 but the dog must be muzzled and kept on a lead in a public place (see s.1(2)(d)). A dog is only "kept on a lead" where the lead is securely held by a person aged 16 years or over, see s.7(1)(b). Kirk has therefore committed an offence under s.1(2)(d) by tying the lead to railings.

(b) A constable has the right to seize the dog under s.5(1)(a)(ii). Under s.5(4) a justice of the peace must order the dog's destruction if Kirk is not prosecuted. If Kirk is convicted, an order must be made for the dog's destruction under s.4(1)(a).

EXERCISE 3

1. Garry Dunne brought the application for judicial review. This followed his conviction by Magistrates in relation to an offence under s.1 of the Dangerous Dogs Act 1991, and a subsequent successful appeal to the Crown Court against that conviction. The prosecution before the Magistrates had been initiated by the Crown.
   (see p. 491j–492b)

2. What is the proper interpretation of the phrase "any dog of the type known as the pit bull terrier" in s.1(1)(a) of the Dangerous Dogs Act 1991, and did the Crown Court at Knightsbridge err in law in its interpretation of that phrase? (see p. 492j and p. 495d–e)

3. (a) Dunne's case was heard by
       (i) the Wells Street Magistrates' Court;
       (ii) the Crown Court at Knightsbridge;
       (iii) Laws J. in the High Court;
       (iv) the Divisional Court of the Queen's Bench Division of the High Court.

   Brock's case was heard by
       (i) the Barnet Magistrates' Court;
       (ii) the Crown Court at Wood Green;
       (iii) the Divisional Court of the Queen's Bench Division of the High Court.

   (b) Both cases arose out of criminal prosecutions. The application for judicial review in *Dunne*'s case and the case stated in *Brock*'s case were both means by which the decisions in the original criminal proceedings could be challenged.

(c) Both Dunne and Brock were convicted at first instance.

(d) Dunne's appeal was upheld in part by the Crown Court at Knightsbridge.
Brock's appeal was refused by the Crown Court at Wood Green, but was allowed by the Divisional Court. (see p. 498h)

(e) No. No indication of any such report appears from any of the *Current Law* citators as of October 1994.

4. Yes. The *All England Law Report* itself makes references to the cases of:

Annan v. Troup   [1993] SCCR 192
Parker v. Annan   [1993] SCCR 195

The *Current Law Legislation Citator 1989/93* indicates the following additional cases:

Normand v. Freeman   [1992] SLT 598
Bates v. D.P.P.   *The Times*, 8 March 1993
R. v. Bezzina; R. v. Codling;   *The Times*, 7 December 1993
R. v. Elvin
Fellowes v. D.P.P.   *The Times*, 1 February 1993
R. v. Walton Street Justices,   *The Times*, 30 June 1992
ex p. Crothers

The Current Law Monthly Parts up to October 1994 indicate the following further cases:

D.P.P. v. Kellett   *The Times*, 14 July 1994
W. v. C.I.C.B.   C.I.C.B., Plymouth, 10 August 1993
McGeachy v. Normand   [1993] S.C.C.B. 951

EXERCISE 4

1. *R. v. Tower Hamlets London Borough Council, ex part Begum*
   (see p. 67f–h)

2. (a) 2 September 1991 before Popplewell J.
   (see [1993] 1 All ER 447, at p. 449b–c, and [1993] 2 All ER 65, at p. 67g–h)

   (b) 28 November 1991 before Rose J.

(see [1993] 1 All ER 447, at p. 449c, and [1993] 2 All ER 65, at p. 67g–h)

(c) 15 and 20 July 1992, before Lord Donaldson of Lymington MR, Butler-Sloss LJ and Staughton LJ
(see [1993] 1 All ER 447, at p. 447b–c, taken together with p. 449h–j, and [1993] 2 All ER 65, at p. 67g–h)
Note that the judgment was delivered on 30 July 1992 after the Court of Appeal had taken time to consider their decision (see [1993] 1 All ER 447, at p. 449h–j)

(d) 18 January 1993 before the Appeal Committee of the House of Lords, Lord Mustill
(see [1993] 1 All ER 447, at p. 456h together with [1993] 2 All ER 65, at p. 67g)

(e) 18 and 19 January 1993, before Lord Griffiths, Lord Bridge of Harwich, Lord Ackner, Lord Slynn of Hadley and Lord Woolf
(see [1992] 2 All ER 65, at p. 65b–c)
Note that their Lordships' opinions were delivered on 18 March 1992
(see [1992] 2 All ER 65, at p. 65b–c)

3. Derek Wood QC, David Watkinson and Leslie Thomas (see p. 68a–b)

4. Three (see p. 67b–c).

5. All five of the judges agreed that the appeals in relation to Garlick and Bentum should be dismissed. These appeals were therefore dismissed unanimously. However, whereas four of the judges were of the opinion that the appeal in relation to Begum should be allowed, Lord Slynn of Hadley dissented, and was of the opinion that Ferdous Begum's appeal should be dismissed. That appeal was therefore allowed by a majority of four to one.

EXERCISE 5

1. The answer to this is to be found in the first paragraph which expands upon the title of the article to tell you that the author is intending to look at legislative and other attempts to integrate women, members of the ethnic minorities and homosexuals into police forces. The article, as its title says, will be comparative and the first paragraph tells you the comparison will be between Britain and America.

Note two further things about the first paragraph. First there is a sub-heading "Introduction" above it. Articles and chapters in books are often helpfully divided into separate sections with sub-headings to tell you about the content of each section. You can use such sub-headings when you want to refresh your memory of a particular aspect of an author's argument. Sadly in this case "Introduction" is the only sub-heading. Remember authors and editors are only human. Books and articles will contain errors of this kind. As a reader you need to be alert to spot them. You would feel foolish if you wrote an essay in which said, "McKenzie outlines the issue which he intends to examine in the section of his article entitled "Introduction," and your tutor subsequently pointed out that the entire article comes under the sub-heading "Introduction." Equally such a mistake might lead your tutor to think that you had not read the article with very close attention. The second thing to note is what McKenzie does not say the article is about. The article is concerned with assessing the effectiveness of various attempts to integrate various groups into the police. The article pays relatively little attention to arguments about why such groups should or should not be integrated in this manner. (There is limited reference to these issues on pages 174–175 of the reprinted article.) This is quite legitimate. Authors will work within a set word limit for either books or articles. Thus they cannot address all possible arguments which pertain to their topic. What is important is that they make the focus of their argument clear to the reader, which McKenzie has done, and that you as a reader understand what you might find information about in the article. This article will tell you more about the effectiveness of attempts to integrate groups into the police. You will have to go elsewhere to find information about arguments as to why such groups should or should not be further integrated into the police.

2. According to McKenzie there are 43 forces in England and Wales. Each of these forces is supervised by a chief constable (called a Commissioner in the case of the two London forces). Each chief constable is in constitutional theory autonomous. The Home Office, the Goverment department responsible for part of the funding of the various forces, issues memoranda about the practice of policing which individual chief constables are legally free to accept, adapt or ignore. Her Majesty's Inspectors of Constabulary inspect forces in order to certify their efficiency. This information can all be found at pages 165–166 in the reprinted article.

Note that although these propositions are in part statements of law McKenzie gives no authority to support his views. There is, however, a reference to a further study, McKenzie and Gallagher, which is said to give more detail. In his alphabetical list of references at the end of his article McKenzie lists McKenzie and Gallagher as being "Behind the uniform: Policing in Britain and America." McKenzie does not say specifically where in McKenzie and Gallagher to look for extra information about the organisational framework of police forces. However, Section 2 of the book is mainly concerned with such matters. If you had looked at that book at pages 56 to 57 you would have found a short discussion of some of the important cases which establish what position the police have within the constitutional frame-work. The two cases discussed on those pages are *Fisher v. Oldham Corporation* [1930] 2 KB 364 and *R. v. Metropolitan Police Commissioner, ex parte Blackburn* [1968] 2 All ER 319. Even here the citations to these law reports are not given. They had to be obtained for this answer by looking them up in a Case Citator.

3. On page 164 of the reprinted article McKenzie argues that, in order to understand policing practices, one needs to understand the internal structures which affect those practices. The organisational framework of the police constitutes part of those practices. An example of the importance of this information can be seen if one turns to page 168 of the reprinted article. Here McKenzie notes that each chief police officer (*i.e.* chief constable or Commissioner) develops their own policy for recruiting, monitoring and retention. The Home Office has only a supportive role. The Home Office cannot intervene directly because of the relationship between them and chief police officers laid down in constitutional law.

4. On page 173 McKenzie says that "[i]n 1992 about 15% of all officers in the UK were women and, in accord with quota thinking, if fair promotion practices were operating one would expect to see that 15% reflected in other grades."

The important phrase here is "quota thinking." One might argue that a reason why a smaller percentage of women are found in more senior police ranks is because large numbers leave to look after children. However, "quota thinking" might then argue that a job structure which does not allow women to return to work, perhaps on a part-time basis, after having children is in itself discriminatory. One might argue that women are not tem-peramentally suited to positions of high authority within the police force. "Quota thinking" would argue that women have an equal array of talents and skills to those possessed by men and thus one would expect them to be found in all senior ranks in equal measure to the percentages found in junior ranks. McKenzie writes that studies have "repeatedly shown" that men and women have equal competencies and that women perform equally well to men in a wide range of tasks (page 171). However, McKenzie cites only one such study in support of his assertions. One might argue that a discrepancy between the percentage of women found in lower police ranks and those found in higher police ranks is a historical anomaly due to now rescinded discriminatory practices. This, unlike the previous arguments, would be an attempt to explain but not to justify the situation. In order to sustain this argument one would need to know more than the article tells us about the statistics for numbers of women in various ranks over the past decades. However, some support for this argument is to be found in the Table 1 in the article which shows an increasing percentage of women police officers over a period between 1985 and 1991. If it takes on average, for example, 20 years from joining a police force to rise to a senior rank even "quota thinking" would lead us to expect now not a percentage of senior officers equivalent to the present percentage of women officers but a percentage equivalent to the percentage of women officers 20 years ago.

In deciding which of these and other arguments we accept we need to answer a number of questions. Do we believe that women do not achieve high rank because they do not have in equal measure to men the qualities that those making appointments consider to be necessary for that rank? If the answer to this question is yes do we also accept that the qualities considered necessary are in fact necessary? Alternatively do we believe that those making promotion decisions are driven by conscious or unconscious bias in deciding that women do not have the qualities necessary for promotion? Do we believe that people making promotions are driven by conscious or unconscious bias in deciding what qualities are necessary for promotion or are simply wrong in deciding what qualities are necessary? "Quota thinking" implies a belief that women have all the same qualities as men or, if they have different qualities, that, perhaps for reasons of over-riding social policy, this is unimportant in selecting them for employment. Plainly this is a position that is adopted by some and not by others. Two things are equally important whatever your final conclusion. One is that you should understand the reasons for "quota thinking;" the other is that you understand the reasons for rejecting such arguments. Only after assessing all sides can you come to your own conclusions.

5. In the final paragraphs of his article McKenzie argues that whereas in the United States illegitimate discrimination is seen to be opposed by "powerful figures" in the United Kingdom "although government figures may publicly disparage such behaviour, for all practical purposes the control and limitation of the unacceptable face of human nature, is left in the hands of a faceless and tiny minority . . . And, on top of that, the penalties for non-compliance with the legislation are derisory" (page 179). Two arguments are thus involved. One is that illegitimate discrimination will be reduced if it is seen as being unacceptable to the powerful. The second argument is that people will change their behaviour in order to avoid being punished.

A number of possible counter-arguments should occur to you. McKenzie notes that "the emancipated woman and the homosexual may both be denigrated on the basis of religious dicta" page 173. It is not difficult to find cultures and religions which find homosexuality and the notion of equality between the sexes abhorrent. Would not a police officer holding those views think it morally right to discriminate? Moreover, if he held those views strongly and if they formed a central part of his belief-system, would he not be likely to continue to hold to those views even though others thought him wrong and even though he were punished? In such cases it is surely necessary to try and directly change the attitude and not simply to try to effect behaviour. A simpler argument is to ask to what extent McKenzie demonstrates that the situation in the USA is in fact more favourable to preventing illegitimate discrimination than that in the UK. There is little in the article which proves this superiority. Page 168 makes a brief reference to contract compliance rules but no statistical or other evidence is adduced to show their success. He does point to the existence of women Chiefs in America (page 171) but 6 women Chiefs out of 17,613 police departments demonstrates very little. Page 175 notes the presence of lesbian police officers in the LAPD but in the context of remarks by the former chief of the LAPD which McKenzie regards as in themselves illegitimately discriminatory. The best evidence for American superiority is found in references to studies of the American "litigation-approach" which McKenzie says show the success of such an approach. However, since the article in the main concentrates on outlining the situation in the UK its conclusions about the USA might well be regarded as a little tendentious.

6. At pages 172–173 McKenzie discusses the effect of the Halford case. Halford succeeded in gaining an out of court settlement when she took action on grounds of sexual discrimination through the Equal Opportunities Commission. McKenzie thinks that more might have been achieved if the case had been determined within the judicial process. At page 178 McKenzie discusses the way in which behaviour can be modified by punishment. Being successfully sued can properly be regarded as punishment. At page 169 notes that there has been a case of an Asian officer successfully suing on grounds of discrimination. McKenzie's belief that successful litigation will change behaviour might, however, be wrong. Employers might take the view that few officers will be willing to undergo the stress of taking action and that where action is taken any awards made might merely be regarded as payment for being able to make the kind of promotion decisions that senior officers prefer to make.

INDEX

The index is meant to be used in conjunction with the detailed list of contents at the beginning of the book. Those interested in looking at the range of careers with a legal content should also refer to the Careers Directory at pages 215–232.